Churrasco

Churrasco

A Theological Feast in Honor of Vítor Westhelle

Edited by
**Mary Philip,
John Arthur Nunes,**
and
Charles M. Collier

☙PICKWICK *Publications* · Eugene, Oregon

CHURRASCO
A Theological Feast in Honor of Vítor Westhelle

Copyright © 2013 Wipf and Stock Publishers. All rights reserved. Except for brief quotations in critical publications or reviews, no part of this book may be reproduced in any manner without prior written permission from the publisher. Write: Permissions, Wipf and Stock Publishers, 199 W. 8th Ave., Suite 3, Eugene, OR 97401.

Pickwick Publications
199 W. 8th Ave., Suite 3
Eugene, OR 97401

www.wipfandstock.com

ISBN 13: 978-1-62032-946-7

Cataloging-in-Publication data:

Churrasco : a theological feast in honor of Vítor Westhelle

    Churrasco : a theological feast in honor of Vítor Westhelle / edited by Mary Philip, John Arthur Nunes, and Charles M. Collier.

    xxii + 196 p. ; 23 cm. — Includes bibliographical references.

    ISBN 13: 978-1-62032-946-7

1. Westhelle, Vítor, 1952-. I. Philip, Mary. II. Nunes, John. III. Collier, Charles M., 1971-. IV. Title.

BX4827.W48 U45 2013

Manufactured in the U.S.A.

Contents

List of Contributors vii
Acknowledgments xi
Introduction xiii

THEORIA

1 Wrestling for Grace   3
   —Oswald Bayer
2 Did Luther's Students Hide the Hidden God?: *Deus Absconditus* among Luther's First Followers   7
   —Robert Kolb
3 The Dynamics of Secularization, Atheism and the So-called Return of Religion and its Significance for the Public Understanding of Science and Religion: Some European Perspectives   17
   —Antje Jackelén
4 Beatitudinal Eschatology: In Space or Time?   29
   —Ted Peters
5 Queering the Erotic: Bernard's and Luther's Use of the Nuptial Metaphor   38
   —Else Marie Wiberg Pedersen
6 Postcolonial Transfigurative Identity: Reading Walcott with Westhelle in Mind   49
   —John Arthur Nunes

POEISIS

7 Created Co-Creator: Symbol of Life in Crisis and Ambiguity   63
   —Philip Hefner
8 The Flavour of "the Other": Re-thinking Differences in Europe, the Ecumenical Movement and Elsewhere   72
   —Claudia Jahnel

9 Wind, Breeze, Hurricane: On Poetry and Theology—Insights from the Perspective of Brazilian Literature   82
   —Roberto E. Zwetsch

10 Remembrance: A Living Bridge   94
    —Mary Philip (Joy)

11 Theology as Tapestry Weaving: From a "Lutheran Core" Through Mediating Devices—and Back   105
    —Luís H. Dreher

12 Knowledge Transfigured by Love: Theological Perspectives of Vítor Westhelle's Thought   114
    —Kathlen Luana de Oliveira

PRAXIS

13 Our Global Diversity—God's Amazing Grace!   127
    —Musimbi Kanyoro

14 Psalm 90: God behind God   133
    —Walter Altmann

15 Experience and Its Claim to Universality: The Nature of Experience   140
    —Reinhard Hütter

16 Classrooms and *Choratic* Spaces: A Meditation on Seminary Teaching   150
    —Kathleen D. Billman

17 Charting a New Vision: Paul's Copernican Revolution for Our Witness to the Gospel   160
    —José David Rodríguez

18 (Re)-Claiming *Oikoumenē*? Ecumenism, Ecology, Empire   172
    —Barbara Rossing

A Prayer   184
—Deanna A. Thompson

List of Vítor Westhelle's Publications   185

Contributors

Walter Altmann is the moderator of the World Council of Churches (WCC) Central Committee. He was the president of the Evangelical Church of the Lutheran Confession in Brazil (IECLB) from 2002 to 2011. A pastor and teacher of the church he has served many parishes in Brazil and also taught at seminaries both in Brazil and in the US. Altmann's theological work is focused mainly on Martin Luther, Latin American liberation theology, and ecumenism.

Oswald Bayer (1939) is professor emeritus of systematic theology at the University of Tübingen, Germany, and the academic director of the Luther Academy Sondershausen-Ratzeburg. An ordained pastor of the Lutheran Church of Württemberg, he was the editor of *Neue Zeitschrift für Systematische Theologie und Religionsphilosophie* (1986 to 2006). His research focuses especially on Luther and Hamann (see Oswald Bayer, *A Contemporary in Dissent: Johann Georg Hamann as a Radical Enlightener* [2012]).

Kathleen D. (Kadi) Billman is the John H. Tietjen Professor of Pastoral Ministry: Pastoral Theology, Professor of Pastoral Theology, and Director of the Master of Divinity Program at the Lutheran School of Theology at Chicago, where she served as Dean from 1999 to 2009. She co-authored *Rachel's Cry: Prayer of Lament and Rebirth of Hope* with Daniel L. Migliore and co-edited *C(H)AOS Theory: Reflections of Chief Academic Officers in Theological Education* with Bruce C. Birch.

Luís H. Dreher is a native of Brazil; he studied theology and philosophy in Brazil, Germany, and the US. He is currently Associate Professor of Philosophy of Religion at the State University at Juiz de Fora. Among his major publications are *O método teológico de Schleiermacher* (1995) and *Metaphors of Light: Philipp K. Marheineke's and the Ongoing Program of Mediation*

Contributors

Theology (1998). He is well known for his writings on philosophical theology, hermeneutics, and the philosophy of religion.

Philip Hefner is professor emeritus of systematic theology at the Lutheran School of Theology at Chicago. He was founder and director of the Zygon Center for Religion and Science (1988-2001) and editor of *Zygon: Journal of Religion and Science*. His article in this book is based on his Rockwell Lectures at Rice University in 2002.

Reinhard Hütter is Professor of Christian Theology at Duke Divinity School and the Rev. Robert J. Randall Distinguished Professor of Christian Culture at Providence College (2012-13). His most recent books include *Ressourcement Thomism: Sacred Doctrine, the Sacraments, and the Moral Life* (with Matthew Levering) and *Dust Bound for Heaven: Explorations in the Theology of Thomas Aquinas*. He is co-editor of the journal *Nova et Vetera: The English Edition of the International Theological Journal* and an ordinary academician of the Pontifical Academy of St. Thomas Aquinas.

Claudia Jahnel is head of the Department for Mission and Intercultural Studies at Mission Eine Welt (Mission OneWorld), a development agency of the Evangelical Lutheran Church in Bavaria, Germany. Her area of expertise includes religion and development, contextual theologies and ecumenism in times of globalization.

Antje Jackelén is Bishop of the Diocese of Lund, Church of Sweden, and Adjunct Professor of Systematic Theology/Religion and Science at the Lutheran School of Theology at Chicago, where she taught (2001-2007) and also served as the director of the Zygon Center for Religion and Science (2003-2007). Jackelén is the author of *Time and Eternity* (2005), *The Dialogue between Religion and Science* (2004), and *Gud är större* (*God is Greater*, 2011).

Musimbi Kanyoro is President and CEO of the Global Fund for Women a public foundation that invests in women-led organizations and women to advance the rights of women and girls worldwide. Prior to the Global Fund she served with the David and Lucile Packard Foundation, the World YWCA and Lutheran World Federation. She currently serves on the Global Committee of the Council on Foundations, CARE, Intra Health and CHANGE.

Robert Kolb is Missions professor of systematic theology emeritus at Concordia Seminary, Saint Louis USA. A widely published and accomplished

Contributors

Lutheran scholar, one of his major contributions has been co-editing the *Book of Concord* with Timothy Wengert. He is the author of several books and articles, notably *Martin Luther, Confessor of the Faith* (2009) and *Bound Choice, Election, and Wittenberg Theological Method from Martin Luther to the Formula of Concord* (2005)

John Arthur Nunes has served as the President and CEO of Lutheran World Relief since 2007, providing leadership for a $49 million organization helping overseas communities living in poverty and marginalization to work their way to sustainable livelihoods.

Kathlen Luana de Oliveira is a Brazilian Theologian, doing her doctoral studies at Escola Superior de Teologia in São Leopoldo. Author of *Toward a Policy of Living Together: Theology, Human Rights, Hannah Arendt* (*Por uma política da convivência: Teologia, Direitos Humanos, Hannah Arendt* [2011]), her research is focused on "Justice, Freedom and Communion: the political density of theological knowledge and the paradoxes of democracy in times of human rights."

Ted Peters is research Professor Emeritus in Systematic Theology at Pacific Lutheran Theological Seminary and the Graduate Theological Union in Berkeley, California, USA. He is author of *God—The World's Future* (Rev. ed., 2000) and *Anticipating Omega* (2008). He co-edits the journal *Theology and Science* and previously served as editor of *Dialog, A Journal of Theology*.

Mary Philip (Joy) is the SEVIS officer at the Lutheran School of Theology at Chicago. Formerly a professor of Zoology (India), she is also adjunct faculty for Theology at Lewis University, Illinois.

José David Rodríguez currently serves as the President of Superior Evangélico de Estudios Teológicos (ISEDET). He is also the Augustana Heritage Chair of Global Mission and World Christianity at the Lutheran School of Theology at Chicago (on leave). Rodriguez recent books include *Romanos* and *La Vocación*. He also serves on the editorial boards of the Association for the Theological Education of Hispanics and the Journal of Hispanic/Latino Theology.

Barbara Rossing is professor of New Testament at the Lutheran School of Theology at Chicago, where she also advises the seminary's Environmental Emphasis. She is the author of *The Rapture Exposed: The Message of Hope in the Book of Revelation* and *Journeys Through Revelation: Apocalyptic Hope for Today*. She served on the executive committee and council of the Lutheran World Federation (LWF) 2003–2010.

Deanna A. Thompson is professor of religion at Hamline University in St. Paul, Minnesota. She is the author of *Crossing the Divide: Luther, Feminism, and the Cross* (2004) and most recently of *Hoping for More: Having Cancer, Talking Faith, and Accepting Grace* (2012). Speaking widely to both church and academic groups, Thompson integrates the scholarly and the personal, especially in relationship to the suffering that invades our lives.

Else Marie Wiberg Pedersen is Associate Professor of Systematic Theology in the Department of Culture and Society in the Faculty of Arts at Aarhus University. She has published widely on medieval and Reformation theology and ecumenism, and is editor of *Gudstankens aktualitet* (*The Immediacy of the Idea of God*, 2010). She is currently working on an English revision of her book *Bernhard af Clairvaux. Teolog eller mystiker?* (*Bernard of Clairvaux: Theologian or Mystic?*).

Roberto E. Zwetsch is a pastor of the Evangelical Church Lutheran Confession in Brazil; he is also a missionary of the Indigenous Peoples in Brazilian Amazon Region. Zwetsch is Professor of Practical Theology and Missiology at Faculdades EST, São Leopoldo, Brazil since 1993. He has published several books and articles, notable being *Missão como com-paixão: Por uma teologia da missão em perspectiva latino-americana* (2008).

Acknowledgments

GRATITUDE, IT IS SAID, is the memory of the heart. Many friends and colleagues, near and far, are due this memory of the heart for helping to make this book possible. However, first and foremost, our sincere gratitude goes to Vítor Westhelle, who has played no small role in our lives, has been integral to how our theologies have been shaped, and to whom this book is dedicated.

Churrasco had its inception one quiet evening in 2011 while sitting with Vítor in his office talking about the impact and influence some people have on others—how lives are changed and given a purpose because someone cared or listened. It just dawned on me that Vítor was one such person. That led to conversation with some friends and colleagues about the possibility of releasing a book to celebrate and acknowledge the contributions of Vítor on the occasion of his sixtieth birthday. Twenty-five months later it has brought us here.

Any attempt in this Acknowledgement fully to recognize Vítor's capacious contribution to the theological academy would be premature. This is not a eulogy. The scope and scale of his impact, in fact, appears to be on a rising trajectory.

Among all with whom he has influence, narrowing down the list of candidates for this volume was no simple task. From the one-hundred-fifty-plus graduate students Vítor mentored in the past 30 years, the two editors alone are included. The past and current colleagues included are friends with whom Vítor worked from the 1980s, be it in Brazil, Kenya, India, the United States, or Europe. They are from various phases and vocational contexts of Vítor's remarkable career. Our sincere gratitude is extended to each and every contributor for giving their time and scholarship despite the stiff deadlines placed on them.

Three of the texts in this collection have been previously published. Reinhard Hütter's essay, "Experience and Its Claim to Universality: The

Acknowledgments

Nature of Experience" was first published in *Communio* 37, no. 2 (2010). Antje Jackelén's "The Dynamics of Secularization, Atheism and the So-called Return of Religion and its Significance for the Public Understanding of Science and Religion: Some European perspectives" appeared in *Ecumenical Trends*, volume 41, no. 4. Barbara Rossing's essay was previously published as "(Re)claiming Oikoumene: Empire, Ecumenism and the Discipleship of Equals" in the book *Walk in the Ways of Wisdom* (Trinity Press International). However, all three texts have been revised and reorganized specifically for this *Churrasco* of a book.

Special thanks to the fastidious Sara Jane Baublitz for her editorial contribution. Our deep appreciation also goes to Wipf and Stock publishers, who accepted the proposal and encouraged the particular nuances that we proposed. A special word to Charlie Collier, the Wipf and Stock editor in charge of this collection, and also one of its co-editors. Thank you, Charlie. You have been amazing!

And to you, dear readers, thank you for checking the acknowledgements page. But read on, will you? This is merely a foretaste of the feast to come!

Introduction

CHURRASCO IS A BRAZILIAN dish that Vítor Westhelle loves. It is similar to a barbecue of a variety of meats. This book is a theological *churrasco*. It is not based on a common theme or themes that are connected. Common themes may be conceived but each of these essays is an individual piece that relates to the author's relationship with Vítor. But more importantly, this collection of essays is not a Festschrift. Festschrift, here in the West, marks the end of a scholar's career, and that is not what we are intending with this volume. It is not an announcement of an end but the heralding of a rejuvenated and vivacious time to come. This mélange of texts is an acknowledgement and celebration of sixty years of the gift of Vítor's life, more than half of which has been dedicated to academia—religious and theological, and secular.

In India and most of the global south, you can reach seventy or one hundred years of age but it wouldn't really be that significant. Even the so-called golden fifty does not matter. But completing sixty years —*shashtiabdapoorthi*[1]—is considered a blessing from God. The sixtieth year is the mirror image of the day that person was born, and if one reaches that age, the person is believed to be in God's favor and will be blessed to enter the new and exciting second cycle of life. It is like a rebirth, where is one is showered with blessings. Thus this platter of theological essays is not a Festschrift, signaling a coda or conclusion, but rather a celebration of this sharp and swanky Brazilian's crossing of a threshold to an even more exciting phase of life.

Back in 1992, LSTC's President William Lesher extended Brazilian pastor and professor Vítor Westhelle a faculty position in place of Carl Braaten who was retiring. It hadn't been that long since Vítor had been awarded his doctoral degree from LSTC and had returned to his home church and

---

1. A word in Malayalam meaning completion of 60 years.

Introduction

his alma mater in São Leopoldo, Brazil, where he was making a name for himself, training future Brazilian Lutheran theologians.

David Nelson, the staff person in the ELCA for inter-church relations with the Evangelical Church of the Lutheran Confession in Brazil (IECLB) was asked by the then-Global Mission Director Mark Thomsen to be in touch with the Brazilian church to find out if they were aware of this call to Pastor Westhelle by LSTC and what they thought about it. The Secretary for Theological Education in the IECLB was the Rev. Harald Malchitsky, and David with some trepidation made the telephone call to Pastor Malchitsky in his Porto Alegre office expecting to hear from him a strong negative reaction to the ELCA making this surprising move so soon after Vítor had concluded his doctoral studies at LSTC. But to his surprise, not only was Pastor Malchitsky fully aware of the invitation extended by LSTC but his response was a moving affirmation of the church's confidence in the brilliance and scholarship of Vítor: If you are taking one of ours we are glad that you are taking one of our best. He added that Vítor would make a terrific contribution to theological education in the ELCA and that students in the US would benefit greatly from this articulate spokesperson of South American Lutheran theology and the Brazilian reality.[2]

Now, twenty-one years later, one can only marvel at the contributions that Vítor has made to theological education not only in the ELCA and the Lutheran School of Theology at Chicago but also to the wider church and the theological/religious academia at large. Over the years, his voice and work have shaped many theologians around the world. Vítor currently spends half the academic year in Brazil and the other half in the US. He holds the chair of Luther research at Faculdades EST in São Leopoldo, Brazil, and is also honorary professor of theology at Aarhus University, Denmark.

What is unique about this volume is its disconnect. Fragments—fissures—best explain Vítor's theology, a uniqueness of those coming from the Third World. The Divine is often located interstitially, in the fissures, cracks, fragments, "sparks of the divine," as David Tracy would call it. Life itself is about fragments. We are fragments each with our own unique shape, color, race, and language, each which has its own place in the scheme of things, in the whole that is being patterned as each move in, as one more piece being put into place, respecting differences yet encouraging translation as a practice rather than a solution. What is envisioned here is something similar to a Derridean teleopoeisis that allows these fragments, these

---

2. I am thankful to Pastor David Nelson who does not tire of telling this story. When asked if I could share the story in the book, Pastor Nelson, whilst writing the sermon for the coming Sunday, took a break and sent me a short write-up of the incident/conversation with Pastor Malchitsky.

Introduction

theological pieces, to communicate with that which is distant and seems disconnected and yet to aim at a completion. We hope these theological pieces that may seem fragments, in the reader, will shift and rearrange, fractionate and reconsider, allowing for a message to come through.

"My life is an open book," would be Vítor's response if you asked him to say something about himself. He would then add: "It is written in Chinese." He couldn't be more right. Both Vítor and Vítor's work does not have a poker face. What you see is what you get. However, there is one catch: you need to have the language. And that is what Vítor's vocation is all about. You can acquire all the knowledge and skills you want, but if you don't have the language, it's all a waste of time. Without language one is lost. Be it teaching systematic theology, philosophy of religion, or faith and fiction, that is what Vítor strives for—language. He is not telling us to acquire a well ordered, complete package that works like a science, but rather reminding us that what matters is in the fissures, in the cracks, in the white fires. And likewise this volume, *Churrasco*, is a collection of essays—fragments from different contexts and with their own flavors—from people all over the world that share this vocation with Vítor and in their coming together say, "Salute dear colleague!" for being our partner, for prodding and challenging us in this search for language.

Luís Dreher reminds us that Vítor Westhelle is a dangerous theologian. As a proclaimer of Jesus Christ, announcing in bold voice and candid rhetoric God's good news for people at life's marginal places, Westhelle's words are necessarily "dangerously-saving." As a teacher and mentor of many, he engenders danger because, at his core, he is a radical theologian. We mean radical in the most passionate and paradoxical sense of the term. First, radical derives from *radix*, denoting what is at the root, foundational and traditional. Vítor's confessional commitments and working familiarity of Martin Luther are *sans pareil*.

We also mean radical in the sense of Vítor's predilection for what is redemptively transcending the tradition, those words from God that are controversially controverting colonialist epistemologies, especially in the form of the Law's devastating negations of theologies of glory; sometimes these *theologiae gloriae* are predicated on a power that organizes itself in rationalities (Foucault). Sometimes they are buttressed by regimes, like Rome's colonialism, which was "seen through" by a centurion (Mark 15:39). In any case, Vítor's theology is dangerous in spite of the fact that it isn't first about soteriology or politics or morality or economic systems or the nature of God (though these are not without implication), but first about God's revelation in Jesus Christ. Referencing another of Vítor's works, *Mark Mattes* notes the spectrum of usability his radicality provides. "That this book cannot easily be labeled a representative of current theological schools is due to its genius."[3]

If Aristotle were reading this volume, he might recognize three broad categories of essays represented: 1) theological *theoria*, a systematic contemplation of the things of God; 2) theological *poiesis*, that consideration of purposeful production done in God's name; 3) theological *praxis*, humans engaged in faith-fueled friction and action. The editors have used these categories to divide the contributions into three parts; however, as with Westhelle's work, these three ways of knowing do not stay put in pat categories. They leak. They defy rationalizing or sequencing, akin to Vítor and *Churrasco*.

Spatiality is a key issue in this volume. Professor Vítor Westhelle has been known to explore dramatically in classroom lectures the ecclesial implications and correlative relationality of temporal and spatial themes, especially in situations of humans living in marginality. He has taught many of us that during the second half of the second millennia—at least the last five hundred years—notions of temporality and spatiality have shaped the dimensions of the Christian worldview; for example, one focus of his lectures has been the ways in which maps have assumed a totalizing placelessness in contrast with the itineraries of old which were more directive and instructive for a distinct journey. Here, for example, is a brief, synthesized summary of Westhelle's thinking:

- "Space has indeed become illusory"[4]
- "Maps have lost the itinerary character they once had"[5]
- Maps have become "homogenous representations of extension, losing the connection with their situatedness."[6]

The breadth of perspectives represented by *Churrasco* demonstrates the broad range of conversation that Vítor's particular Lutheran radicalism is inspiring. It's as diverse as the intellectual engagements of the man it honors, from classic, Greco-Germanic argumentation to iconoclasti, constructive mysticism. In fact, as he has insisted, all traditions of truth necessarily bear their opposite within them.

Oswald Bayer sets the tone for the volume when he takes us homiletically to a deepest, darkest moment along life's cross-marked journey, when

3. Mark Mattes, review of *Scandalous God* in *Lutheran Quarterly* 21 (2007) 464.
4. Vítor Westhelle, "Re(li)gion: The Lord of History and Illusory Space," *LWF Studies* 4 (1994) 90.
5. Ibid.
6. Vítor Westhelle, "The Way the World Ends: An Essay on Cross and Eschatology," *Currents in Theology and Mission* 27.2 (2000) 89.

Introduction

the whispering voice deprecates us oppressively: "Your life was worthless, it is of no value. Throw it away!" God's promises to Jacob and to Jonah in their despair are delivered to us in baptism. The theology of the cross—recurrent thread in this volume—comes alive in the preached Word of God, which Luther declaimed was the best test of theology.

Robert Kolb traces and masterfully delineates five components of the theology of the cross: 1) as a burden to help crucify the flesh, 2) as eschatological battle evidenced in the suffering of church, 3) as the means of atonement through Jesus death and resurrection—albeit, 4) exhibiting a weak and foolish (1 Cor. 1:18-25) epistemology as contrasted with human wisdom and 5) as distinguishing the hidden God and the revealed God. Professor Kolb then introduces us to some names (some new to most of us) and views of some of Luther's first theological descendents with regard to this hidden God—Johannes Brenz, Erasmus Sarcerius, Caspar Crucifer, Cyriakus Spangenberg, Tileman Heshusius, Johannes Wigand. Kolb uses these second- and third-generation Lutherans to illumine the genealogy of a concept Westhelle introduces in *The Scandalous God*—namely, "the evasions of the scandal"—ways in which "contemporary theologians strive to evade and escape the scandal of the cross."

Antje Jackelén, the bishop of Lund, Sweden, offers an ecclesial-theological consideration of faith in the public sphere, not shying from its myriad—and sometimes frightening—forms. The complex cultural interplay between secularism and a rising religiosity is traced by Jackelén in a manner that respects this same inside/outside dialect; for example, note even the way in which she suggests that "with the fall of modern theism even atheism became an impossible position." The healthy and helpful components of this lively and refreshingly contemporary discourse are surfaced by this former colleague in the Systematic Theology department at the Lutheran School of Theology at Chicago.

Ted Peters and *Kathleen Billman*, from distinct starting points and through two analogical frames, engage Westhelle's conceptual frameworks of spatiality. Peters analyzes the turn to the spatial, away from a linear view of time which is complicit with a "European colonialist consciousness" leading to marginality. Westhelle opts for a focus on "little stories and the space they occupy in everyday life." Those are the places of realized eschatologies, the pluralized *ta eschata* is purposeful, full of God's purpose now. "Beatitudinal Eschatology" constitutes Peter's counterproposal. Reading Matthew 5 he sees the promise of a proleptic exchange between today's marginalization and "life in the center of God's domain tomorrow."

Else Marie Wiberg Pedersen is inspired by the powerful concluding pages of *The Scandalous God*, in which Vítor ponders the "mad economy"

Introduction

of an empty tomb filled with women bearing gifts of fragrant spices. So moved, Wiberg Pedersen plumbs the uses of the biblical nuptial metaphor by Bernard of Clairvaux and Martin Luther. Each in their own way offers additional glimpses of a "grace-side economics" in their gender-crossing interpretations of the Song of Solomon (Bernard) and Isaiah (Luther). In continuing the exegetical tradition of Origen, which combined a twofold erotic reading of the nuptial mystery (individual soul bride and the Word; collective bride church and Christ), Luther and Clairvaux not only illumine "the importance of love as the source and end of life in the relational exchange between God and humans," but their gender-crossing exegesis also "meets many of the requests made by feminist and postcolonial theologies about recognition of difference and the other."

John Arthur Nunes is similarly moved by Vítor's work to attend to questions at the intersection of theology and postcolonial studies; however, Nunes redirects our focus from allegorical exegesis to the "transgressive vision" of Nobel laureate Derek Walcott. Nunes admires the "hybrid mischief" of Walcott's poetry—at once reflecting Walcott's classical education as well as his love for everyday Caribbean life—and Nunes espies in Walcott's poetry a cousin to Martin Luther's bilingualism, that is, his proficiency in both rarefied academic discourse and the simple, even crude, vernacular of the ordinary Germans of his day. The key here, according to Nunes, is the fecundity of hybridity for contemporary Christian theology. The hybridity of Luther's and Walcott's linguistic creativity is brought forth to renew our appreciation of the extraordinary hybridity at the heart of the gospel: Jesus Christ as the God-Human. The transgressive character of basic christological doctrine is thus held up as a crucial resource for those who would work to move the church beyond the destrutive habits of a colonial Christianity and to return it to its native habitat—service of the marginalized.

In the second part of this volume, we open with *Philip Hefner's* poeitic response to a critique Vítor leveled a decade ago. Hefner invokes a compelling aspect of Vítor's *deus obsconditus* as part of an *apologia* and response to that critique. His key concept "created co-creator" was evaluated by Westhelle to be too centrist and too teleological. We anticipate that this may not be the final word in this conversation, but the reader may enjoy Hefner's conclusion drawn from Westhelle's own conceptual framework: "God is hidden from us in this experience, God is not absent from our struggle. (Hefner: 7)"

We hope *Churrasco* to be a tasty volume especially as it includes the "The Flavor of 'the Other.'" *Claudia Jahnel* takes us beyond mere external tolerance of the Other as she argues compellingly for the reality of a "cultural interweaving . . . full of transgressions, exchange processes, and syncretism."

Introduction

The Holy Spirit calls us transculturally, gathers the human in a unique bricolage, enlightens formerly narrow-minded identities with genuine love for the neighbor, and sanctifies and knits together the human community formerly full of fragmentation.

Roberto Zwetsch includes Westhelle's "dangerous" translation of what the NRSV calls "to the ends of the world" (Romans 10:18); namely, to the "margins of *oikoumenē*." Interspersing his argument with beautiful poetry he advocates for this performative language as both expressive of spirituality and creative of reality. Such faith is anchored in the surprise of the incarnation, the encounter with "the *un-expected*, the *un-suspected*, the *ineffable*, the *unspeakable*." While Zwetsch provides readers with affirmations of life in this world, he does not ignore opportunities to introduce subversion and the cross, especially for the sake of showing solidarity with people living in tragic situations which oppress.

Mary Philip (Joy) takes us to the hilly regions of Meghalaya while she enlivens the concept of anamnesis by reflecting on the demanding, risky, even dangerous power of remembrance to help put back together—to re-member—our broken pasts into present and future wholes as well as to lead us into the service of those in need of a similar reconciliation, a similar re-membering. Philip draws upon the work of Derrida and Benjamin to develop an understanding of remembrance as that which opens up *choratic* space—a living bridge—between past and present. To illumine how remembrance might forge constructive links between past and present, Philip concludes by telling the story of the living bridges of Cherrapunji, India. There, natural organisms—roots, branches, and flora—are enmeshed and adapted to the environment through multigenerational efforts to build transformative crossings to a hopeful future.

In his appeal for contextualized theology, *Luís Dreher* is rooted in the theology of the cross: "God speaks and acts in hidden ways which we cannot control and dualistically separate." Variations of "danger" are used a dozen times as Dreher takes us on a comprehensive tour of the primary theological themes showing up in his vocational mentor, Westhelle: from apocalypticism to Gnosticism, time and space, essentialism and marginalization. This is a theologian who digested Westhelle's way of working with the W/word and now reverberates with his own appropriation, and ecstatically so.

With evocative poetic interspersions, *Kathlen Luana De Oliveira* sees Vítor's theology and contributions through a the lens of "a bird-like look." Mystically, this "look" seems to be both this contributor's own looking at his work, as well as Vítor's own way of seeing radically as he goes to the origins. He "goes inside the words and sees something that was already there but was not told yet." This is as much theological disposition as it is method,

Introduction

and Kathlen Luana De Oliveira takes it as artwork: bounding within the wondrous and marvelous, bursting boundaries, embracing experience, a "knowledge transfigured by love."

In the third and final section of the volume, we turn to praxis-oriented contributions. In her appeal for contextualized theology, *Musimbi Kanyoro* aligns her identification as similar to Westhelle's: in celebration of diversity, rather than attempting to domesticate and dominate the Spirit's wondrous fission. In an essay most explicitly engendering the place of women, Kanyoro elucidates three considerations for our global engagement: 1) be prepared to be disturbed by the chasmic socio-economic gap that divides humanity globally; 2) be ready to be in conversation concerning the place of privilege and power those in the north experience; 3) claiming God's hope and refusing fear will lead to risk-taking for the sake of celebrating diversity.

Walter Altmann, in his reflective contribution, is sermonic without being sermonizing. He ingeniously interweaves Psalm 90, allowing the psalmist and Aniceto, an indigenous leader, to both speak. Ruptures are revealed. Wisdom is discerned and distinguished from cleverness. Repentance is called for. Joy erupts. "Our faith and our theology must be human and ecologically responsible" if it is God's incarnate work in the world. This juxtaposition is seamless and challenges the readers not only to prayer and but to action, dangerously so.

Reinhard Hütter offers a careful consideration of the nature and universality of human experience and, with an assist from Thomas Aquinas, demonstrates the indispensability of the virtues of humility and magnanimity for any human life filled with hope, which is to say passionately and openly oriented toward the future. Hütter concludes by drawing on his careful account of experience to show that those who seek after what it might mean to partipate in God's own life would do well to attend to the lives of the saints. For it is the saints who manifest with unique clarity what it means to have lives opened up to the future of divine charity.

Kathleen D. Billman, who has taught alongside Westhelle, reflects on key learnings from both him and their students on the narratological dimensions of faith. In this imaginative telling and listening, alternate meaning can emerge, burgeoning in what Westhelle has defined as "space between spaces." Billman sees this space between space as a space of remembrance, where hope and despair sit side by side. While this essay is an affirmation of the vocation of a seminary teacher, it is also a salute to a dear colleague.

José David Rodríguez' inclusive vision—an inclusivity advanced by multiple contributors in this volume—proffers a prophetic alternative to human dividedness; it is a Pauline vision as revolutionary as Copernicus' marked by mutual respect and ample, salvific space for all ethnicities. Old

Introduction

sins, albeit, continue to blur God's vision, like idealizing or idolizing one culture over another or bowing to the gods of the marketplace. Rodriguez argues for a Spirit-empowered reclamation of "the values of solidarity and equality." His highly contextual essay reflects Westhelle's commitment to orthopraxis—especially with respect to solidarity with the suffering and living together as the community called the church.

And with regard to life together, after a considered investigation into the historical, biblical and political usages of *oikoumenē*, Barbara Rossing's essay registers reservations that might be surprising to readers comfortable with the received connotations of the term. Rossing doubts *oikoumenē* viability for positive ecclesiology. The etymological baggage of empire may be real also in our own context, she indicts: "Any attempt to reclaim or redefine the word *oikoumenē* for the agenda of ecumenism must begin by repudiating the imperial trajectory of the word, including the church's own imperial legacy." Under the encroaching reality of globalization, one application for Rossing may be, in a Westhellian way, to exploit the eschatological dimensions of the *oikoumenē*. Her concluding metaphor is verdant and redemptive, if not for the term, then certainly God's people.

After the final contribution, *Deanna A. Thompson* offers a prayer as a poignant and radical invitation to you and to me to hope for more, to be in fellowship with the creator and the created order even in the face of adversity and the harshest realities.

Vítor rarely uses the word "conclusion." He prefers to use the phrase "in the offing." That is how we would like to come to the end of this theological *churrasco*, this skewer of loving contributions in honor of Vítor—with *saudades*, longing for more.

The table is set. Let us keep the feast!

THEORIA

1

Wrestling for Grace[1]

OSWALD BAYER

In Gen 32:23–32 we hear the story of how Jacob wrestles at the Jabbok, how he wrestles for grace. It is an intensely riveting, immensely dramatic story, a story about a life-and-death battle for recognition—a difficult story that in a subtle, even cryptic fashion speaks about the threat to our life, but—thanks be to God!—also to our salvation.

> The same night [Jacob] arose and took his two wives, his two female servants, and his eleven children, and crossed the ford of the Jabbok. He took them and sent them across the stream, and everything else that he had. And Jacob was left alone. And a man wrestled with him until the breaking of the day. When the man saw that he did not prevail against Jacob, he touched his hip socket, and Jacob's hip was put out of joint as he wrestled with him. Then he said, "Let me go, for the day has broken." But Jacob said, "I will not let you go unless you bless me." And he said to him, "What is your name?" And he said, "Jacob." Then he said, "Your name shall no longer be called Jacob, but Israel [that is, one who fights with God], for you have striven with

---

1. Sermon preached by Oswald Bayer on Gen 32:23–32 at the Cathedral in Ratzeburg on October 8, 2010.

> God and with men, and have prevailed." Then Jacob asked him, "Please tell me your name." But he said, "Why is it that you ask my name?" And there he blessed him. So Jacob called the name of the place Peniel [that is, face of God], saying, "For I have seen God face to face, and yet my life has been delivered." The sun rose upon him as he passed Penuel, limping because of his hip.[2]

It is not a matter of course if we acquire blessing and the sun rises upon us. It is not a matter of course if we do not founder and perish in the dangerous transitions of our life, but are rather preserved and saved.

What we are told about Jacob, the patriarch of Israel, is after all the story of our own life, characterized by more or less threatening and dangerous transitions: out of the narrow cervix into this earthly life under an open sky. Kindergarten, enrollment at school, beginning our working life, marriage, the birth of children, times when life is marked by the death of those closest to us, and whatever other demarcations and transitions we may find in our respectively different life stories, inescapable, unavoidable at any rate is the last transition—crossing the ford, through the water, perhaps at night, perhaps alone. A time when we might become scared and terrified—especially if our past catches up with us, as in the case of Jacob, the deceiver. Especially if there is reason to be afraid that Esau, the deceived brother, will now finally avenge himself, reason to be afraid that your wicked deed will come back like a boomerang, that its curse will turn you into one who is not blessed, but cursed, not someone for whom the sun rises, but for whom it does *not* shine and who plunges into darkness. A time when we might become scared and terrified, "when the foe shall taunt and assail us" (LSB 768, 3), when the great accuser and scaremonger whispers to us: Your life was worthless, it is of no value. Throw it away!

None of us can say that we never have such dark thoughts, that our life is always bright and that we have a cheerful answer to everything. We live in a world that is not devoid of deception and fear, not without threats, torture, murder, terror, and war. We live in a world where we cannot escape the question Wolfgang Borchert asks in "The Man Outside" as he returns from the eastern front into a bomb-gutted Hamburg: "Were you loving in Stalingrad, dear loving God, were you loving then, huh?"

In the place of God's clear love and grace, in the place of the bright sun of his mercy, a dark, mute, implacable fate seems to prevail instead. Not a person, whom you could address by name, but a nameless thing. And it's not something I can ignore—it bothers me, badgers me, afflicts me, attacks me. "And a man wrestled with him." Jacob doesn't know *who* it is. Yet it is

---

2. This and all following Scripture quotations are taken from the ESV.

precisely this uncertainty and namelessness that is unbearable. Just who is this enemy that attacks me? Attacks me with *external* tribulations, blows of fate, with hostilities, harassments, character assassination? Or with *internal* "Anfechtungen," with the guilt and burden of my own past and the fear of my own future? Or is it—in, with, and under these external and internal hostilities—the destroyer of life, that is, the devil? Or is it God himself, who, as it seems sometimes, does not let his face shine on me, but hides it from me, does not hear me, does not answer me, does not help?

What to do? Lay down my weapons? Give up? Do I become hardened? Mute? Depressed or frivolous? Jacob knows that it's all or nothing; he goes for broke: If I perish, I perish; but first I want to fight for my life, defend myself. Jacob wrestles against curse and damnation, wrestles for grace, for blessing; he wrestles for these things in desperate defiance and wrings a blessing from his enemy: "I will not let you go unless you bless me." If you will not bless me, if you will not turn your face to me, if you will not give me courage and strength, then I am done for. This Jacob is *wrestling* with a terrible power; he does not let go of his enemy, but simultaneously he completely surrenders to him: If you will only bless me! For without you I am nothing. As Jochen Klepper writes in his hymn, "Without God I am a fish on land, without God a droplet in the heat. Without God I am just grass in sand and a bird whose wings no longer beat. When God calls me by my own name here I am water, fire, earth and air.[3]"

Jacob *is* called by God by his own name; he *is* blessed; God has let himself be coerced. How can this be? How can the omnipotent God let himself be defeated by a powerless, mortal human being—like Jesus finally conceded defeat to the impudence and quick-wittedness of the Syrophoenician woman? Let us make this as clear as possible to ourselves by recalling our Baptism.

In Baptism, God has promised himself into our power, has delivered himself into the Word of his pledge: "I am with you always: In my goodness I will give you whatever you need; in my mercy I deliver you out of all your troubles!" And now God stands in the Word; he wants to be taken at his Word, this pledge: "You have said, 'Seek my face.' My heart says to you, 'Your face, LORD, do I seek'" (Psalm 27:8). We may, yes, we should grasp God at his pledge, appeal to it, whenever we have to wrestle with him, whenever he—and with him the whole world and our own heart—becomes dark to us in the transitions, in the crises of our life, whenever he hides his face from us, "nor to thy supplication an answering voice be found" (TLH 520,9). It is then, yes, then that we should, that we may under no circumstances give

---

3. Translator's own attempt at an English rendition of the German hymn.

in and abandon ourselves to resignation and tiredness of life, but must put up resistance —with precisely that weapon, which God in Baptism himself placed into our hands, or more precisely, into our ears and hearts: with his promise to be there, to encompass you on all sides with his protection and to hold you in the palm of his hand, in short: with his promise to bless you.

God gave us this promise when we were baptized in his name. He "delivered" (Col 1:13) us from all darkness and all uncertainty and transferred us into his triune fellowship; he rescued us from the jaws of fear and wrapped us up in his mercy; he called us by our name, made us to be unmistakably individual people, by setting us in his presence, calling to us and pledging us to himself by his triune name, with the name that we may call on in joy and sorrow, the name by which he assuredly lets himself be found.

We can do nothing better than to remember this pledge in all the vicissitudes of our life—not least in the dark hours when we cross the ford, at night—to take hold of it, to defend ourselves with it against everything that assails us, to cling to it and believe with it and to hope that no life is futile or plunges into oblivion, but that the sun rises for every man and woman, even if we limp because of our hips. Then we can sing—like Jonah from out of the belly of the fish: "I praise my God, who brings me up from the depths that I may live." Amen.

— Translated by Karl Böhmer

2

Did Luther's Students Hide the Hidden God?
Deus Absconditus among Luther's First Followers

ROBERT KOLB

IN HIS *THE SCANDALOUS God* Vítor Westhelle begins with a discussion of "the evasions of the scandal," an exploration of ways in which contemporary theologians strive to evade and escape the scandal of Christ's cross.[1] Such attempts to sidestep or ignore the implications of Luther's *theologia crucis* did not begin in this generation. The opinion has sometimes been expressed that "Luther's followers in the sixteenth century very seldom talked about their theology as a theology of the cross, and they preserved this new orientation for addressing theological topics only partially."[2] Luther's distinction of the Hidden and Revealed God provides one critical point on which the more important, second, part of this observation may be tested.

Since *theologia crucis* became a standard topic for Luther research approximately a century ago, at least five distinct, though related, aspects of this hermeneutical approach of the Wittenberg reformer have become clear. The cross as the burden which aids believers in "crucifying their

---

1. Westhelle, *Scandalous God*, 3–15.
2. Kolb, "Luther on the Theology of the Cross," 444.

flesh," especially in the course of practicing their earthly callings,[3] became enshrined as a topic in Philip Melanchthon's *Loci communes*.[4] The cross as the suffering of the church and its members under the continuing assault of Satan's deceiving in his eschatological battle against God's truth (John 8:44) drifted into some obscurity although it remained prominent in second generation, "Late Reformation" Lutheran thinking.[5] Luther's treatment of God's method of atoning for human sin and reconciling his chosen people to himself through the "weak and foolish" (1 Cor 1:18–25) means of Christ's death and resurrection,[6] remained a standard component of later Lutheran dogmatics, though since the nineteenth century much debated and disputed.[7] Though the "weak and foolish" epistemology of faith or trust in the Crucified and Risen One and in his Word—in contrast to human reason— was still regarded as paradigmatic it was not always with emphasis on the weakness and foolishness of the method and its message. Dialogue with opponents of the Lutheran confession, within and outside Christendom, required resorting to rational argument and philosophical logic. Perhaps the most fragile part of Luther's original "theology of the cross," a centerpiece of the Heidelberg Theses which in 1518 launched the concept, was the distinction of the hidden from the revealed God (*Deus absconditus/revelatus*).[8] It functioned as Luther's theodicy, or better yet, as his refusal to indulge in justifying God, a kind of anti-theodicy. Westhelle comments, "It is a way of stopping at the point where reason wants to take over and explain faith away... If it comes to it, it is better to blame God, this hidden and ineffable God (*deus absconditus*), than to try to account for God's ways, to justify God."[9] To quote Klaus Schwarzwäller, in the reformer's most extensive treatment of the Hidden and Revealed God, his *On Bound Choice* [*De servo arbitrio*], "Luther stops at the boundary that God's Godness draws... he surrenders himself completely to the God that meets him there."[10] This is Luther's means of resisting the temptation to exercise control oneself, his way of letting God be God, a hard task for theologians in all ages.

---

3. Wingren, *Luther on Vocation*, 50–63.

4. *Corpus Reformatorum*, Bretschneider et al. [henceforth CR], 21:528–36 (2nd ed.) and 934–55 (3rd ed.).

5. Leppin, *Antichrist und Jüngster Tag*, 206–63.

6. Kolb, "Resurrection and Justification, 39–60.

7. Forde, *Law-Gospel Debate*, 3–134.

8. Cf. Forde, *On Being a Theologian of the Cross*, 69–95.

9. Westhelle, *Scandalous God*, 53–54.

10. *Theologia cruces*, 160.

Part of the problem that scholars encounter when they assess Luther's "hidden God" comes from his imprecise usage of the term. He did not know that he was setting forth hermeneutical principles that would be used half a millennium later. Sometimes "the hidden God" refers to the Creator who is beyond the grasp of creatures, particularly sinful human creatures; this Hiddenness embraces those aspects of God that simply cannot be comprehended by human creatures. Some facets of this Hiddenness lie totally outside the realm of human perception; other facets appear on human horizons, usually as terrifying, inexplicable, threatening: the ugly God who does not correspond to his revealed promises and to human expectations for a good God. Sometimes Luther uses the term in another way, however: for the god refashioned "in our own image" that sinners substitute for the true God. However, in a third sense Luther also describes as "hidden" the ways in which God's revelation in Jesus Christ and in Scripture do not appear obvious but rather seems "weak and foolish" to "reasonable" expectations of human beings. God comes *sub contrario*, "under the appearance of the opposite [of his gracious intentions]."

The true test of a Lutheran doctrine takes place in the sermon: can the idea be preached? Luther himself advanced his *theologia crucis* originally in academic theses for disputation,[11] but it appeared in other genres, including biblical commentary.[12] Early on, a month before the Heidelberg disputation, March 17, 1518, Luther experimented with thoughts of the Hidden and Revealed God in a sermon on John 9, specifically on Jesus' explanation that the blind man suffered blindness not because of his own or his parents' sin but "to reveal the glory of God." Luther called his sermon "foolish" and thanked God for making him this kind of fool. Christ makes blind all who see, he concluded; all the wise and clever he makes foolish. Only from Christ, "our righteous, faithful God," do we receive light and illumination. Without using the term, he made hearers dependent on the Revealed God, not on their own conceptions of "power, skill, wisdom, righteousness, holiness, purity, etc." "God turns everything on its head." He regards those who appear wise and powerful to the world as an abomination but embraces instead those who recognize their ignorance and sin.[13]

The sermon continued: Christ himself had emptied himself and taken on the form of a servant, dying in obedience to his Father (Phlm 2:5–8). Christ came, not as God nor as Lucifer, who sought to refashion himself into God's image, nor as some great human personage; he came as "a fool,

---

11. WA 1:353–74, LW AE 31:39–70.
12. WA 40,3:9–475; see Kolb, "Luther's Theology of the Cross," 69–85.
13. "Zwei deutsche Fastenpredigten," WA 1:267,4–268,18.

mocked, despised, ridiculed by the entire people, bearing all our misfortune ... so that we might follow him freely."[14] Luther played on the allegorical possibilities of any story of a blind person by identifying the man in this story with every sinner, who is blind and cannot see God in his hidden holiness. After citing Augustine's observation that the devil said that Adam's transgression had opened human eyes to good and evil, Luther shifted to dealing with the Hidden God who terrifies: he concluded that the eye that must be torn out (Matt 5:29) is the eye that views itself as abandoned by God. Believing eyes perceive God's presence and love behind and despite the experiences that reason views as evil, the experience of the cross, which is "God's reliquary," "his last will and testament." For God brings his people near to him by sending them "disaster, tragedy, fear, cares, troubles, poverty, opposition, ... sickness ... and at the end of life the devil, in the final struggle, who will plague you unceasingly and terrify you so greatly that you have to despair." That, Luther concluded, is the way God works.[15]

Several of Luther's early followers treated this passage in commentaries published to aid pastors in preaching to their people. They envisaged these printed works as tools for busy parish preachers in their preparation for regular pulpit duties.

Johannes Brenz (1499-1570), reformer of Schwäbisch Hall and later in Württemberg, had heard Luther in Heidelberg in 1518. He never studied in Wittenberg but knew Luther's and Melanchthon's works well and supported their cause enthusiastically while remaining a somewhat independent thinker. His commentary on John 9, however, came rather close to Luther's concept of the *Deus Absconditus*. The disciples' questions called Job's friends to Brenz's mind.[16] However, Brenz did not deny God's punishment for sin. With an argument against the sinlessness of infants, probably reflecting engagements with Anabaptists, he maintained the propriety of punishment even for children's sins, recalling the threat of the visitation of sins to the third and fourth generation in the Decalogue (Exod 20:5). Nonetheless, afflictions can also manifest God's way of working, as was the case with Job. Whoever rejects the cross impatiently is rejecting God's glory, Brenz concluded. Therefore, "if I am the most rejected and powerless person possible and am afflicted with the cross, I will suffer the offense in my rejection and most despicable death," and through it I will see the light of the world in the cross. For Christ is present in his person and as the Word of God. In his

14. WA 1:268,39–269,20.
15. WA 1:269,24–271,40.
16. In his commentary on Job, *Hiob cum piis et evditis*, e.g., 14b–15b, 45b–52a, 295b–297a, 311b–331b, Brenz confronts the mystery of the evils that befall the people of God and affirms God's presence and his use of evil to test and strengthen faith.

light and from his Word believers can "pass from death, sin, and every misfortune into righteousness, life, and every heavenly blessing."[17] Although he adopted other elements in Luther's *De servo arbitrio*,[18] Brenz did not employ Luther's terminology of the Hidden and Revealed God, but he led readers at this passage to confront God's mysterious ways of acting, albeit without mentioning the scandal that it causes to human reason.

Erasmus Sarcerius (1501–1559), at the time court preacher in Nassau-Dillenberg, found Jesus' disciples typical of those who associate suffering with punishment for sin, like Brenz comparing them to Job's friends. Instead, Jesus had explained that this man's blindness was designed to glorify God, demonstrating to the pious the power and ultimate triumph of their liberation through Christ's cross. The impious do receive suffering as punishment for their sin, but not the pious. They sometimes suffer to give God glory and manifest his working and power.[19] Sarcerius did not go further, presenting the Hidden God, who works *sub contrario*. He did not try to explain how or why God works in this way. He tamed but did not obliterate Luther's approach to the text.

Luther's Wittenberg student and colleague Caspar Cruciger (1504–1548) treated this passage, beginning with the affirmation that calamities are not all punishments of sins. Indeed, the Decalogue threatens to visit the sins of parents upon their descendants (Exod 20:5-6, Deut 5: 9-10), but Ezekiel 38:1-9 promises liberation from the curse through repentance. Indeed, calamities in general stem from the sin of the first parents. The world's contempt for God and the devil's rabid savagery threaten especially the church. And "God wants our recognition of our infirmity to grow and to draw forth our faithfulness to him; he wishes to arouse our invocation of God" through suffering. Afflictions also testify to our immortality and future glory, as well as to God's teaching. Through them "we become like the image of the children of God: Abel, Isaac, Isaiah, Jeremiah, John the Baptist were types of Christ." Afflictions can indeed also be punishments for certain sins. Often, however, they show that the obedience of the saints is performed because of God and that the church's protection lies in God's, not human, hands.[20] Cruciger used the example of Job to demonstrate

---

17. *In D. Iohannis Evangelion . . . Exegesis*, 171b–173a.

18. *In D. Iohannis Evangelion . . . Exegesis*, 106b, [John 6:29], 195a, [10:14–15], 255a [15:5], 244b [14:17], 268a–b [14:2], 265a–266b [15.2], 274a–275a [15:16]. Cf. Brecht, *Die frühe Theologie*, 169–70, 199–201, 213–14, 238.

19. *In Ioannem Evangelistam*, 383.

20. *In evangelivm Iohannis*, 429–35. Although sometimes attributed to Melanchthon, this commentary was composed by Cruciger, see Wengert, "Caspar Cruciger," 417–41.

that God does act through evils to elicit prayer and faith and to show his glory. Though not so direct in describing the evils that befall believers, and without describing God's hiddenness, Cruciger helped readers confront the mystery of God's way of working without venturing excuses or explanations for why he works "contrary to human wisdom." It is sufficient that he gives consolation through Christ.[21] Cruciger, like Brenz and Sarcerius, preserved something of Luther's willingness to confront the scandal of God's presence in the midst of evil.

In his expression of despair over confronting the Hidden God and his way of doing things, particularly in connection with the election of the faithful, in *De servo arbitrio*, Luther turned to Romans 11:33–36, with its acclamation of God's wisdom and inscrutability, as he stepped back from trying to fathom the depths of God's way of working.[22] In his lectures on Genesis, in his last decade, the Wittenberg professor applied this passage to those situations, historical and contemporary, in which believers experience evil but in which they should nonetheless be confident that God is present with them, sometimes for reasons totally unfathomable to the faithful.[23] His sermon on the epistle for Trinity Sunday of May 27, 1537, nearly two decades after the Heidelberg Disputation, his most detailed exposition of this passage, confronted the grandeur of God's revelation of Christ but did not explicitly address the mystery of human suffering and believers' experience of evil. This sermon spoke of the inaccessibility of God's inner essence to human reason, apart from whatever the Holy Spirit reveals. Human reason dare not be abused by presuming to seek more knowledge than is found in God's Word or to peer into God's secret plan for salvation in Christ.[24]

Melanchthon's first commentary on Romans, 1523, identified the rhetorical function of Romans 11:33–36 as an *exclamatio*, indeed an *admiratio*, praising God for gospel of justification by grace through faith. He did not venture into the larger mysteries of the Hidden God.[25] In his reworked 1532 commentary Melanchthon explained that in this passage God was reining in human arrogance and the attempt to master God's counsels with human reasoning. The apostle admonished readers not to apostatize but rather to acknowledge God's wrath, as seen in the rejection of peoples, and his

---

21. Ibid., 435–43.

22. WA 18:784,6–785,38, LW AE 33:289–92.

23. WA 43:395,8–22, LW AE 4:358; WA 43:72,37–73,9, LW AE 3:276; WA 44:637,18–30, LW AE 8:79.

24. WA 21:509,6–30, 511,18–512,2, 518,6–520,20. See Kolb, "Unsearchable Judgments of God," 30–49.

25. CR 15:484–85.

mercy, in disseminating his Word throughout the world.[26] Melanchthon's final comment on Romans, in 1556, again celebrated the wonders of God's promise but it also confronted the question of why so few are saved, why the church is "dissipated" and oppressed, why the impious enjoy glory, riches, virtue, wisdom, etc. Here Melanchthon reflected the struggles of his later years in bowing before the mysteries of evil, clearly affirming the inability of human reason to answer such questions, while directing readers to the revealed Word of God. He strongly rejected any attempts to enter into the labyrinths of disputation where one becomes prey for the devil's machinations. Instead, believers turn to God in prayer.[27]

Echoing Melanchthon, Sarcerius asserted that the height of the riches of God's wisdom and knowledge destroyed the conviction of human reason and fleshly wisdom that works and their merits can justify sinners and win them forgiveness of sins. Human reason depends on the Holy Spirit to acquaint it with God's wisdom (1 Cor 2:6–16).[28] Sarcerius defined justification by faith as the theme of the entire epistle and in this case avoided any real development of the hiddenness of God while focusing on the impossibility of human reason to grasp God's grace in justifying sinners.

Johannes Brenz recognized that Romans 11:33–36 constituted the climax of Paul's lament over the apostasy of his own people in Romans 9–11. Indeed, God was able to reveal his mercy to all through his concluding all under sin (Rom 11:32), and that demonstrates his almighty power. Nonetheless, presumptuous questions over God's mysterious plan for dealing with sinners have no place. Believers avoid questions about the salvation of some and not others, or about why God sent his Son to the cross when he could have accomplished salvation in other ways, or why he did not reveal himself through miracles alone, or even why he has plants grow slowly and at different tempos instead of having them produce their fruits at once. But particularly the question of why Caiaphas remained unconverted and the heathen were coming to Christ vexed Paul and all believers. Only acknowledging God's majesty and glory, as Paul did, appropriately reacts to these questions,[29] Brenz then turned to the Revealed God, without using the term, and praised God's plan for salvation in Christ and his sending the Holy Spirit

---

26. CR 15:701–702, cf. the translation of the 1540 revision of the 1532 text, *Commentary on Romans*. Translated by Fred Kramer. 2nd ed., Saint Louis: Concordia, 2010. 208.

27. CR 15:997–98.

28. *In epistolam ad Romanos*, x4a–x8a.

29. *Erklerung der Epistel S. Pauli*, 726–31.

to reveal him. For him this served as sufficient answer to such questions for those who recognized the depths of the riches of God's wisdom.[30]

Cyriakus Spangenberg (1528-1604), son of the reformer of Nordhausen, Johann Spangenberg, and a devoted disciple of Luther, was pastor in Mansfeld when he preached a long series of sermons on Romans in the 1560s. He defended Luther's teaching on the bound will and the election of those whom the Holy Spirit would make the faithful as the reformer had developed his views in his *De servo arbitrio*.

Spangenberg turned his sermons on Romans into a commentary on the epistle. There he recognized the context for the closing verses of Romans 11 in Paul's struggling with Jewish failure to acknowledge Jesus as the Messiah, but he connected the question of why God placed this fate upon his chosen people with the ultimate theodical question, why God permitted the snake to deceive Eve, and other questions that defy answering (in much the same manner as Brenz had): why the Almighty God concluded that his Son must be sent to the cross when he could have saved sinners in other ways; why God did not send his Son while Adam still was living; why God did not make Jesus more attractive to the world; why he has plants grow as they do. Reason wracks its brain over such questions, without result. Spangenberg chose to focus on God's mercy in sending Christ to save sinners.[31] At great length, with aid from numerous Bible passages, from Jesus Syrach and the Wisdom of Solomon, and from Ambrose, Gregory the Great, and Theodoret, Spangenberg exulted in the riches of God's wisdom, particularly in his plan to redeem his chosen people, while insisting that God's counsels and plans lie far beyond human reason's ability to comprehend.[32] This sermonic exposition of Romans 11 concentrated on the question of God's predestination of the elect. Like Luther, Spangenberg refused to give an answer; unlike Luther, he did not wrestle with the scandal but simply submitted to the wise but inscrutable counsel of God.

Lectures at the University of Jena provided the setting for Tileman Heshusius's (1527-1588) comment on Romans, published in 1571. In this passage, according to Heshusius, Paul broke off his "disputation concerning God's gracious election and justification of human beings through faith." He admonished readers to refrain from seeking answers regarding the divine majesty outside the revealed Word of God and to avoid asking why God rejected Saul, Joash, and Judas, why he loved Jacob and hated Esau, why he permitted the Gentiles to go so long without the gospel, why the impious

---

30. Ibid., 731-33.
31. *Auslegung der Letsten*, FFf1a-FFf2a.
32. Ibid., FFf2a-GGg1a.

prosper, why the devil can act rabidly. Heshusius insisted on a strict distinction between what God has revealed and what he holds secret and argued against a concept of contradictory wills in God.[33] Heshusius distinguished God's revelation from what he had not revealed but restricted his discussion of what he hides from human beings to the core theodical questions, evading pressing existential questions and not struggling in Luther's manner with the questions of how evil can exist and why some are elect and others not.

In contrast to these others in the Wittenberg circle, Johannes Wigand (1523–1587), at the time bishop of Pomesian in Prussia, published his commentary on Romans in 1580. He pointed to the "mystery of the gracious reception no human being could invent but God himself has revealed to us" in Christ on the basis of Romans 11:33–36 but did not venture near addressing the confounding mystery of how God works *sub contrario* at this passage.

Wigand illustrates the phenomenon of those who strove to be faithful to their Wittenberg mentor but who chose selectively what they could put to use in any given instance. Luther himself, of course, did not use the distinction of the Hidden and Revealed God at every turn in his writings, and in the selected focal points for this brief study, his disciples employed the distinction in various ways. Some did indeed confront the theodical dilemmas posed by daily life and by theological rumination. When, for instance, Brenz, Spangenberg, and Heshusius did, they followed Luther in turning the attention of their readers immediately from the mysterious presence of God beyond their explanation to focus on the Revealed God, in Jesus Christ. In this way they demonstrated one aspect of Luther's abiding influence, the usefulness of his bold confrontation with the mysteries of God's working *sub contrario* in the midst of the eschatological assaults on his people.

BIBLIOGRAPHY

Brecht, Martin. *Die frühe Theologie des Johannes Brenz*. Tübingen: Mohr/Siebeck, 1966.
Brenz, Johannes. *Erklerung der Epistel S. Pauls an die Ro[e]mer/ Erst/ mals durch den Ehrwirdigen Herrn Johan Bren/tzen/Probst yu Studgarten/ in Latein aussgan/gen/ Vnd jetzunder in die Deudsche Sprach gebracht/ Durch Jacobum Grettern/Dienern der Kirchen yu Schwa[e]bischen Hall*. Translated by Jacob Gretter. Frankfurt: Peter Brubach, 1566.
———. *Hiob cum piis et evditis . . . comentarijs, ad Hebraicam ueritatem ita translates, ut nulla porrò obscuritas Lectorem poßit offendere*. Hagenau: Johann Secer, 1527.

33. *Explicatio epistolae Pavli*, Aaa1a–Aaa2a.

———. *In D. Iohannis Evangelion, Ioannis Brentij Exegesis, per authorem iam primum diligenter reuisa, ac multis in locis locupletata*, 2. ed., Hagenau: Johannes Secer, 1530.
Forde, Gerhard O. *On Being a Theologian of the Cross: Reflections on Luther's Heidelberg Disputation 1518*. Grand Rapids: Eerdmans, 1997.
———. *The Law-Gospel Debate: An Interpretation of Its Historical Development*. Minneapolis: Augsburg, 1969.
Heshusius, Tileman. *Explicatio epistolae Pavli ad Romanos*. Jena: Güünther Hüttich, 1571.
Kolb, Robert. "Luther on the Theology of the Cross." *Lutheran Quarterly* 16 (2002) 444.
———. "Luther's Theology of the Cross Fifteen Years after Heidelberg: Luther's Lectures on the Psalms of Ascent." *Journal of Ecclesiastical History* 61 (2010) 69–85.
———. "Resurrection and Justification: Luther's Use of Romans 4,25." *Lutherjahrbuch* 78 (2011) 39–60.
———. "The Unsearchable Judgments of God: Luther's Uses of Romans 11,33–36." *Luther-Bulletin, Tijdschrift voor interconfessioneel Lutheronderzoek* 15 (2006) 30–49.
Leppin, Volker. *Antichrist und Jüngster Tag. Das Profil apokalyptischer Flugschriftenpublizistik im deutschen Luthertum 1548-1618*. Gütersloh: Gütersloher, 1999.
Luther, Martin. *Luther's Works*. Vol. 3. Edited by Jaroslav Pelikan. Saint Louis: Concordia, 1995.
———. *Luther's Works*. Vol. 4. Edited by Jaroslav Pelikan. Saint Louis: Concordia, 1995.
———. *Luther's Works*. Vol. 8. Edited by Jaroslav Pelikan. Saint Louis: Concordia, 1995.
———. *Luther's Works*. Vol 31. Edited by Harold J. Grimm. Philadelphia: Fortress, 1957.
———. *Luther's Works*. Vol 33. Edited by Harold J. Grimm. Philadelphia: Fortress, 1957.
Melanchthon, Philip. *Commentary on Romans*. Translated by Fred Kramer. 2nd ed., Saint Louis: Concordia, 2010.
Sarcerius, Erasmus. *In epistolam ad Romanos, pia & erudite scholia, pro Rhethorica dispositio, ad perpetuum coherentiae filum, conscripta*. Frankfurt: Christoph Egenolph, 1541.
———. *In evangelivm Iohannis Apostoli Enarratio*. Strassburg: Crato Mylius, 1546.
———. *In Ioannem Evangelistam ivsta Scholia summa diligentia, ad perpetum textus cohaerentiae filum*. Basel: Bartholomäus Westheimer, 1540.
Schwarzwäller, Klaus. *Theologia cruces: Luthers Lehre von Prädestination nach De servo arbitrio, 1525*. Munich: Kaiser, 1970.
Spangenberg, Cyriakus. *Auslegung der Letsten Acht Capitel der Episteln S. PAVLI an die Ro[e]mer*. Strassburg, 1569.
Wengert, Timothy J. "Caspar Cruciger (1504–1548): The Case of the Disappearing Reformer." *Sixteenth Century Journal* 20 (1989) 417–41.
Westhelle, Vítor. *The Scandalous God: The Use and Abuse of the Cross*. Minneapolis: Fortress, 2006.
Wingren, Gustaf. *Luther on Vocation*. Translated by Carl C. Rasmussen. Philadelphia: Muehlenberg, 1957.

3

The Dynamics of Secularization, Atheism and the So-called Return of Religion and Its Significance for the Public Understanding of Science and Religion

Some European Perspectives[1]

ANTJE JACKELÉN

EUROPE AND THE DYNAMICS OF RELIGION AND ATHEISM

Europe's history is marked by linguistic, cultural and religious diversity. The collective term "the Christian West" does not do justice to that fact. The

---

1. Text from a lecture given for the Paul Wattson Lecture series at the University of San Francisco on February 27, 2012.

past fifty years have brought significant changes to the scene of European diversity. The ongoing process of European integration has brought different cultures closer to each other. Exchange programs have increased the awareness of national and cultural diversity. Migration puts pressure on the development of integration programs while at the same time exposing discomforting levels of xenophobia in modern well-to-do societies.

In this situation, two trends in the religious world have been causing debate—secularization on the one hand and the so-called return of religion or God on the other hand. In Sweden, people had become used to secularization expressing itself mainly as indifference toward religious questions and rites. However, in recent years, like elsewhere, even Sweden has seen the rise of a more self-conscious atheism. It is articulated by a vocal—sometimes aggressively vocal—minority. With the "return of God" (the new visibility of religion) and the new atheism, two apparently opposite trends operate at the same time. Nevertheless, they are part of one and the same dynamic.

The interplay of the return of religion and the atheist crusade—to borrow *Der Spiegel*'s[2] words—creates challenges, especially for philosophers, theologians and sociologists interested in trans-disciplinary research and dialogue. On the one hand, we see a growing interest in existential and religious questions, often combined with a great deal of ignorance in religious matters; in both Eastern and Western Europe there are whole generations that for different reasons have grown up in religious alienation. On the other hand, we are seeing new vitriolic attacks on religion. Compared to much of the classic critique of religion these new attempts often lack in acuity and depth of thought. However, what they lack in intellectual rigor, they tend to compensate with prophetic zeal. The arguments used often boil down to a description of religion and believers as being irrational and prone to violence in their behavior, simplistic and dogmatic in their worldview. A rather funny generalization, at least from a perspective of a bishop in the Church of Sweden to which an average of 70 per cent of Swedes belong, is Richard Dawkins statement in an interview with the Star Tribune in Minneapolis. When he was asked, "Imagine for us a world without religion. What does it look like?" he responded: "Perhaps it would look like modern-day Sweden."[3]

---

2. In a special issue entitled "Weltmacht Religion. Wie der Glaube Politik und Gesellschaft beeinflusst" ("World Power Religion: How Faith Influences Politics and Society"), *Spiegel* again addressed the theme of religion. This time, the cover story read "'Gott ist an allem schuld!' Der Kreuzzug der neuen Atheisten" ("'God is to blame for everything!' The crusade of the new atheists.")

3. Miller, "Dawkins."

AN EXCURSION: THE DYNAMICS VIEWED THROUGH THE LENS OF CONTEMPORARY LITERATURE

Novels often prove helpful in understanding shifts and motifs in cultural developments. Even though a glance at one example cannot be used for a systematic argument, I think it provides some useful insights.

Brazilian writer Paulo Coelho's books have been on top of bestseller lists in many countries. Spirituality plays an important role in his writings. His novels often come across as a plea for a spirituality released from formal religion. He likes to set up his stories in Europe and he has a special taste for journeys in general and unusual pilgrimages in particular. Many of his main characters are exposed to encounters with the desert and in the desert as well as to significant dreams. Coelho's fans praise his ability to open up for existential questions. Some liken him to a midwife assisting with an initiation—somebody who helps readers encounter the sublime inside themselves. Others admire the way he shapes the interplay of facts and magic. Nevertheless, as so often, that which looks original, smart, deep, and inspiring to the admirers is simple nonsense in the eyes of the critic.

Coelho's international breakthrough came with *The Alchemist*. Dreams, signs, and legends are weaved together in a rather innocent way in that book. In a more recent book, *The Witch of Portobello* (2006, English 2007), he goes much further in presenting a full-blown alternative spirituality. The main character is born in Sibiu, Transylvania (Romania) by a Roma mother. She is adopted by a wealthy Lebanese couple. After her childhood in Lebanon she comes to London as a refugee. Well-established there, she works as a real estate broker in the Middle Eastern desert landscape. Athena, as she calls herself, is a pilgrim, however of a very special kind. As a believer she is rejected by the established church: she is excommunicated by the Roman Catholic Church when she gets divorced. The gifted young woman slides into what goes by the term witchcraft: dancing sessions leading to trance, dramatic initiation rites, clairvoyance, and a meshing of identity with the so-called 'great mother.' There is a severe critique of established religion, in this case of Christianity. Established religion comes across as rigid and dogmatic. It is a lot more about being against than about being for: affirming things and people. In *The Witch of Portobello*, traditional religion is portrayed as both intellectually and spiritually dissatisfying. It is anti-intellectual because it clings to traditions that mirror worldviews from a time long past. It is anti-spiritual because it suffocates genuine spiritual hunger with pre-determined and licensed patterns. Witchcraft thus presents itself as a good way out—a way to freedom beyond all rational and spiritual straitjackets.

Coelho confronts us with the European wrestling with its own intellectual and spiritual heritage. His critique of religion overlaps in parts with the critique of Richard Dawkins and others. There is one decisive difference, though. Whereas Dawkins dismisses all kinds of religiosity as equally dangerous and unnecessary, Coelho urges his readers to think seriously about spiritual needs and desires.

If Coelho has caught the gist of the European struggle with its rational and its spiritual heritage appropriately, this has some bearing on the religion-and-science dialogue. So far, the main ambition of religion-and-science dialogue has been to make things intellectually fit. Much energy is invested in the effort of finding a coherent and adequate language that does justice to the progress of science, while at the same time allowing for the communication of a religious worldview, and rightly so. Yet, in light of Coelho's authorship, we may have to acknowledge that making things intellectually fit is necessary, but not sufficient. In the end, intellectual coherence will only reach halfway.

People want and need to see that things fit spiritually, too. This is a hard challenge to meet, however. It is easy to err, both on the side of spirituality and on the side of rationality and thus to build in distortions of science or religion or even of both from the very beginning. Fritjof Capra and Dana Zohar on the side of spirituality and Richard Dawkins as well as Daniel Dennett on the side of rationality may serve as examples here. The latter operate within a rather peculiar paradigm, where the level of defeat of religion serves as an indicator of the progress of cultural evolution in humankind. None of this would appeal to Athena, that is, to an intelligent, well-educated person in search of wholeness, providing space for both, rationality and spirituality and allowing philosophy, science and theology to cross-fertilize.

It is indeed difficult to do justice to the full integrity of both rationality and spirituality. However, the situation is not hopeless. Even though emphasis has been on the intellectual perspective, the last thirty years of dialogue between religion and science have also generated concepts and models that have the potential of making things fit not only intellectually but even spiritually. I see that potential, for example, in Philip Hefner's concept of the created co-creator and in Ted Peters' and Martinez Hewlett's attempt to develop a theology of evolution that can serve not only as an effective rebuttal of Intelligent Design and creationism, but also as a catalyst of hope.

In days to come, the dialogue between religion and science must become both intellectually and spiritually fit in ways that surpass what we have so far. In order to make a difference, this dialogue must be vital in the academic world, but it must reach out beyond academia into the public spaces of church and society.

If Coelho's characters are the typical seekers of our time, we need to be able to address individuals who are well-educated, who wish to live independent of authoritarian structures, who are skeptical of pure rationality, and whose prime criterion of truth is "what feels right for me." In Søren Kierkegaard's characterization of stages, these are people who belong to the aesthetic stage—a level that is respectable in itself, but falls short of reaching the ethical and the religious stages.

People like Athena have developed a deep skepticism of both the radically rational and the radical secular. Often, they are also deeply unconvinced of what they perceive as traditional religion. Since they have not reached the ethical stage yet, they open the doors widely for irrationality—which is why we see in Coelho the victory of alchemy over chemistry, magic over physics, astrology over astronomy, and phrenology over physiology.

SECULARIZATION

These observations suggest that neither secularization nor its opposite are unequivocal phenomena. Simple theories of secularization have proven wrong. It is not true that where modernization goes in, religion must go out. And each and every step forward for science and technology is not a step back for faith. The relationship between secularization and modernization needs to be revisited.

Such revisiting will have to include some creative thinking about the public, personal, and private character of religion. In secularized societies such as Sweden, religion is often declared to be private and nothing but private. In fact, the privacy of religion is looked upon as a condition for public democratic consensus. The underlying assumption is that religion kept behind the locked doors of a private home is fine, but religion that slips out into the public square causes trouble and would be a threat to democratic freedom.

In the light of the developments of the past thirty years or so, the privacy position seems rather outmoded. We have been seeing a deprivatization of religion instead. In part, this is a consequence of migration and globalization: religion becomes more visible as a marker of ethnic and cultural identities. Today, we can see processes of deterritorialization of religion and a growing global denominationalism.[4] The consequences of the rule *cuius regio eius religio* of the 1555 Augsburg peace, according to which the sovereign of a region had the power to decide the religious affiliation of all its

---

4. Casanova, "Political Challenges."

inhabitants, have become exceedingly blurred. It is only now that religious denominations go really global.

The new visibility of religion has called into question one of the creeds of modernity—that the modern is inextricably linked with secularization. Secularization led to a critique, a weakening and sometimes the abolishing of authoritarian structures. It brought about the end of the Constantinian époque for the church. However, it also paved the way for a post-secular understanding of modernity in which the return of religion may be more significant than the breakdown of ecclesial structures.

THE NEW ATHEISM

In Sweden, the atheist association some years ago shifted name to "The Humanists" —suggesting that atheism is the authentic face of humanism. Apart from the confusion and frustration this creates for other associations devoted to the ideas of humanism in its traditional sense, these humanists practice a rather eclectic reading of tradition. One is not surprised to find that their list of famous names in the history of humanism omits Erasmus and Philip Melanchthon, for example, but mentions Bertrand Russell and Richard Dawkins.

This narrow (at best) and distorting (at worst) interpretation of humanism relates to an equally narrow or distorting understanding of religious faith. It tends to neglect the overlap between a humanist and Christian agenda that has existed for centuries. Christians have always been able to support large parts of the ideas and programs of humanism. For a long time, it has been fully possible to be a humanist and a non-believer as well as to be a humanist and a believer. In line with a more traditional understanding of humanism, I argue that Christianity and humanism in fact need each other for the sake of their own vitality. Humanism will remind Christianity of its need to relate to the universally human—a reminder that Christianity can never be an affair for insiders only. Christianity will insist that concentration on the human, even the universally human, will end up in a blind alley, if it degenerates into human navel-gazing, oblivious of the rest of nature/creation.

Policy statements of the Humanists reveal a strong belief in reason, particularly in reason opposed to faith. The corollary of this fundamental belief is the assumption of strong friendship between humanism, science and technology. This in turn means, in the logic of the Humanists, that religious faith has an equally strong friendship with irrationality, anti-science and anti-technology. Even though empirical evidence shows something different, this portrait of religion is hardly questioned by critical humanist reason.

The merits of rationalism in the advancement of science and human rights cannot be disputed. Nevertheless, as historical research has shown, rationalism does not hold the exclusive right to either science or human rights. Progress tends to come about when different forces interact in constructive tension rather than by domination of just one idea. Rationalism has done no better than Christianity in protecting humankind from violence and cruelty, regardless whether it ruled under the flag of revolution or colonialism. Atheistic rationalism has no convincing track record as a remedy against war and injustice. Even rational people fall into guilt. And guilt and shame are experiences that involve more than reason. They require reconciliation and healing in a way that surpasses that which reason and reasonable care can offer.

Both faith and reason are powerful resources that can bring about miraculous things when they are at their best and can lead to disaster at their worst. Use and misuse are always close neighbors. Science and faith have accomplished brilliant things; at the same time atrocities have been committed in the name of both. That is why critical and self-critical examination is required over the whole range.

In my view, the new atheists have got a serious problem: they are not radical enough to be able to cope with the challenges facing humanity. The main difficulty is not their scurrilous portrait of religion as irrational, simplistic, dogmatic, prone to violence, and caught in a pre-scientific worldview whose prime feature is a dualism between natural and supernatural. Their main problem is the bleakness of the alternative they offer: a sort of second coming of European Enlightenment philosophy. Today's globalized and technological world needs something more than a rehash of old Western stuff. Just think of Athena!

This is not to deny the merits of Enlightenment. There is an obvious aspect of freedom in Immanuel Kant's famous definition of Enlightenment as the ending of self-inflicted incapacity. The same is true of his famous appeal "Sapere aude"—dare to use your own reason. Kant makes clear that lack of enlightenment is not a question of a deficit of rationality but a deficit of courage.

This interplay of reason and courage hints at what I see as the Achilles' heel of enlightenment: the autonomy of reason. How autonomous can reason ever be? Corrupted and vacillating reason does not correspond to the ideals of enlightenment, yet it is a familiar phenomenon in daily life.

The concept of autonomous reason residing in an autonomous self has been subject to much criticism and revision by both theorists and social activists. Sometimes such critique has ended up in the opposite ditch: an understanding of personal and social identity as nothing but social construction. In the wake of the Enlightenment, it can no longer be denied that knowledge is associated with power and that the inner life we call religion also is public and political.[5]

These insights have helped overcoming the Eurocentric patterns of interpretation in enlightenment philosophy. Moreover, we know today that the mainly Cartesian anthropology that has come to be associated with the Enlightenment is outmoded from the perspective of both contemporary theology and modern science.

Therefore, a second coming of Enlightenment philosophy served by new atheists will not do a good job. The dualistic concepts it is based on are badly equipped to deal with the challenges of our time.

BEYOND MODERNITY

In late modernity, emphasis has shifted from an understanding of reality as something basically static to the concept of a fundamentally dynamic reality, structured by the categories of space, time, and language. Rationality is perceived as more inclusive and complex in character. We have left positivism behind. We understand that there is hybridity in the air we breathe. This makes us more interested in the complex and particular than in the universal und uniform. We expect more insight from inspecting the seams that keep together the garment of knowledge we call our civilization than from pure admiration of the magnificence of the whole.

When it comes to philosophy and theology, it is our growing familiarity with contemporary voices that have been nourished in other cultural and philosophical contexts than those of the West that has opened our eyes to see syncretism also in the heart and history of Western philosophy and theology. In theology, Asian, African and Latin American voices have raised the consciousness that a *theologia absoluta et pura* cannot be the norm for doing theology. The norm must be a theology that can motivate and nourish hope. This does not happen by means of an absolute theology, but rather by means of a resolute theology—a theology resolved to pursue the critical and self-critical reflection on the contents and effects of religious traditions. Such a theology will not worship purity as a value in itself, it will be prepared to get dirty in its earthy business.

The 1960s saw the culmination of the so-called God-is-dead-theologies. In their wake, new God-language was born. Here are some examples:

---

5. Cf. Robbins, "Introduction," 12.

"God is more than necessary" (the German theologian Eberhard Jüngel), "God without being" (the French theologian Jean-Luc Marion) and "God the event" (the American philosopher John Caputo). This language covers ground that lies beyond an abstract theism, because theism as abstract idea is always concerned with the necessity of God.

What we need today is a more rigorous enlightenment and a softer ontology: an enlightenment that is enlightened about the risks of freezing into dogma and a more open philosophy and theology that takes seriously that we are always exposed—exposed to the undecidability that marks the essence of being (the great achievement of quantum physics) and to the contextuality that requires perpetual translation between texts and contexts under the spell and the promise of the ambiguity of language.

This in turn has consequences for atheism. In the words of Italian philosopher Gianni Vattimo: "The end of metaphysics and the death of the moral God have liquidated the philosophical basis of atheism."[6] Vattimo observes that with the fall of modern theism even atheism became an impossible position, because it is the negation of theism. If God is more than necessary there is no point in the atheistic critique that wants to get rid of the idea of God by showing that it is a non-necessary idea. If the foremost statement about God no longer is that God is or exists, then also the negation of God's existence becomes a rather pointless exercise. The atheism that is a mirror image of theism has lost its base. This is quite obvious as long as atheism relies on arguments that are close to positivistic, that rely on a dualistic worldview where natural and supernatural as well as immanent and transcendent are each other's opposites, and that is stuck with the idea of an exclusively abstract, authoritarian, transcendent God. Atheism needs new theoretic foundations. Atheism tends to regard faith as an inferior way of knowing. Thus it fails to see that faith is meant to be about relationships of trust and confidence and about hope.

Jürgen Habermas gives us some clues that point in the same direction. Reason that takes seriously its own critique and its own limits cannot help but transcend itself toward something other/different. This happens without any previous or explicit theological intention.[7] Therefore, concludes Habermas in his well-known conversation with then-Cardinal Ratzinger, it is in the interest of both philosophy and democracy to handle carefully

---

6. Quoted from Robbins, "Introduction," 17.

7. "Ohne anfänglich theologische Absicht überschreitet sich auf diesen Wegen eine ihre Grenzen inne werdende Vernunft auf ein Anderes hin . . . " Habermas et al., *Dialektik*, 29

those cultural sources that feed citizens' consciousness of norms/values and to facilitate open and complementary processes of learning.[8]

THE ROLE OF THEOLOGY

Theology has a role to play in the public spaces of our time. For its own sake it needs to be exposed to interdisciplinary and public discourse. It is impossible for theology to succeed in its critical and self-critical task without relation beyond its own horizon. Excellence requires constant reflection on how concepts and definitions interact with and in different contexts.

Deliberate interplay in and with public contexts can be helpful to theology in detecting possible abuses of religion. When things go wrong with religion they tend to go badly wrong, because religion is such a powerful force. Therefore, theological reflection on the level of public intellectual discourse provides a better protection against possible misuse of religion than the restriction of religiosity to the private sphere.

Furthermore, theology is expected to contribute constructively to many central issues of our time. In response to a number of problems we often see new and maybe unexpected alliances. "In many parts of the world, secular greens and religious people find themselves on the same side of public debates: sometimes hesitantly, sometimes tactically, and sometimes fired by a sense that they have deep things in common," *The Economist* reported.[9]

Sociobiologist E. O. Wilson, his critical attitude toward religion notwithstanding, appeals to religious communities for the sake of the earth. His book *The Creation: An Appeal to Save Life on Earth*,[10] is a fictitious letter to a Baptist pastor. The message is: "Pastor, we need your help. The Creation is the glory of the earth. Let's see if we can't get together on saving it, because science and religion are the most powerful social forces on Earth. We could do it."[11]

British researchers have examined how people discuss ethical questions. Their analysis indicates that people often raise theological questions and that these questions are often misunderstood by the experts as well as by media. Experts usually stick to one technical or legal question at a time and ignore the broader existential questions; media often treat the same questions as emotional and irrational talk. The consequence is a serious gap in communication. This can be a rather serious situation in democratic

8. Ibid., 32f.
9. "Faith upon the Earth," *Economist*.
10. Wilson, *Creation*.
11. Wilson, "Interview."

states, since democracy is dependent on successful public communication. The British researchers who had examined communication concerning genetically modified food concluded: "Theological perspectives may now be indispensable in helping explain to largely secular institutions the sources and dynamics of conflicts now threatening to paralyze the development of what is being posited as a key technology for the twenty-first century."[12] If they are right, then the public role of theology is not wishful thinking of a handful believers but a necessity for a democratic society.

This is a challenge for all those who are used to arguing: a democratic, multi-cultural society requires a neutral, religion-free public center. The research from Britain suggest instead: precisely in order to function as a democratic and multicultural democratic society, theological discussion needs to be part of the public sphere.

Good solutions in many areas require cooperation between the best scientific, technological, and theological knowledge and skills. Religion, its doctrinal expressions, and its rites are robust and changeable at the same time. New challenges will shape new alliances across religious communities. What we mean by ecumenism will change. In the process, the religious geography of this world may be up to some surprising developments. I believe that many of these will be good developments.

BIBLIOGRAPHY

Casanova, José. "Political Challenges from Religion in the 21st Century." Paper presented at the conference "Religion in the Twenty-First Century: Transformations, Significance and Challenges," Copenhagen University, September 19–23 2007.

Coelho, Paulo. *The Alchemist*. Translated by Alan R. Clarke. New York: Harper Collins, 1993.

———. *The Witch of Portobello*. Translated by Margaret Jull Costa. New York: Harper Collins, 2007.

Deane-Drummond, Celia, et al., editors. *Re-Ordering Nature*. London: T. & T. Clark, 2003. "Faith upon the earth: In many parts of the world, religious groups and environmental scientists are teaming up—albeit sometimes reluctantly." *The Economist*, September 20, 2007. http://www.economist.com/node/9832922.

"Gott ist an allem schuld!" Der Kreuzzug der neuen Atheisten ("'God is to blame for everything!' The crusade of the new atheists"). Special issue of *Der Spiegel* 22 (May 2007).

Habermas, Jürgen, and Jospeh Ratzinger. *Dialektik der Säkularisierung*. 7th ed. Wien: Herder, 2007.

Miller, Pamela. "To scientist and writer Richard Dawkins, religion is nonsense and humanity would be better off without it." *Minneapolis Star Tribune*, November 3, 2006. Online: http://richarddawkins.net/articles/274-atheist-firebrand

---

12. Deane-Drummond et al., *Re-Ordering Nature*, 22.

Robbins, Jeffrey W. "Introduction." In John D. Caputo and Gianni Vattimo, *After the Death of God*. New York: Columbia University Press, 2007. (Original: Vattimo, Gianni. *After Chrisitanity*. Translated by Luca d'Isanto. New York: Columbia University Press, 2002.

"Weltmacht Religion: Wie der Glaube Politik und Gesellschaft beeinflusst." ("World Power Religion: How Faith Influences Politics and Society"). Special issue of *Der Spiegel* (2007).

Wilson, E. O. *The Creation: An Appeal to Save Life on Earth*. New York: W. W. Norton, 2006.

———. "Interview with E. O. Wilson." By Kim Lawton. *PBS Religion and Ethics Newsweekly* (November 17, 2006).

http://www.pbs.org/wnet/religionandethics/episodes/november-17-2006/eo-wilson/3349/

4

Beatitudinal Eschatology

In Space or Time?

TED PETERS

TIME IS BOTH FRIEND and thief. As a friend, time allots to each of us the years that make up our life story. Time allots to our people centuries to construct meaningful traditions that permit cumulative creativity to build monuments of achievement and identity. As thief, however, time is constantly passing, ever eroding, ever destroying, ever forgetting. Time is merciless. Time steals from every entity its future through relentless rusting, corroding, weakening, dissipating, and dissolving. "Time, like an ever-rolling stream," we sing; "Soon bears us all away."[1]

Vítor Westhelle says he does not like time. Or, perhaps a bit more precisely, he does not like the role time plays in the dominant Western eschatology. Theologians such as Paul Tillich and Wolfhart Pannenberg follow their mentor Augustine by promoting a linear understanding of time and, worse, they make universal history their central category for understanding reality. A linear universal history leads to one and only one future, one and only one hegemonic eschatology.

---

1. See Peters, "Eschatology," 348.

THEORIA

When we focus on linear time and a consummate eschatology, we marginalize and render something invisible, namely, space. In particular, we render invisible the separate spaces of marginalized peoples. By turning our attention away from time and toward space, argues Westhelle, our gaze will suddenly include the separate territories where meaningful events happen in the lives of peoples left out of the picture drawn by linear history and a single encompassing eschatology.

It may appear that what we have here is a competition between a temporal eschatology and a spatial eschatology. Perhaps we might label the first position: *linear eschatology*. The alternative position, the Westhelle position, could be labeled: *spatial eschatology*. Neither of these satisfies me. I would like to propose a third position, one that synthesizes the best of the two. I will label this: *beatitudinal eschatology*. In what follows I would like to delineate these three positions, comparing and distinguishing them. It will be my suggestion that what distinguishes them is not the contrast between time and space, between calendars and maps. Rather, what is decisive is the role that eschatological imminence plays in each of the three.

LINEAR ESCHATOLOGY

Westhelle complains that Western theology, especially since Augustine, has narrowed the domain for divine action to historical and eschatological time. This historical time is singular; it presupposes one single universal history with one single final outcome. More specifically, European theologians along with their North American disciples presume that time is linear; and they restrict God's activity to linear history ending at some point in the future with an eschatological consummation. The end time means *end* both as *finis* and as *telos*, both as conclusion and as purpose. What this leaves out is space, space for living and space for meaning. "The emphasis, practically exclusive on the axiological and the teleological senses of the term, has left out of the picture the spatial dimension of eschatology."[2]

Westhelle is certainly correct in observing how temporality and history play a decisive role in the worldview constructed by Western theologians, especially European theologians. "The medium of God's revelation is primarily history and not nature," we find asserted in the German *Evangelical Catechism for Adults*.[3] Paul Tillich, similarly, holds that "the Church which gathers from all nations, is the end of all religious nationalism and

---

2. Westhelle, *Eschatology and Space*, 69.

3. *Evangelischer Erwachsenenkatechismus*, 218; cited by Westhelle, *Eschatology and Space*, 10.

tribalism. . .up to the end of history."[4] Continental theology, especially German language theology, places our faith within a framework of Western history punctuated with God's revelatory and redemptive actions that promise a final *eschaton*. Time runs in one direction, from the past through the present toward a future yet-to-be-determined by God.

"History is the most comprehensive horizon of Christian theology," writes Wolfhart Pannenberg.[5] History for Pannenberg is not merely linear temporality. Rather, it is culture, hermeneutically understood. With terms such as *Traditionsgecshichte* or *Überlieferungsgeschichte*, Pannenberg refers to the history of the transmission of traditions. Cultural history provides us with the cultural consciousness of the present and our present anticipations of the future. More than bare linearity, history is cumulative; and eschatology is consummative. Human meaning is contextual, and the most comprehensive context of meaning is the entire history of God's creation consummated by God's *eschaton*. The single future of all creation is what draws all disparate histories into a single universal history, *Universalgeschichte*.

History is the primary category within which we place everything, even nature. "The cosmos not only *has* a history; it *is* a history,"[6] writes Antje Jackelén. The entire cosmos is historical. This means the cosmos with everything in it will meet the one God eschatologically.

We today have God's promise for an eschatological future. It is not here yet. It is coming. Does this mean it will come as a date on the calendar? If not tomorrow, then some day in the future? If the *parousia* has been delayed, as some claim, must we simply wait? Is this what linear time means?

Apparently, this is Westhelle's interpretation of the first position. Westhelle objects because the concept of linear time combined with a single universal history belies the fact that this so-called universal history is the construction of European colonialist consciousness. It places Europe in the middle of the stream of this history, because European eyes are blind to other histories and other peoples in other places. By denying local histories—the histories of tribalism and nationalism—the concept of universal history culminating in a single eschatology denies the existence of separate places in separate times. In order to bring the margins to the center, Westhelle adopts a postcolonial approach to theology.

"While colonialism dominated and displaced the *Other*, postcolonialism emplaced and empowered the *Other*. . . . Postcolonialism indicates a crossing over, transgression of the boundaries, the *eschata*, of the colonial

---

4. Tillich, *Theology of Culture*, 39.
5. Pannenberg, *Basic Questions*, 1:15.
6. Jackelén, "Cosmology and Theology," 143, author's italics.

world, simultaneously incorporating some of its values and accomplishments while abandoning others in a dynamic process. This process called as 'hybridization' thus has an eschatological twist to it."[7] It is the European metanarrative that Westhelle objects to; and he believes he can destabilize this metanarrative by turning from time to space.

SPATIAL ESCHATOLOGY

Westhelle wants to turn away from linear time with its universal history and its encompassing eschatology. He wants to " . . . focus attention . . . on little stories and the space they occupy in everyday life."[8] He turns away from time and toward space. But the space he turns toward is not Isaac Newton's container space. Nor, is it outer space, the cosmos. Rather, Westhelle turns toward spaces in the plural, toward terrestrial territories and smaller locations that determine the consciousness and identities of local peoples. It is the specificity of separate spaces that draws Westhelle's attention. With the term *space* he means "the awareness of objective and more or less as measurable confinements of geographical, social, psychic, and epistemological domains."[9] Not just land in the objective sense, but space in the subjective or psychic or cultural sense. Although he does not say it, Westhelle is describing the special space we all call "home."

Events happen within these spaces, according to Westhelle. This is the door he walks through to spatialize eschatology. No longer is eschatology singular and universal; rather, it is territorialized and localized. "With the territorialization of eschatology. . .one should speak not as much of the *eschaton* in singular as in the plural: *ta eschata*. These *eschata* are limits, margins that are (1) either set by individuals or systems, or (2) are by them suffered while liberation represent the blessed crossing of them of which the ultimate is death itself."[10] The concept of eschatology is here applied to the limits within which our spatial communities find themselves; and it is applied to their transgression or their conquering.

One theme of the eschatological promise bequeathed to us by the teachings of Jesus in the New Testament is the great reversal: the last will be first and vice versa. The stresses of an oppressed community yield a hope for a specific or concrete reversal. Such an event of reversal constitutes an eschatological event. "The first (*protoi*) will be the last (*eschatoi*) and the

7. Westhelle, *Eschatology and Space*, 77.
8. Ibid., 119.
9. Ibid., 3.
10. Ibid., 82.

last first. The *eschaton* is the location in which a reversal occurs. It is not so much something to be awaited for as it is something already and presently near."[11] The eschatological transformation occurs now, politically and socially, when a reversal takes place.

Westhelle brings the unrealized future into the present. Each event of transgressing limits constitutes an eschatological event for a particular space. "Eschatology is an experience embedded in everyday life when an irretrievable loss has been experienced and lament ensues, yet also entailing the ineffable promise that unveils a hopeless birth of hope."[12] Or, "Eschatology is. . .not primarily about cosmic catastrophes or abstract speculations about time and eternity; it names the experience of a crossing in which the messianic is an occurrence in time that becomes *kairotic*, and in spaces, *choratic*. Such messianic experience in space and time entail a faint promise of a *weak epiphany,* not a cosmic Armageddon."[13] Although he dismisses C.H. Dodd and Rudolph Bultmann for flirting with Gnosticism,[14] Westhelle appears to me to embrace a variant of realized eschatology.

However, ascribing a realized eschatology to Westhelle might be a bit premature. This is because he works with a paradoxical epistemology. He works with the Theology of the Cross, the *theologia crucis*. Things are not what they seem. 'Paradoxical' means that what we see in this world actually points to what we should hear, the Word. 'Asymmetry' means that what appears on one side of the binary categories is not mirrored in the other but is shaped in it—or perhaps by it—in unexpected ways. Westhelle says "*This argumentative devise is called irony: a rejection of analogical reasoning with apparent analogical correspondence.*" Applied to our topic here, this suggests that a comprehensive metanarrative such as a theology of history culminating in a grand eschatology, which cannot avoid relying upon analogy, ignores the irony of the cross. This applies even to the relationship between nature and creation. Westhelle, in contrast to Pannenberg or Jackelén, would not place nature within a universal history leading to a universal *eschaton*.

The view we have of *nature* is the blindness we have to *creation*. Analogical correspondence between these two is truncated. The "mechanism" through which we link creation and Creator cannot be grasped externally, because we are implicated in it through and through; we cannot observe it from a transcendent standpoint (*sub species aeternitatis*).[15]

11. Ibid., 81.
12. Ibid., 132.
13. Ibid.
14. Ibid., 62.
15. Westhelle, *Scandalous God*, 97.

THEORIA

This epistemological employment of the *theologia crucis* suggests that Westhelle is doing more than simply making a move away from European metahistory toward local or spatial self-understandings of marginalized communities. Our very understanding of God's relationship to the world is due to paradox or irony, not to an analogical construction. When we look at the world, we need to listen to the revelatory Word that hides. We need to attend to the revelation that God and even God's eschatological plan is mystery. Eschatological presence is still realized for Westhelle, it seems to me; but this realization is not unambiguous. It maintains its paradoxical and ironic character.

BEATITUDINAL ESCHATOLOGY

What have we said so far? Linear eschatology relies upon universal history culminating in a single eschatological event that unifies previous disparate histories. Its strength is that it looks forward to an eschatological consummation which confirms our faith in the God of Israel as the God of all reality. The weakness, according to Westhelle, is that its universal vision constitutes a hegemonic metanarrative that marginalizes humble spaces not yet on the radar screen of the European theologians who formulated this idea of eschatology. An additional weakness, in my judgment, is the idea of the delayed *parousia*. It is the idea that the apocalypse is a date on our calendar and that we are simply waiting for the future to happen.

In place of linear eschatology, Westhelle offers a spatial eschatology. The merit of this position is that it honors what is local, geographically or territorially discreet, separate, humble, and in need of respect and dignity. Westhelle's motive here is to destabilize the metanarrative of linear eschatology. By taking time away and substituting space, linear eschatologists—if there is such a term—are left empty handed. They have lost their time because Westhelle has replaced it with his space. Due to a change in the recipe, Westhelle's eschatological desert will emit multiple tastes for multiple taste buds. More important than the conceptual change here is the moral shift, that is, drawing our attention to the *Other* who had previously been marginalized. No longer is eschatology a metaphysical or conceptual matter; it is now a moral matter.

What comes next? Between these two—and to some extent a synthesis of these two—I proffer the idea of beatitudinal eschatology. On the one hand, beatitudinal eschatology begins with universal history and a single eschatological fulfillment for all of creation. On the other hand, it treasures the purity of heart among the humble in their specific time and place. Like the widow's mite, it treasures the small while glorifying the magnificent. We still deal with a metaphysical or ontological treatment of reality, but it is tied inextricably with the moral dimension of human living.

Beatitudinal eschatology begins by recognizing that God has promised an apocalyptic scale transformation of the present creation into the new creation. Further, it recognizes that this transformation is cosmic in scope, embracing all creation of all time and all places. The eschatological event is not local only; it is universal and total and whole, and complete. Still further, the time of the consummate *eschaton* is not located on the calendar. It is almost, but not quite fully, present. It is imminent without being consummate. The totality of transformation is as close to us right now as the next moment is. In fact, it is the next moment emitting power and grace and transformation into the present moment.

The future is more real than the present. The future of God is the ground of all being, the support for all that exists. To exist is to have a future. It is the power of God's future that provides the present moment with its dependent reality. Without the power of God's future at work in the present, we would simply drop into non-being, into non-existence. The ground of our being is not the past or the present, but rather the power of God to grant the present moment a future.

Still more importantly, the future that God grants us moment by moment is redemptive, transformative. Each moment God releases us from past bondages and opens up a freedom for unprecedented newness. The promised eschatological kingdom of God or new creation is the ground of all being; and God's promised future releases into the present moment a transformative reality which is, in fact, reality. God's future is more real than our present.

Jesus tried to communicate this in his Beatitudes. These are very familiar. But, take a moment to look at some of them again. Matthew 5:3–9 reads: "Blessed are the poor in spirit, for theirs is the kingdom of heaven. Blessed are those who mourn, for they will be comforted. Blessed are the meek, for they will inherit the earth. Blessed are those who hunger and thirst for righteousness (*dikaiosune*), for they will be filled. Blessed are the merciful, for they will receive mercy. Blessed are the pure in heart, for they will see God. Blessed are the peacemakers, for they will be called children of God."

Note the proleptic structure. In most cases, Jesus begins with a present moment and then ties it to the future. Or, perhaps the logic is the reverse: the future determines the significance of the present. The future will be imbued with mercy, therefore, those who are merciful today belong to the future. The future will be imbued with righteousness—actually the term *dikaiosune* can be translated 'justice' or 'justification' as well as 'righteousness'—therefore, those who thirst for justice today will find their thirst quenched in the kingdom of God. In other words, the future God has promised is present today, perhaps in a fragmented way, when we find ourselves poor in spirit, mournful, meek, pure in heart, hungering and thirsting after justice, merciful, and striving to make peace. The future God has planned for all of creation is present right now in the lives of those who live, unknowingly, beatitudinally.

The proleptic structure includes a strong dose of the reversal. The eschatological banquet which Jesus employed in so many of his parables reinforces what the Beatitudes say. The parable of the wedding feast provides an illustrative example (Matthew 22:1–14; Luke 14:16–24). A householder (king in Matthew's version) plans a banquet for his son's wedding. Snobs were invited. But, the snobs gave excuses for not attending: one had just purchased new property needing examination; another had just purchased five oxen needing care; and a third had just gotten married and wanted to be attentive to his new wife. The wedding host rescinded the initial invitations and instead invited "the poor and maimed and blind and lame" along with those living along "the highways and hedges" (Luke 14:21,23). The last replaced the first in the parable; and this portends a parallel reversal at the advent of God's eschatological kingdom. Or, to say it beatitudinally, one's life on the margins today may be exchanged for life in the center of God's domain tomorrow.

A beatitudinal epistemology hints at a *theologia crucis*. Those about whom Jesus speaks seem to press on with their beatitudinal living within an unacknowledged paradox: today's thirst for justice and heartache at injustice is a thirst the imminent Kingdom of God slakes. What we experience every day is the heartache at the absence of justice; but this heartache at the absence marks the very presence of God's eschatological future. This is the case whether the thirsty one is aware of it or not. In part, the pronouncement of a beatitude makes visible what has been invisibly the case all along. Jesus' Word illuminates what we previously thought was visible but now interprets it with an ironic depth, with a proleptic yet paradoxical mystery.

CONCLUSION

Westhelle does not like time. Well, more precisely, he does not like the kind of time at work in metanarratives of history that leads to a single metaeschatology. To subvert this universal notion of time, Westhelle turns our gaze toward spaces in the plural, toward territories where marginalized peoples make their home. The weakness in Westhelle's shift is overcompensation, I believe. Surrendering time on behalf of space goes too far. History and eschatology must remain temporal categories, I think. Still, the eschatological reversal which means so much to Westhelle must be brought from the frame to the center, from the conceptual frame to the center of our daily living. The third model, beatitudinal eschatology, accomplishes this, in my judgment.

Maranatha.

BIBLIOGRAPHY

Jackelén, Antje. "Cosmology and Theology." In *The Routledge Companion to Religion and Science,* edited by James W. Haag, Gregory R. Peterson, and Michael L. Spezio. New York: Routledge, 2012.

Jentsch, Werner, et al., editors. *Evangelischer Erwachsenenkatechismus: Kursbuch des Glaubens.* Gütersloh: Gerd Mohn, 1975.

Pannenberg, Wolfhart, *Basic Questions in Theology.* 2 vols. Minneapolis: Fortress, 1970–1971.

Pannenberg, Wolfhart, *Theology as History.* Edited by James M. Robinson and John B. Cobb, Jr. New York: Harper, 1967.

Peters, Ted. "Eschatology." In *Essentials of Christian Theology,* edited by William C. Placher, 347–65. Louisville: Westminster John Knox, 2003.

Tillich, Paul. *Theology of Culture.* Edited by Robert C. Kimball. New York: Oxford University Press, 1959.

Westhelle, Vítor, *The Scandalous God: The Use and Abuse of the Cross.* Minneapolis: Fortress, 2006.

———. *Eschatology and Space: The Lost Dimension in Theology Past and Present.* New York: Palgrave Macmillan, 2012.

5

Queering the Erotic

Bernard's and Luther's Use of the Nuptial Metaphor[1]

ELSE MARIE WIBERG PEDERSEN

WHEN ASKED IF I would contribute to this *churrasco* prepared in appreciation of my friend and colleague Vítor Westhelle, I was deeply honored. But then appeared the problem: what meat should I serve this gifted poetic theologian of the cross and friend of the heart? To offer simply a theology of the cross would demand a treatment of the subject in another key. Yet, I am inspired by Westhelle's conclusive "coda" in his *The Scandalous God*, in which he expounds how the women at the empty cross and the empty grave were laboring to fill the emptiness and "spread scent countering the miserable odor of death . . . in the midst of apocalypse, a work of another economy, a mad economy (call it 'grace-side economics') that spends for a gift that cannot be returned: spices for a dead and decaying body."[2]

---

1. This article is an abbreviated and altered version of a paper delivered at the Seminar "Nuptial Imagery and the Erotic," University of Aarhus, Denmark, 1 March 2012, in which Vítor Westhelle took part.

2. Westhelle, *Scandalous God*, 176.

This essay is an attempt to offer examples of such a grace-side economics by way of fluid uses of the nuptial metaphor, which in long stretches of Christian tradition has been seen as the most sublime expression of the divine-human relationship. With its erotic love poetry and nuptial imagery, the Song of Solomon inspired and provoked exegetes wanting to explain this carnal love poem's presence in the Christian canon. Read through the *quadigra*, the erotic poem expressed what allegorically could only be understood as God's love relation to humans. Prominent exegetes such as Origen, Gregory of Nyssa, and Gregory the Great all interpreted it as a dramatic *epithalium*, a wedding song, identifying it as *theologia*, and employed its nuptial imagery and erotic semantics as a means[3] of transforming the bodily sense to the spiritual, the physical to the metaphysical, in order to combine the two realms, the divine and the human in a complex of the three orders of life: *theoria* (the seeing of God), ethics, and the physical.[4] They considered the nuptial imagery from Hos 2:19–20; Jer 2:21; John 3:29; Matt 9:15; 2 Cor 11:2; Eph 5:27; Rev 19:9 and 22:2 the most sublime among God metaphors. The metaphor of groom was perceived as a depiction of the intimate love bond between God and humans,[5] in contradistinction to the metaphors "master," signifying human status as creatures, and "father," signifying human status as adopted children,[6] not displaying such intimacy. The carnal imagery pointed to its opposite, the spiritual, as well as to the union of those different, God and humans, while each part in the nuptial drama alternated between "gender loose" bride and groom. I therefore contend that this imagery meets many of the requests made by feminist and postcolonial theologies about recognition of difference and the other.

QUEERING THE EROTIC: A HETEROLOGY[7] OF SHAMEFUL LOVE

From Jewish exegetes Christians learned to interpret the image of the bride and groom allegorically as a conjugal love bond between God and God's people. Combining this interpretation with Pauline formulations on the

---

3. Gregory of Nyssa, CC 773 N S 27, z 1ff.. See Bjerre-Aspegren, *Bräutigam, Sonne und Mutter*, 65.

4. Gregory the Great, "Exposition of the Song of Songs N. 8–9," Turner, *Eros and Allegory*, 222–23.

5. Gregory the Great, "Expos. N. 7," in Turner, *Eros and Allegory*, 222.

6. Gregory the Great, "Expos. N. 8," in Turner, *Eros and Allegory*, 222.

7. The term "heterology" is Edith Wyschgorod's for Foucault, in *Ethics of Remembering*, 37.

relation between Christ and the Church (2 Cor 11:2, Eph 5:22–32), Christian exegetes counted the Song among the biblical writings that treated most deeply the mystery of the relation between the church/the believer and God in Christ.

Especially the Song's vivid language of kissing and swelling of breasts is constantly utilized as hermeneutical and pedagogical tools to explain the loftier things of faith in a constantly gender-crossing language. The erotic language forms a meta-narrative as a means to transcend the human world, to see beyond the carnal words to an inner understanding.[8] The language of familiar "shameful love" is a way to God's holy love,[9] in a *humilitas-sublimitas* movement, God's self-humiliation by speaking words that raises human comprehension.

Monastic exegesis continued Origen's twofold interpretation with its emphasis on the spiritual-erotic drama between either the individual bride soul and the Word or the collective bride church and Christ. Over the centuries commentators provided three different interpretations: the ecclesiological (the church as the bride of Christ, the bridegroom), the individual (the soul as the bride of the Word, Christ), and the mariological (Mary as the bride, at once virgin mother of Christ and church/faithful disciple).

BERNARD OF CLAIRVAUX AND THE QUEERING OF MARRIAGE

The allegory was used to emphasize the erotic tension of the text as an eroticism of the words and concepts inherent in the Song.[10] Many medieval exegetes struggled to de-eroticize the sexual words of the text by overemphasizing its spiritual sense, but Bernard kept the complexity of the text and its meaning, highlighting the ambivalence of what later was called "the rhetoric of sexual difference."[11] It was retained not as a question of sexuality or spirituality, nor as a simple question of sublimation of sexuality, as the typical modern discourse would reduce it to be.[12] Bernard refined the erotic imagery of the nuptial longing in order to accentuate the Christological, soteriological, and eschatological character of Christian belief.

Like in his treatise *On the Loving of God*, Bernard sets out to interpret the double commandment of love of God and neighbor. Echoing John and

8. Gregory the Great, "Expos. N. 2," in Turner, *Eros and Allegory*, 217.
9. Gregory the Great, "Expos. N. 3," in Turner, *Eros and Allegory*, 217–18.
10. Matter, *Voice of My Beloved*, 33.
11. Johnson, *Critical Difference*, 13. Cf. Matter, *Voice of my Beloved*, 33.
12. Cf. Foucault, *History of Sexuality*, 17–35.

Paul, Bernard understands God as love (1 John 4:8), and love as the gift of God (Eph 2:8).[13] God-talk logically must be about love, because God in and out of love gave humans themselves in creation and *a fortiori* gave them God-self in salvation through Christ on the cross.[14] The love of God and the cross are constantly combined in the double understanding of Christ as *donum et exemplum*, because "charity *gives* charity . . . Where it signifies the giver, it takes the name of substance; where it means the gift, it is called a quality."[15] Hence, the love of neighbor and enemy are extensions of God's love turned into benevolence,[16] neither tied to a particular sex or gender. It is a disinterested love (*amor castus*) aimed at the total other, God, neighbor or enemy, as its only measure.[17]

Concurrently, Bernard's theology of love is formulated in a continuously gender-crossing discourse.[18] God transcends the human and mundane, including sex and gender, being father and mother in a constant interplay with the equally gender-crossing believer. Following Origen's sexual ambiguity, Bernard sets up a true wedding drama, in which the bride and groom change roles, the breasts first applied to the bridegroom. By honoring the bride "with the nurturing sweetness" of his breasts, the groom has prompted her boldness, convinced of his goodness and forgetful of his majesty.[19] But through this feeding of love and mercy, the bride's (male or female) breasts are equally filled with love and desire through the kiss of the bridegroom, her breasts filled with the milky abundance of love and grace in order to imitate Christ's love.[20]

Bernard's monastic interpretation is mimetic.[21] The Song's nuptial imagery and its erotic discourse are an encoded theological discourse, employed to pattern the life of love that those praying will be able to imitate.

---

13. De Diligendo Deo (Dil) XII:35: "Deus caritas est. Dicitur ergo recte caritas, et Deus, et Dei donum." Winkler, *Bernhard von Clairvaux* I:74–145 (134). Cf. Sermones de Cantica Canticorum (SC) 83:4. For an exposition of Bernard's theology, see Pedersen, *Bernhard of Clairvaux*.

14. Dil V: 15 and Dil III:7; XV:39. Cf. SC 43:4. Bernard often quotes 1 Cor 2:2 and Gal 6:14 in his opera.

15. Dil XII:35.

16. Dil I:1 and VIII:25. Winkler I:139.

17. Dil XV:39. For a more detailed treatment of Bernard's and Luther's understanding of faith and grace, see Pedersen, "The Significance of the *Sola Fide*," 20–43.

18. Thanks to Caroline Walker Bynum's groundbreaking book, *Jesus as Mother*, the attention of medievalists and theologians alike was drawn to the gender crossing language of Bernard and the Cistercians.

19. SC 9:4.

20. SC 9:6.

21. Cf. Turner, *Eros and Allegory*, 140–42.

THEORIA

The theology of love, described through the metaphor of the erotic marriage, the ultimate otherness of the celibate monk's life, indeed has a sociopolitical aim.

He explicates human love as ideally an imitation of Christ's love. Employing the monastic social life as his frame and the conjugal image of the Song as his hermeneutical key, Bernard spells out the triune God's love for humans as what should pattern inter-human communal life. While Christ as the divine Word performs as the bridegroom, the individual Christians as Bernard or his monks and the church perform as the bride.[22]

Bernard warns against mistaking the eroticism of the words for an eroticism of the body (*amor sui* and *amor mundi*). The text is the body, but the physical body is not the text. The Song, so easy for the unlearned to misread as an "indecent" theology,[23] is only for those who are able to read it as a contemplative text, a *theoricus sermo*, the purpose of which is to transmit the insight that life is a graceful gift to humans whose task is to receive it. This is where God's grace plays the central role. Humans need God to drag them along (Song 1:4) by way of divine grace and mercy, expressed in God incarnated and crucified.[24] In an utterly anthropomorphic language, Bernard describes how the love of God is exchanged in the swelling breasts of the spouses while the bride in the regal marriage's wonderful exchange (*stupenda mirabile*) receives the happy kiss (*felix osculum*) of forgiveness, grace and peace, exchanging unbelief with faith, being justified through faith (*iustificati per fidem*).[25] Soteriologically, God's gifts are forgiveness of sins and the promise of grace. But "the kiss itself is nothing else but the mediator between God and humans, the human being Jesus Christ.[26]

In Bernard's understanding, love is *the* socializing factor in life, taking place in a circulation of love between God and humans. With the Trinity as a sublime love affair in an eternal kiss and the bridegroom's breasts of patience and forgiveness abundantly flowing with grace to humans through the kiss of love, Bernard sets up a program for a life in love in a constant giving and receiving. Humans can only enter this relationship by receiving the gift.[27]

---

22. For an in-depth exposition of Bernard's performance of gender, intersecting male and female, see Engh, *Performing the Bride*.

23. This term was coined by Althaus-Reid for an updating of liberation theology by way of postcolonial and queer approaches in her book, *Indecent Theology*.

24. SC 20–21. See Winkler V:114–307.

25. In SC 2:3 and SC 2:8. Winkler V:74. Cf. SC 9.

26. SC 2:9.

27. Dil XII:35: "caritas dat caritatem, substantive accidentalem. Ubi dantem significant, nomen substantiae est; ubi donum, qualitatis." Winkler I:134.

LUTHER ON LOVE AND EROS

To Luther, the most precise picture one could paint of God would be one of love, as the precise painting of love would be one of God, for "love is a picture of God per se"—the living God burning like "an open fire and passion [*brunst*] of love," as Luther wrote in his sermons to 1 John.[28] Whereas God's substance is love, humans are endorsed with the quality to love. In a cocktail of John and Paul, Luther explicates how God is love, and how those who are in love are in God as God is in them, so that God and they will become "one cake" in the divine "oven of love."[29] This means that humans are called to show love and serve in love, love of neighbor, and since God is nothing but love, pouring it abundantly into us, we should let our hearts move to acting in love to our neighbor, in a circulation of love. So much so, that "the one who loves the neighbor, has Godself," and should also love enemy for Christ's sake, he who gave himself on the cross.[30] Like Bernard, Luther accentuates God's being the reason for love: God loved us first, and through divine love and the acting of love humans become God's children, deified, and united with God.[31]

The other focus of the sermons on John 1 is that of restoring the right balance between faith and love. As in a Chalcedonian "without confusion, without separation,"[32] Luther determines the relation between faith and love as not the same, yet interrelated. Faith constitutes the human relationship to God (*coram Deo*), and love the inter-human relationship (*coram hominibus*).[33] Connected by grace and forgiveness, given by God to humans, these relations should be exercised also between humans (cf. Our Lord's Prayer: "Forgive us our trespasses").

---

28 WA 36:416–77, here: 424. The term "brunst" is a strongly carnal expression for "passion."

29. WA 36:422–25. Luther combines 1 Cor 13 and 1 John 4 to underline the unity in love between God and humans by the image of a cake (ein kuche), thus alluding to the Eucharist.

30. WA 36:431–34: "Si diligit proximum, is habet deum ipsum" (431).

31. WA 36: 437–38, and 461–62. An emphatic expression of deification is found in Luther's formulation: "Wer in liebe bleibet ... ist nicht mehr ein lauter mensch, sondern ein Gott ... Den Gott is selber inn im ..." (438) [Who remains in love ... is no longer simply a human being, but a God ... since Godself is in her].

32. WA 36:454.

33. WA 36:447.

THEORIA

MARRIAGE AS A HAPPY EXCHANGE

Like Bernard, Luther utilizes the nuptial metaphor both for the love between God and humans and the inter-personal love between humans. In his "Sermon on the Double Justice"[34] he uses it at two levels, in relation to the *iusticia aliena et infusa*, and in relation to the *iusticia nostra et propia*. The happy exchange of Christ's justice with our sin takes place in the first, in which the human bride receives all that belongs to Christ the bridegroom, the gifts of grace and faith, while Christ takes away sin from the bride. The bride and bridegroom become one flesh (*una caro*) in this common ownership, just as Christ and the church become one spirit (*unus spiritus*).[35] The very same paradigm we find in *The Freedom of a Christian*, when Luther likens the union of the soul and Christ with that of bride and bridegroom in Eph 5:32 (not Hosea 2 as some will have it!).[36]

In my reading, Luther, like Bernard, understands the happy exchange in a slightly asymmetrical way (cf. his exposition of Hosea 2).[37] Whereas the bridegroom is the fullness of all good and gives all good things to his bride out of grace and mercy,[38] his spouse has it only partially and must progress in imitation of Christ's unselfish love: the external justice "is not totally infused at one time, it begins, proceeds and is perfected through death,"[39]—echoing Bernard's *On Loving God*. More is needed since humans live in a social setting.[40]

Yet, there is also symmetry in the exchange. Luther, who always operates dialectically, uses his dialectics of the inner and outer human, of spirit and flesh, of gift and example, of the alien justice and own justice, and of the *coram Deo* and the *coram hominibus* to explicate life's two dimensions: the God-human relation and the inter-human relation. Whereas Christ is gift (*donum*) in the first justice, he is example (*exemplum*) in the second, in which humans become Christ-formed by doing works of love. Luther stretches the nuptial imagery to explain the reciprocal bond of love coming from God. This is where symmetry between Christ, the bridegroom, and

---

34. WA 2:145–52.

35. WA 2:145, Luther employing Eph 5:29ff.

36. WA 7:54: "[Fides] animam copulat cum Christo, sicut sponsam cum sponso," Luther employing Eph 5:32. LW 31:351.

37. Luther's comments to Hos 2 in LW 18, 13: "The groom gives his bride *not a gift but himself*, the deepest love of his heart and all his property. He goes ahead of his bride; he seeks her out, etc." My emphasis.

38. Cf. Luther's comments to Hos 2. LW 18, 14.

39. WA 2:146.

40. WA 7:59 and 64.

the believer, the bride, is found in a truly reciprocal responsiveness. Referring to the nuptial exchange in the Song 2:16 and Jer 7:34, Luther identifies Christ's *gift* of justice as an exclamatory "I am yours" in the flesh (*incarnation*), which is responded to by the bride's *act* of justice (love of neighbor) as her exclamatory "I am yours" in the spirit (*sanctification*), while crucifying the flesh.[41]

Again, we find the exact same dialectical paradigm in *The Freedom of a Christian*, where Luther, after having unfolded the freedom in Christ through faith (inwardly), emphasizes the serfdom in Christ through love. In all actuality, the human being is a social being, always in relation to Christ and the other in a circulation of love.[42]

MARRIAGE AS AN IMAGE OF THE POLITICAL AND ECONOMICAL

In his commentary to the Song, Luther uses all his effort to transpose its nuptial frame to a political and economic frame. Discarding all medieval interpretations as immature and strange, Luther de-sexualizes and impersonalizes the poem, employing it as a *Fürstenspiegel*: it is King Solomon's honor of God for his good and peaceful governance.[43]

Luther uses the Song to encourage the Lutheran princes to stay with and fight for the evangelical principles.[44] The Song, he emphasizes, is *not* a love song but an encomium of political order,[45] an entirely figurative poem about good government,[46] being exercised only in intimate union between the God of mercy and the whole people of God, the bride represented by the king: "He is kissing me."[47] Discarding the interpersonal eroticism of the poem, Luther converts it to a political and economic eroticism. In his hermeneutics, the kisses—"held in less esteem" by him—are signs of God's love and favor of the government, not of an individual soul. Still, God's kisses are real and present, he assures his princes, though not obvious on the outward due to the afflictions of real politics and economy. They are after all

---

41. WA 2:147. Quoting Rom 6:19 and Phil 2:5ff., Luther accentuates the justification that leads to sanctification.

42. See especially the German version, *Von der Freiheit eines Christenmenschen*, 7–27 (27). Cf. WA 2:742–58 and WA 50: 641–43.

43. LW 15,191. Cf. Luther's interpretation of Magnificat, LW 21, 295–358.

44. LW 15:191.

45. LW 15:194–95.

46. LW 15:196. Cf. Bernard, SC 1:8.

47. LW 15:193. Cf. Bernard, SC 1:5.

"kisses of his mouth," God's Word given to both governments (*politia*) and households (*economia*).

Luther does enter the bedchamber of the newly married couple, but his discourse is kept asexual, drawing on another kind of eroticism, the erotic endeavor for good governance: "just as when a groom brings his bride into his chamber, he certainly does not do so from hatred of the bride!"[48] In the same vein, Luther flatly states that the breasts of the bridegroom symbolize Christian doctrine and the preaching of the words of the gospel in contrast with those of the law. In his account, totally stripped of hot kisses and swelling breasts, the nuptial drama has been strictly economized and politicized.

LUTHER AND QUEERING OF THE MARRIAGE[49]

Let me end this exposition of Luther's use of the nuptial imagery by pointing to the fact that he does not simply follow a new track as he does in his interpretation of the Song. Luther actually follows the tradition from Origen and Bernard much more extensively than most think.[50] Hence, we find the same discourse of gender crossing in Luther's use of the nuptial imagery, although in his comments to quite another text, the prophet Isaiah. Here, Luther interprets the bridal metaphor ecclesiologically: the bride symbolizes the church (Ephesians 5).

But Luther goes even further when in his exposition of Isaiah 61:10 he does not simply identify Christ with the bridegroom and the church with the bride, but also, like Bernard, identifies believers with the bridegroom. In the marriage union of faith, humans take on the role of Christ: "Thus all of us who believe are by faith bridegrooms and priests."[51] Humans perform both as bride and bridegroom by way of faith. Reflecting on Isaiah 66:9, Luther applies the same dual nuptial identity of bride/groom to Christ, in a reciprocal movement of life and death, of giving and receiving. He says that He is the author of begetting: "I, however, do not appear to be fertile. On the contrary, I, God, am sterile, yes, dead and crucified. But I keep my method of bearing for myself. I give others the power to bring forth, and I can bring forth too. I am both Bridegroom and Bride. I can beget and give birth, and I can give others the power of begetting."[52]

48. LW 15:198.
49. I owe this formulation to Kleinhans, "Christ as Bride/Groom," 132.
50. I disagree with Kleinhans, "Christ as Bride/Groom," 128, who claims a generic, and indeed unsubstantiated, difference between Luther and the "medieval mystics."
51. LW 17:342.
52. LW 17:406.

What is employed here is a discourse that is indeed pregnant with divine eroticism, yet untying the nuptial imagery from specific sexes and gender roles, while displaying otherness. Luther uses the text in a de-stabilizing and fluid way, loosened from any creational order of sexes or cultural bindings on gender. The marriage is queered and set free for the Christian or any creature to become fully human in the social and political play.

CONCLUSION

At the core of Bernard's and Luther's theology is an understanding of God as the being of love. They agree in this ontological understanding, as they agree in their theological semantics of a *caritas* love, at times in expressly carnal language. By way of a fluid and gender-crossing use of relational metaphors, especially the nuptial imagery, they emphasize the importance of love as the source and end of life in the relational exchange between God and humans. There is no doubt that both Bernard and Luther perceive God as the very being of love, and see this love operating in a sublime circulation as love abundantly flowing from the heart of God to the heart of humans, the incarnated and the crucified Christ/God being the gift and example of that. In my view they in each of their contexts display a *theologia caritatis* in a sublime combination of *theologia cordis* and *theologia crucis*, a theology of love spelled out in the sharp reality of life with its poles of the deepest pain and the highest bliss. God became fully human (*Mensch/homo*) to be heterologically recognized as a human in life and death among humans.

BIBLIOGRAPHY

Althaus-Reid, Marcella. *Indecent Theology. Theological Perversions in Sex, Gender and Politics*. New York: Routledge, 2000.

Bjerre-Aspegren, Kerstin. *Bräutigam, Sonne und Mutter. Studien zu einigen Gottesmetaphern bei Gregor von Nyssa*. Malmö: Gotab, 1977.

Bynum, Caroline Walker. *Jesus as Mother. Studies in the High Middle Ages*. Berkeley: University of California Press, 1982.

Engh, Line Cecilie. "Performing the Bride. Gender and Self-Representation in Bernard of Clairvaux's *Sermones super cantica canticorum*." PhD diss., University of Oslo, 2011.

Foucault, Michel. *The History of Sexuality: An Introduction*. New York: Penguin, 1978.

Johnson, Barbara. *The Critical Difference*. Baltimore: John Hopkins University Press, 1984.

Kleinhans, Kathryn A. "Christ as Bride/Groom: A Lutheran Feminist Relational Christology." In *Transformative Lutheran Theologies*, edited by Mary J. Streufert, 123–34. Minneapolis: Fortress, 2010.

Luther, Martin. *Von der Freiheit eines Christenmenschens. Von weltlicher Obrigkeit. Sermon von guten Werken.* 2nd ed. Gütersloh: Chr. Kaiser/Güterloher, 1998.

———. *Luthers Werke. Kristische Gesamtausgabe.* (WA).57 vols. Weimar: Böhlau, 1883ff.

———. *Luther's Works. American Edition.* (LW). 55 vols. Saint Louis and Philadelphia: Concordia and Fortress, 1955

Matter, E. Ann. *The Voice of My Beloved. The Song of Songs in Western Medieval Christianity.* Philadelphia: University of Pennsylvania Press, 1990.

Pedersen , Else Marie Wiberg. "The Significance of the *Sola Fide* and the *Sola Gratia* in the Theology of Bernard of Clairvaux (1090–1153) and Martin Luther (1483–1546)." *Luther-Bulletin*, Jahrgang 18, 2009.

———. *Bernhard af Clairvaux. Teolog eller mystiker?* (*Bernard of Clairvaux. Theologian or Mystic?*). Copenhagen: Anis 2008.

Turner, Denys. *Eros and Allegory. Medieval Exegesis of the Song of Songs.* Kalamazoo, MI: Cistercian, 1995.

Westhelle, Vítor. *The Scandalous God: The Use and Abuse of the Cross.* Minneapolis: Fortress, 2006.

Winkler, Gerhard B. *Bernhard von Clairvaux. Sämtliche Werke lateinisch/deutsch I-X.* Innsbruck: Tyrolia-Verlag, 1990–99.

Wyschgorod, Edith. *An Ethics of Remembering: History, Heterology and the Nameless Others.* Chicago: University of Chicago Press, 1998.

6

Postcolonial Transfigurative Identity
Reading Walcott with Westhelle in Mind

JOHN ARTHUR NUNES

THE POETIC VISION OF Derek Walcott is transgressive. This is poetry in which is hidden a theological purpose: Walcott's transgressivity is going somewhere, each "turn" towards transfiguration and truth. Vítor Westhelle's understanding of hybridity provides an interpretive key to this conclusion, an echo of the truth of the Gospel of Jesus, the redemptive turning toward humanity of the hybridized God-man (*communicatio idiomata*), the Only-begotten, uncreated creator, the ultimate Outsider and Insider. In his very self he redefines and redeems identity for those others living in marginality.

> Derek Walcott considers himself a poet by vocation: "My calling as a poet is votive, sacred, out-dated, if you will, but it was a cherished vow taken in my young dead father's name, and my life is to honor that vow. I believe that through all adversities I have been blessed."[1]

Exploring one of Westhelle's preferred ideas, poetics, a favorite theologian of his, Oswald Bayer, affirms "the essential relevance of poetry" as

---

1. Baer, *Conversations with Walcott*, 85.

a devotional practice within the sphere of a divine calling. We interpret Bayer to suggest that poetry serves as a strategic art (*techne*) inasmuch as it expresses theology, especially when theology is plotted "as a way of navigating between metaphysics and mythology."[2] If theology is a critical and self-critical reflection on the human response to God's sacrificial love for creation, then poetics is helpful since its language is reflectively hybrid. Metaphorical words speak bi-directionally; poetry addresses both the philosophical reasoning about the "what" and the "why" of humankind within this universe (metaphysics) *as well as* a human community's narratological self-understanding—those stories that codify human origins and its pathway through the world (mythology).

Westhelle's illuminating distinction between *poiesis* and *praxis* gives further nuance and guidance to our reading of the theological aspects of Walcott's work: *poiesis*, in this usage, describes those creative acts determined to produce a tangible outcome nurturing intellectual life. Westhelle contrasts this with *praxis*, which describes the deeds done having had communal impact, though necessarily producing a material product.[3] So, Walcott's output nurtures the life of the mind, leading to action, both theological and intellectual, in the tradition described by Ngũgĩ wa Thiong'o (b. 1938): "An intellectual is a worker in ideas with words as the primary means of production."[4]

Though Walcott's poetic production has been prolific and seems to exude confidence, this success does not preclude the equally real burden of a vocation that neared vexation over the course of his career. Witness the epiphanic appropriation of his calling, predictably cryptic, semiotic, indirect, and passionately grief-laden and laced with divine themes:

> Then suddenly, from their rotting logs, distracting signs
> of the faith I betrayed, or the faith that betrayed me—
> yellow butterflies rising on the road to Valencia
> stuttering "yes" to the resurrection; "yes, yes is our answer,"
> the gold-robed Nunc Dimittis of their certain choir.
> Where's my child's hymnbook, the poems edged in gold leaf,
> the heaven I worship with no faith in heaven,
> as the Word turned toward poetry in its grief?
> Ah, bread of life, that only love can leaven!
> Ah, Joseph, though no man ever dies in his own country,

---

2. Bayer, "Poetological Theology," 163.

3. See Westhelle's careful distinction, as applied to ecclesiology, in *Church Event*, 32–34.

4. Ngugi wa Thiong'o, "Interpreters," 45.

the grateful grass will grow thick from his heart.⁵

Such artistic agonizing was not rare for Caribbean intellectuals in the mid twentieth century—a time in the developing world of radically rising critical consciousness (Portuguese, *conscientização*).⁶

A HYBRID TURN

Walcott's biographical context in St. Lucia consists of a racially mixed ancestry: Dutch, African, English. Language, culture, and ethnicity are woven together in much of the Caribbean context to create a mélange: a multilayered, multilingual, multiethnic hybridity. Early in his career, Walcott reflected viscerally on the seeming impossibility of a particular postcolonial situation requiring a binary ethical choice:

> I am who am poisoned with the blood of both,
> Where shall I turn, divided to the vein?⁷

Walcott, himself, is a pilgrim wanderer, even more, a mongrelized nomad reflecting on being at home nowhere—"I had no nation now but the imagination. / After the white man, the niggers didn't want me / when the power swing to their side."⁸ He describes his situation: "Schizophrenic, wrenched by two styles / one a hack's hired prose / I earn my exile."⁹ A complex flux for this artist to live and work: "I am a kind of split writer. I have one tradition inside me going one way and another tradition going another. The mimetic, the narrative, and dance element is strong on one side, and the literary, the classical tradition is strong on the other."¹⁰

Such hybridity, Baugh concludes "is cognate with the dualism of Walcott's yearning for a plain style in his poetry, and his instinct for metaphorical richness and elaboration."¹¹ Predictably, linguistic implications flow from cultural hybridity.

---

5. Walcott, *Collected Poems*, 510.
6. See Freire, *Pedagogy of the Oppressed*.
7. The proximate context for this citation is the Mau-Mau uprising and suppression in Kenya. Walcott, "Far Cry from Africa," 18.
8. Walcott, *Collected Poems*, 350.
9. Walcott, "Codicil," 61.
10. Quoted in Baugh, *Derek Walcott*, 60.
11. Ibid.

THEORIA

A LINGUISTIC TURN

As in hybrid situations broadly, and in Walcott's case specifically, ethnic identity is further complexified not only by the exigencies of both colonial and postcolonial[12] class structures, but language usage bears directly the mark of competing identities. "To change your language you must change your life."[13] St. Lucia offered its wealthier (and often "mixed") citizens a formal, regimented system of "classical," canonical education.[14] In a backhanded compliment, some critics considered it a compliment to approve Walcott's language skills as even superior to British English. His hybridity has also subjected his language to negative critique from both sides: "he has been called too Western by some Afrocentric critics and too Afro-Caribbean by some Eurocentric critics."[15] Undeterred, and with a panache reaching exuberance, Walcott delights in both deflated (vernacular) and inflated (highbrow) language practices: "I'd rather be pompous than dull, rather go for the big swipe than the timid, decent drawing-room gesture."[16]

Though Derek Walcott's creative impulse was inspired and fired by the context of the Caribbean, it was also stifled and stymied by the same context due to the difficulty of artists to sustain themselves there, "I watch the best minds root like dogs for scraps of favor" The exercise and expression of the artistic craft in this environment of economic exploitation, of illiteracy regarding the formal arts, of intellectual provincialism, intensified by segregating social stratification, seems to have contributed to Walcott's

---

12. I am working with the following definitions of Colonial and Postcolonial: *Colonialism* represents a nationalistic ideology with a purportedly civilizing mission, often reinforced by a religious framework, legitimating the total or partial invasion and suzerainty of another's land and people—extending beyond geography to their relationships, soul, intellect, and imagination—accruing usually to the occupier an economic and/or military advantage.

Postcolonialism represents a critical and self-critical intervention of colonialism's invasionary proposals and practices to the extent that colonialist structures are destabilized and transformed, whereby a transfigured identity is re/claimed, asserted, and recognized.

13. Walcott, "Codicil," 61.

14. "From England, he [Walcott] has appropriated an old-fashioned love of eloquence, an Elizabethan richness of words and a penchant for complicated, formal rhymes. In fact, in a day when more and more poets have adopted a grudging, minimalist style, Mr. Walcott's verse remains dense and elaborate, filled with dazzling complexities of style. Shakespeare, Hopkins, Marvell, Keats, Auden, and Eliot—these are just some of the influences one can discern in his work; Homer, Virgil, Dante, and Ovid—some of the allusions." Kakutani, "Books of the Times."

15. "Derek Walcott." http://www.enotes.com/derek-walcott-essays/walcott-derek-78954.

16. Derek Walcott in Baer, *Conversations with Walcott*, ed. William Baer, 82.

conceptualization of himself as schizophrenic, destined toward two lives, "the interior life of poetry," and "the outward life of action and dialect."[17] This double-mindedness, I contend, was prompted not only by ethnicity, but also by the breach between his popular culture of St. Lucia and the high literary culture of England.

Walcott's generation of writers were conversant in the literature of empires—Greek, Roman, British—as well as being apt in the indigenous "slang." Mastering this European language presented this poet with a profound existential crisis cutting to the vein between "this African and the English tongue I love?"[18] Such excellence and affection for the language, viz. *Omeros*, led to his 1992 Nobel Prize in Literature. Again, not without cost, but with *Anfechtung*, to invoke Martin Luther's despair, with angst exemplified in, if not amplified by, the dilemma of multiple hybridities.

In spite of Walcott's often pedantic insistence on complex rhyming schemes, and his rarefied—at times, nearly ornamental—vocabulary, his main characters are often ordinary and unlikely, with mouths full of foul talk and plainspoken patois unavailable in any conventional dictionary. Transgression!

This is not unfamiliar to those within the Lutheran tradition. Martin Luther, likewise, worked to keep linguistically connected to common folk. Casual dinner comments, and other *obiter dicta*, gathered in the compendia of his "Table Talk" display Luther's language as intellectual, but hardly highbrow, and undoubtedly earthy, even crude to politically correct ears. Certainly capable of going toe-to-toe with weighty academics, Luther was a master also of *haute vulgarisation*—taking complex thoughts and making them simple. For example, with respect to a common complaint concerning God's overly severe condemnation of Adam, Luther says, "Our Lord God is always in the wrong, no matter what he does ... God is said to have gone too far. On the other hand, God freely forgives all sins, even the crucifixion of his Son, provided men believe, and this is also regarded as going too far."[19] Complex theology wrapped in linguistic simplicity. With an ear to the popular piety of the pew, Luther speaks directly and comprehensibly, exhibiting a propensity for common folk.

Walcott, likewise, in *Dream on Monkey Mountain*, introduces us to his "heroes." These are often outdoor people subsisting and surviving on an

---

17. Walcott, *Twilight*, 4. See also William Baer's interview which exposits Walcott's intention with this statement of dialectic.

18. Walcott, "Far Cry from Africa," 18.

19. Luther, "Table Talk," 105. This specific table talk reference is Number 587.

ordinary Caribbean landscape and seascape. They sound like the biblical cast of outcasts associating with Jesus, dismaying the pharisaical:

> poor fishermen, derelicts, eccentric persons, saxophonists, alcoholics, transvestites, workers, common people. There is also a remarkable grocer who dreams of returning to Africa and leading the exodus to the new Jerusalem. There are peasants, charcoal-burners, coal-carrying women, carpenters, cripples, felons, paupers, priests.... dancers, singers musicians, dreamers, philosophers, artists.[20]

In the poet's poetry (*Another Life*):

> Provincialism loves the pseudo-epic,
> so if these heroes have been given a stature
> disproportionate to their cramped lives,
> remember I beheld them at knee height,[21]

In many and various ways mainstream writers and scholars have tended to under-regard the rhetorical twists, euphonic devices, and comic turns-of-phrase of non-dominant cultures, opting instead to interpret language more often with a propositional gravitas. While Walcott did receive in St. Lucia a classical, British education, he was additionally a student of the people—their inflection, their patois, their Africanisms, their demotic character, their blended everyday speech, what Henry Louis Gates designates as signifyin(g).[22]

Readers of Walcott's work who read between the lines (cf. intelligence, Lat. *inter-legere*) see him engaged in a hybrid mischief depositing theological terms side-by-side with ordinary speech. This literary playfulness represents theological transgressivity, a liberating arena for the oppressed to speak. Postcolonial poets unsilence the voices from "below." For example, historically among African-Americans in the United States, especially in everyday settings, there have been many lively levels of vernacular speech: "street corner bantering, beauty-shop boasting, cotton-patch moaning, jump-rope rhyming, prayer-meeting testifying, family-reunion storytelling ... "[23] Like the Caribbean, these linguistic modes and semantic occasions necessarily nurture the slipperiness of word meanings affording a compensatory communicative advantage to those who are otherwise disadvantaged. Revised, non-standard communication honors a rich verbal

---

20. Walcott in Baer, *Conversations with Walcott*, 79.
21. Walcott, *Another Life*, 40.
22. See Gates, *Signifying Monkey*.
23. Nunes, "Preaching and Colloquial Voice," 6.

dexterity that humanizes the outcasts, aggrandizes the underling, heroicizes the oppressed, even as it complexifies stultifying, high-brow semiotics. The dynamic language practices of postcolonial poets are liberational, transfigurative, and revelatory.

A POETIC TURN

The poetic turn of the hybrid signals, foreshadows, and represents a linguistic and transgressive move that transfigures suffering and reveals identity, but not without struggle: "Poetry, in a way, is a quarrel with God, one which I imagine God understands."[24]

Walcott appears as one haunted by religion, suffering from divine things[25] tied to God's luring of this poet towards a transgressive poeticism, "the Word turned toward poetry in its grief."[26] I maintain that postcolonialism represents more than an academic tool for theological assessments, literary analyses, or socio-political appraisals; these themselves are worthy enterprises.[27] But postcolonial poetry's primary engagement is as an intervention, stemming phenomenologically from the experience of those in resistance to a colonial reality. In that sense I borrow from R. S. Sugirtharajah (b. 1947), who defined postcolonialism as "an interventionist instrument which refuses to take the dominant reading as an uncomplicated representation of the past and introduces an alternative reading."[28]

---

24. Walcott in Baer, *Conversations with Walcott*, 84.

25. To borrow from Reinhard Hütter's captivating title, *Suffering Divine Things: Theology as Church Practice*: Jesus " . . . rebuked Peter and said, 'Get behind me, Satan! For you are setting your mind not on divine things but on human things'" (Mark 8:33).

26. Walcott, *Collected Poems*, 510.

27. As an ardent proponent of the liberal arts and learning, Luther often advised young people to study languages, rhetoric, poetry, suggesting that such erudition was related to the "grasping of sacred truth and for handling it skillfully and happily." *Luther's Correspondence*, 176-77; cf. *Luthers Werke*, vol. 3, 49-50; *Luther's Works*, vol. 49, 32-35. Soon after Luther outlined his theology in the 1518 Heidelberg Theses, he wrote to his old teacher Trutfetter, "I believe simply that it is impossible to reform the church if the canons, the decretals, the scholastic theology, the philosophy, the logic as they now are not uprooted and another study installed" (*Luthers Werke*, vol. 1, no. 74). Luther's "other study" would be that of renaissance humanism in which rhetoric was a major component; see Rosin, "The Reformation, Humanism, and Education, "301–18.

28. Sugirtharajah, *Bible and Empire*, 3.

THEORIA

HIDDEN GOD TURNING HYBRID PERSON

What might constitute the alternate reading provided by postcolonial poetry of Christological reflection? Westhelle connects the dots: "Hybrids transgress. They transgress margins, their own habitat by transfiguring themselves."[29]

The "hybrid" nature of Christ—fully human, fully divine—breaks transgressively into this world, turning hearers toward the living Word, even as a baby wearing dirty diapers; in full hiddenness this God-man fully reveals a transfiguring redemption on a vile instrument of public punishment, a cross.

Dietrich Bonhoeffer surfaces this dilemma as he notes the actual transgressive, counter-cultural tone of Jesus, unsurprisingly at odds with colonial cooptation: " . . . [He] did things which, at least from the outside, looked like sin. He became angry, he was harsh to his mother, he escaped from his enemies, he broke the Law of his people, he stirred up revolt against the rulers and religious men of his country. He must have appeared a sinner in the eyes of men. Beyond recognition, he stepped into man's sinful way of existence."[30]

The words of the Incarnate Word, Jesus, cut transcendingly and transgressively against Greek philosophies, Jewish pieties, Roman expediencies, and all contemporary impositions of *prima facie* sensibilities. In every instance, the Jesus we see in the Gospels is both iconoclast and icon, a stranger, a servant, and a sufferer, unrecognized by powerbrokers, yet dying and rising even for those unable to recognize God's turn toward humankind.

Some forms of liberation theology—a first cousin to postcolonial theology—assert emphatically a Christ who radically empties himself (Phil 2:8). I take exception with Leonardo Boff, who notes in Jesus Christ an absence of human personality. This goes kenotically overboard, lacking transgressivity, and is finally unable to establish a transfigurative identity for postcolonials. In Boff's discussion of Jesus' self-emptying and giving over of himself entirely to God, he concludes that "Jesus does not possess what the Council of Chalcedon taught: He was lacking a 'hypostasis,' a subsistence, enduring in

---

29. Westhelle, "Margins Exposed," 86. Westhelle, however, places a premium emphasis on the role of transgressivity in mimesis and strategic, transgressive essentialism. This will not function as a focalizing theme in this work. The context of the quotation referenced in this citation reflects Westhelle's concern: "However, the point is not to surrender their own selves in the transgressive roles they play, for when they do so, they egress existence as such and are only accessible in the tradition of the memory of the victims of which we have plenty. They can pretend an identity which is not false but is intentionally and deceptively always something else, transfigured."

30. Bonhoeffer, *Christ the Center*, 108.

himself and for himself."³¹ While Boff explicitly notes Jesus' life of extreme service for others, I find his theory untenable at this point because of its peculiar contradiction that the humanity of Jesus—which, while unable to grasp the fullness of his messianic identity—was indeed able to grasp the depth of human suffering and thus actually live for the sake of the other. My problem with Boff's view is not its rejection of Chalcedon as much as his totalizing application of "self-emptying" to the extent that any individual personality of Jesus seems to have been evacuated. What remains? There is seemingly no *there* there in the human person, himself.

At this point, with respect to the *genus majestaticum*, it is Westhelle's classroom lectures that led me to align my postcolonial Christology with the Tübingen school's crypticism over against the Giesen school's kenoticism; while the latter solution seemingly prevailed within Western academic theology, it left, according to Westhelle's teaching, a creeping trail of monophysitism infecting Lutheran christology.

Concealment, not deferral, of the divine nature transgressively and ironically stands as the oppressed's most revelatory source of speech. Jesus was recognized most coherently by a "secular" centurion, an avowed enemy of Jesus' people, instrumentalized by the state to be an executioner, an agent of the empire, an outsider who stood facing Jesus, but literally "stood nearby opposite of him" (*parestekòs ek enantías*, Mark 15:39). The irony signaled in this narrative is who recognized Jesus: an outsider from the "nearby-opposite," from those disparaged, most odious to the self's sensibilities, a semi-other, offensive precisely because of his haunting similarity—neither familiarly the same nor totally the other.³² Yet, this centurion confesses all of whom Jesus, the outside/insider, is—"this man was the Son of God." At the place of suffering, a stranger is the one who having seen (*Idòn*, Mark 15:39), recognized, in the fullness of divine suffering, the One who was "beyond recognition." John Caputo summarizes "the 'other' is the one who tells the truth on the 'same.'"³³ Such transfigurative truth-telling, especially by outsiders like Walcott, stands as the root of a poetic transgressive confession of Jesus: God's *telos*, working in the world, on behalf of all who bear the Name.

---

31. Boff, *Jesus Christ Liberator*, 196.

32. Herbert Anderson notes the difficulty posed by "the Proximate Other" ... "a term we have devised to describe the one who is like me and yet different from me. It is a term we use when the qualities between Us and Them are mixed. We are unsettled by the Proximate Other because we see ourselves in the one who seems to be totally Other." From the opening paper of a meeting of the International Academy in Practical Theology in Seoul, Korea, titled, "Seeing the Other Whole."

33. Caputo, *What Would Jesus Deconstruct*, 29.

BIBLIOGRAPHY

Baer, William, editor. *Conversations with Derek Walcott* Jackson: University Press of Mississippi, 1996.

Baugh, Edward. *Derek Walcott*. Cambridge: Cambridge University Press, 2006.

Bayer, Oswald. "Poetological Theology: New Horizons for Systematic Theology." Translated by Gwen Griffith-Dickson. *International Journal of Systematic Theology* 1:2 (1999) 163.

Boff, Leonardo. *Jesus Christ Liberator: A Critical Christology of our Time*. Maryknoll: Orbis, 1978.

Bonhoeffer, Dietrich. *Christ the Center*. Translated by Edwin H. Robertson. San Francisco: Harper, 1978.

Caputo, John. *What Would Jesus Deconstruct: The Good News of Postmodernism for the Church*. Grand Rapids: Baker Academic, 2007.

Freire, Paulo. *Pedagogy of the Oppressed*. Translated by Myra Berman Ramos. New York: Continuum, 2006.

Gates, Henry Louis, Jr. *The Signifying Monkey: A Theory of African-American Literary Criticism*. New York: Oxford, 1988.

Hütter, Reinhard. *Suffering Divine Things: Theology as Church Practice*. Translated by Doug Stott. Grand Rapids: Eerdmans, 1997.

Kakutani, Michiko. "Books of the Times: Collected Poems: 1948–1984 by Derek Walcott." *The New York Times*, January 15, 1986. Online: http://www.nytimes.com/1986/01/15/books/books-of-the-times-355486.html.

Luther, Martin. *Luther's Correspondence II*, edited by P. Smith and C. M. Jacobs. Philadelphia: United Lutheran, 1918.

———. *Luther's Works*. Vol. 49. Edited by Jaroslav Pelikan and Helmut Lehmann. St. Louis: Concordia, 1972.

———. *D. Martin Luthers Werke: Kritische Gesamtausgabe, Briefwechsel*. 3 vols. Weimar: Böhlaus, 1885.

———. "Table Talk." In *Luther's Works*, vol. 54, edited by Helmut T. Lehmann. Philadelphia: Fortress, 1967.

Nunes, John. "Preaching and Colloquial Voice." *Concordia Pulpit Resources* 12.4 (2002) 6.

Rosin, Robert. "The Reformation, Humanism, and Education: The Wittenberg Model for Reform." *Concordia Journal* 16 (1990) 301–18.

Sugirtharajah, R. S. *The Bible and Empire: Postcolonial Explorations*. Cambridge: Cambridge University Press, 2005.

Thiong'o, Ngugi wa. "The Interpreters: Writing, Language and Politics." In *Multiculturalism and Hybridity in African Cultures*, edited by Hal Wylie and Bernth Lindfors, 45. Trenton, NJ: Africa World, 2000.

Walcott, Derek. *Another Life: Fully Annotated*. Boulder, CO: Lynne Reinner, 2004.

———. *Collected Poems: 1948–1984*. New York: Farrar, Straus & Giroux, 1986.

———. "Codicil." In *The Castaway and Other Poems*, 61. London: Jonathan Cape, 1965.

———. "A Far Cry from Africa." In *Collected Poems: 1948–1984*, 18. New York: Farrar, Straus & Giroux, 1986.

———. *What the Twilight Says*. New York: Farrar, Straus & Giroux, 1998.

Westhelle, Vítor. *The Church Event: Call and Challenge of a Church Protestant*. Minneapolis: Fortress, 2010.

———. "Margins Exposed: Representation, Hybridity and Transfiguration." In *Still at the Margins: Biblical Scholarship Fifteen Years after the Voices from the Margins*. London: T. & T. Clark, 2008.

POEISIS

7

Created Co-Creator
Symbol of Life in Crisis and Ambiguity

PHILIP HEFNER

OVER THE YEARS, I have been privileged to carry on conversations with Vítor Westhelle on the concept of humans as God's created co-creators—an idea I first broached nearly thirty years ago in *Christian Dogmatics*.[1] I hope to honor professor Westhelle on this anniversary by contributing another segment to this conversation.

In 2004, he brought his characteristic incisive critique to bear upon the idea when he wrote:

> However, the limitation of this concept is its neatness. It suppresses that which cannot be suppressed. This otherwise straightforward concept fails to give a realistic description of the human in situations of being on the edge that points to an end where there are no alternatives or negotiations.[2]

I am grateful for this critique, since heretofore my representation of the created co-creator and the ensuing discussion has indeed proceeded as if

---

1. Hefner, "Creation," 325–28.
2. Westhelle, "Poet, the Practitioner, and the Beholder," 747–54.

it were a "straightforward concept." Since the beginning, however, I have wanted to probe the more ambiguous and darker sides of the created co-creator, explore the edges where the unsuppressible lives. This volume affords an appropriate place to begin this exploration.

The concept of created co-creator attempts to integrate scientific knowledge into Christian theology. In contrast to the more usual practice of starting with physics and cosmology, the created co-creator focuses not on origins, but on human existence. Philosophically, it begins with anthropology rather than cosmology; scientifically, it begins with evolutionary biology, primatology, and anthropology, rather than physics and cosmology; its literary genre is memoir and personal narrative, rather than philosophical-theological treatise.

With this in mind, exploration of the concept conveys the sense of our experience of ourselves as creators—not in abstract ideas, but in experience. Experience is the domain of the unsuppressible, the ambiguous and inexhaustible substrate that underlies human existence. We ought not let this experience be overwhelmed by an impersonal concentration on creation, cosmology, and physics. We cannot settle for subsuming human experience into an amorphous concept of physical nature. Mine is a human-centered beginning-point, anthropocentric, but not to be confused with anthropocentr*ism*.

CRISIS, LIMINALITY, AND AMBIGUITY

Our experience of ourselves as creators is confronted by what I call a crisis of technological civilization: since the natural systems of the planet are fully conditioned by our technology, we are faced with the challenge of interfacing and harmonizing that technology with the enormously complex natural world; we are faced with innumerable decisions and unavoidable errors that are frequently life-threatening to humans and other citizens of the planet. Creating is an expression of who we are as humans and also a crisis of culture and identity.

The created co-creator concept exists totally under the conditions of this crisis, and for this reason, it can never be understood as straightforward. On the contrary, it is our entrée into the domain of the unsuppressible, the ambiguous and the tragic dimensions of human existence. The crisis constitutes a kind of liminal experience through which we are ushered into the ambiguity and even tragedy in which the unsuppressible takes shape. At issue in the crisis is how we express our creatorhood and whether we can create in ways that are commensurate with our ideal of what we are and ought to be—whether we have the capability and whether the situation in which we live allows us to exercise our creating adequately.

To recapitulate the argument: the created co-creator is rooted in our experience of ourselves as creators and also in the experience of the crisis of our creating. This experience is exhilarating, exhausting, and poignant. In addition to the rush of the flow of creating, we also know a double ambiguity: our actual creating seldom lives up to our visions of what it could be and it is frequently entangled in finitude and destruction. Creating is intrinsic to who we are and at the same time a betrayal of who we intend to become.

Worldviews that deny our co-creatorhood and thereby disallow our experience as creators are not helpful—they distract us from the life-forming struggle to create authentically. These denials mask ambiguity and attempt to flee tragedy. When we must expend so much of our time and energy, for example, arguing whether genetic engineering or reproductive technologies are to be allowed at all, we face up neither to the hard work of setting goals and developing criteria for strategies of creating in these areas nor to the inescapable ambiguity that accompanies creating.

CREATED CO-CREATOR AS METAPHOR AND SYMBOL

I do not propose the image of the created co-creator as a scientific description, however, nor as any kind of literal statement. I propose it as a metaphor and as a symbol, and we must ask what difference this makes.

In both metaphor and symbol, new meanings are created by beginning with a literal image and insisting that there is more meaning to be gained than literalness alone can deliver. Metaphor and symbol express the conviction that the finite and the literal are more than science and technology can take the measure of. They take us, as Mihalyi Csikszentmihalyi has written "out of the present, out of ourselves."[3] They point to possibilities to which our literal descriptions are not sensitive. The literal deals with what is, the metaphorical and the symbolic deal with what can be.

Metaphor

We put the human created co-creator as metaphor in this manner: Humans as created co-creators are metaphor for the meaning of nature, the meaning of creation. We can know the human factor of this metaphor quite literally, but the other factor—nature and its meaning—is beyond us, larger and

---

3. Csikszentmihalyi, "Consciousness for the Twenty-First Century" 17–18.

more complex than our minds can conceive. As human created co-creators we are fully natural, and our emergence within natural processes of evolution is the subject of innumerable scientific studies. Most strikingly, the human creature is aware of itself and interprets itself—we know of no other creature on this earth that struggles to determine the meaning of its own being. Humans recognize that they are possessors of a normative nature that is more than their empirical existence. This recognition is the ground of all moral sensibility. The human creature, in other words, takes the measure of its own being, imagines what it can and should become, and acts to advance that becoming. We actually participate in creating our own becoming. The metaphoric process suggests that the human created co-creator is an epitome of the entire natural world. "Epitome" means representative example and also compact, intense microcosm of the whole. If nature is about becoming aware of itself and creating itself anew, then humans are not isolated in their nature, they are rather the space in which nature becomes most self-aware, the space in which nature takes its own measure, and imagines what it can and should be and shares in its own creation.

There is more to be said, however. Paul Ricoeur speaks of the tension and the self-destructing elements in the metaphoric process. Without this process of self-destructing, new meanings are not engendered.[4] Even though the literal component of the metaphor is essential and the starting-point of the process, it is the literal that self-destructs. This can be seen in at least two points in respect to the image of the created co-creator. First of all, the human creature is literally a bundle of physical-chemical processes. Nobel laureate Francis Crick makes this the core of his study of human consciousness, entitled *The Astonishing Hypothesis*.[5] This physical-chemical literalness self-destructs in the claim that what happens in these processes is the telos of the natural world, the epitome of the processes that actually appear most vividly in *Homo sapiens*. If it is to carry the weight of this large interpretation, the literal neurobiology must go beyond itself and contradict itself.

A second self-destruction is that of worldviews or self-images. Particularly in our western traditions, we have seized upon our self-awareness and freedom to interpret ourselves as qualitatively superior to the rest of nature. We have interpreted our creative capacities literally as the basis for distinguishing ourselves from nature, so that the terms "nature" and "human" are two rims of a chasm which is very difficult for us to cross. This dualism self-destructs when the profound relationship of belongingness

---

4. Ricoeur, *Interpretation Theory: Discourse and the Surplus of Meaning*, 50–51.
5. Crick, *Astonishing Hypothesis*.

between humans and the natural order is unveiled in the metaphor. For the arrogance of anthropocentrism, this collapse of dualism feels like destruction. A genuinely new image emerges of what it means to be human—not by muting our creativity but by re-interpreting it.

For our religious interpretations, this metaphoric process and the self-destruction of the metaphor are equally significant. The metaphor speaks of how God planned the creation. It also gives new meaning to the talk about the image of God. For most of our Christian history, we have interpreted the image of God as a divine reinforcement of our superiority to all other species, a theological blessing of our self-serving agency. When this dualism collapses, there opens up for us the inexhaustibly rich vista of how the image of God far from separating us from the rest of nature in fact bonds us to the rest of nature.

Here we touch upon genuinely new understandings of human becoming and of our experience of being creators. We do not, by and large, view ourselves as an epitome of the natural world or the creation of God, nor do we conceive our creating within the becoming of the natural world. If we did, we would see that our becoming and the becoming of nature are not different becomings, but rather dimensions of the same process. If we did, dualisms between human and nature would not dominate our thinking as they do now.

A next step in understanding flows from what I have said thus far: conceptualizing human life within the processes of creation and orienting our goals and destiny toward those of the creation. If indeed we are part of the creation's becoming aware of itself and freely imagining and creating its identity, then the goal of our creating is defined in terms of that same creation—that is where our destiny lies. Whatever we have been created for, it has something to do with God's purposes for the whole creation—in, with, and under the creation, and not apart from it.

Symbol

While metaphor is this-worldly, symbol opens up the dimension of transcendence. Paul Tillich set this forth in enumerating four basic characteristics of a symbol:

> A symbol "points beyond itself to something else."
> It "participates in that to which it points."
> A symbol "opens up levels of reality which otherwise are closed to us."

It "unlocks dimensions and elements of our soul which correspond to the dimensions and elements of reality."[6]

Placing the created co-creator in this context produces additional insights. For now, let us say that the symbol points to what the metaphor unveiled: human purpose and destiny within the creation, as well as the ambiguity that accompany purpose and destiny.

Participation in nature, with the dualisms of nature and culture abolished, is critical. When we accept our own status as created co-creator and explore it deeply, we immediately recognize that we do in fact participate in this triad of relationships: human, nature, and culture. We are not separated from them. *We are actually embodied in the facts of being created and creating our worlds.* Medicine and the natural environment are two realms in which this embodiment is conveyed to us in particularly vivid ways. As we grow in our understanding of both health and illness, we become aware that we are embodied in the nature of our bodies and also in our cultural practice of medicine, through which we not only gain self-understanding, but also intervene in our own evolution, either to cure disease or to improve our bodies. Reproductive technologies, for example, are not merely speculations for us, or bodies of information we master in medical schools, they are the actual ways in which we conceive babies and bring them into the world—these technologies "are us." When we consider the technologies of pharmaceutical medicines and agricultural production, for example, we recognize that these technologies are also "us," and they live within us, not just outside.

What levels of reality are opened up for us? Relatedness and embodiment are one important level of reality that is opened up for us by the symbol. We gain an awareness of our relatedness to the entire history of the universe and its evolution. At a second level, we recognize that the dualisms which dominate our thinking testify that we are estranged at the center of our being, estranged within the very relationships that constitute us as humans. We know that we belong essentially to the world in which we live, but also that we are estranged from it. This belonging/estrangement equation is an expression of the ambiguity that enfolds us.

The symbol of created co-creator does not convey detached knowledge about ourselves, so much as *it touches the deepest dimensions of who we are and our mutuality with the natural and social world in which we live. This is what it means to say that the symbol goes to the depths of our soul.* It reveals not only the soul's connectedness to the rest of the world, but also our existential inability to experience that connectedness apart from the simultaneous

---

6. Tillich, *Dynamics of Faith*, chapter 3.

conditions of estrangement from our very own being and from the world to which we are essentially connected. We are thereby estranged also from God the creator. This is the creation God has undertaken, and we belong to it, but we are also estranged from it. We find it often abhorrent that God has created us this way.

CREATED CO-CREATOR AS RELIGIOUS SYMBOL

At this point we enter into the religious depth of the created co-creator symbol. In Tillich's framework a religious symbol points beyond itself to ultimate concern, to that which grasps us ultimately, that which poses the issues of life and death, being and non-being. As we face the ambiguity and tragedy in our struggle to be human as created co-creator, we encounter ultimacy at two points: in our *creating* and in our search for *accountability* in that creating.

Our creativity raises the question, "How and where is our creativity sourced? Is its source only in our genes and their processes? Or is it something larger and deeper? In our creativity we are always finding newness—in the world and in ourselves. To what is this newness to be referred?

Associating human activities of creation with ultimacy, a depth or a "*More*" (William James' term)[7] is pervasive in human history. Creating results in the emergence of the new, which deepens the tie with ultimacy. Agriculture, choosing political leaders, procreation, fighting wars are only a few of the activities that have been interpreted by linking them with myths of creation. Eliade notes, for example, that in India "not only does the construction of the house take place in the centre of the world, but in a sense repeats the creation." "Mythical time," including the time of the original creation, "can be repeated *ad infinitum* with every new thing humans make."[8]).

And what is our potent creativity *for*? What is it supposed to accomplish? To what is it accountable? This turns out to be the question of the accountability of our lives. In turn, the question of accountability is the question of the meaning and purpose of our lives. Questions of accountability are intrinsic to the created co-creator symbol, and they, too, bring in the reality of the More. Consequently, creating can become an obsession, whether it is creating a business-empire or a symphony, and it can become a taboo, as when religious leaders anathematize art that parodies dogma or

---

7. James, *Varieties of Religious Experience*.
8. Eliade, *Patterns in Comparative Religion*, 380.

when society outlaws human cloning. Both anathema and obsession signal that our creating work intersects with norms and imperatives that we consider to be transcendent.

If we hide from ourselves the ultimate reality that encounters us in our experience as created co-creators, we court disaster. The created co-creator becomes dangerous; it turns against itself with demonic consequences. Only in the acknowledgment of the ultimate ground of our being as created co-creators can we attain responsible and enriching co-creatorhood. For Christians, this is God-talk, because we believe that God is the source, and God is the final locus of accountability.

GOD REVEALED IN THE CO-CREATOR

Since the symbol points to and participates in this transcendence, this "More," the symbol of the created co-creator roots *us* in this transcendence, as well. This is, of course, the question of God. Since we share in transcendence only through fragments of experience, in this case, our experience of being creators, we cannot claim to understand the fullness of God or even the ability to frame an adequate concept of God. Nevertheless, we do ask, what does that fragment allow us to see of God?

If the complex, self-generative nature of the creation suggests something about God's purposes, could it suggest also something of the nature of God? If self-generation, autopoeisis—the making of ourselves—is written into the very substance of nature, as well as into the fundamental code of human nature and technology, we must consider that it is a clue to the nature of reality and, therefore, to the nature of God. The same is to be said about the apparent fact that we are not given the meanings of nature and human life—not by nature nor by God—but apparently have to discern meaning; we have to create that meaning, and we must decide what is truer or less true about our own creations. This is also a clue to the nature of God. Finally, the fact that rearranging nature and society, thereby bringing new possibilities into existence, is basic to human nature may also be a clue to the nature of God.

One of the classical assertions about God in traditional religions is that God speaks the difficult word that places people on the pressure point of life, won't let them off, and compels them to deal with hard reality. The crisis of technology and culture that I have spoken of is a pressure point for us today. It is the crisis of the co-creators who have proven to be fallible and are uncertain about their creating work. We cannot deny our co-creating nature or escape this pressure point, because our very being is expressed on that point. Even though we may say that God is hidden from us in this experience, God is not absent from our struggle—indeed, our struggle takes place within the very being of God. It is God's redeeming presence in the creation that empowers our struggle on the pressure point.

We see dimly, through the limits of the fragment of experience that has been given to us. In this essay, I have focused on one such fragment—our experience of ourselves as creators. We find ourselves on a journey, whose ending we do not know. Our hope and our strength lie not in our knowledge or in our vision. The source of our hope and our strength lies in the conviction that our perilous journey is not taking us away from God, but rather unites us with God. The accountability that we carry is to create in ways that are appropriate to the creation and to the God whose we are. For Christians this journey will follow the figure of Jesus Christ.

BIBLIOGRAPHY

Crick, Francis. *The Astonishing Hypothesis: The Scientific Search for the Soul.* New York: Charles Scribners, 1994.

Csikszentmihalyi, Mihalyi. "Consciousness for the Twenty-First Century." *Journal of Religion and Science* 26 (1991) 17–18.

Eliade, Mircea. *Patterns in Comparative Religion.* Cleveland: World, 1963.

Hefner, Philip. "The Creation." In *Christian Dogmatics*, vol. 1, edited by Carl Braaten and Robert Jenson, 325–78. Minneapolis: Fortress, 1984.

James, William. *The Varieties of Religious Experience.* New York: Longmans, Green, 1908.

Ricoeur, Paul. *Interpretation Theory: Discourse and the Surplus of Meaning.* Ft. Worth: Texas Christian University Press, 1976.

Tillich, Paul. *Dynamics of Faith.* New York: Harper, 1958.

Westhelle, Vítor. "The Poet, the Practitioner, and the Beholder: Remarks on Philip Hefner's 'Created Co-Creator.'" *Journal of Religion and Science* 39 (2004) 747–54.

8

The Flavour of "the Other"

Re-thinking Differences in Europe, the Ecumenical Movement and Elsewhere

CLAUDIA JAHNEL

WELL-BALANCED IN TASTE AND flavour, the elite coffee from Melitta. Experience the fire of Brazil, the heat of East Africa, the hot temper of Central America and the mildness of the Columbian Highlands—a blend of world coffees—combined into the finest, most flavourful and irresistible variety. Don't be surprised if you feel pleasantly stimulated and revitalized after the first cup. It's the result of the melange!"[1]

1. THE CLOSENESS OF "THE OTHER"

One issue Europe as well as other parts of the world is wrestling with in various forms is the fact that "the other" has come closer.[2] This closeness

---

1 Indirectly cited from: http://www.melitta.de/de/01_produkte/t1_02_01_00.html.

2 The awareness of the compression of time and space and the closeness of "the other" as well as its multidisciplinary discussion has been furthered by scholars of the

involves the serious challenge to deal with "the other" in such way that the differences don't become destructive and violent forces. The Melitta-Coffee-Company, whose internet-spot is quoted above, reveals a very special, but, in a way, also very typical solution to this challenge. The TV-spot of Melitta shows the "white" Melitta-coffee-man together with several "colored" people, representing the different brands of coffee—stemming from Brazil, East-Africa, and Columbia etc. The color of the men's skin and various cultural accoutrements combined with ethnic music create an atmosphere of exoticism, power, sensuality, naturalism, rhythm, and fire. In order to make the product and its consumption more exotic, and thus more attractive, the whole range of colonial stereotypes are reactivated. Within this colonial nostalgia "the other" serves as an ornamental accessory,—while the real difference between the colonizer and the colonized disappears.

Other companies use similar strategies. The fashion shop "United Colors of Benetton," for instance, shows a group of people, a community of differences—in color, age, tradition, and culture—but united under the one dominant company "Benetton."

This mixing and melting of cultural elements, cultural cross-overs and blendings—the "global melange"[3]—is a prominent vision of living together today. It has become "trendy" to be a hybrid cosmopolitan, a world-citizen or a nomadic traveller through the cultures, someone who knows, eclectically lives out, and thereby homogenizes the cultural differences.[4]

2. ASYMMETRIES REGARDING THE CONSTRUCTION OF "THE OTHER"

Yet the critical question to be asked here is: Within this cultural interplay, who is the one "consuming," receiving an advantage from this mixture? And who is being consumed? It seems that the "exoticized other" predominantly serves the needs and desires of the metropolitan citizen, the one who possesses the purchasing power. And it is his or her life and life-style that are enriched by the mixture of cultural elements, while "the other" is being consumed.

Thus the vision of enriching hybrid cultures that is prevalent in much of our consumerist world comprises an asymmetric relation, an unequal

---

so called "globalisation" like David Harvey, Roland Robertson, Manuel Castells and others; yet it is by no means a new phenomenon as migrations have always been taking place.

3 Nederveen, "Der Melange-Effekt," 101.
4 Bronfen and Marius, *Hybride Kulturen*.

distribution and use of power and of the possibilities to enjoy the diversity.[5] At the same time, the real differences are excluded, the very "concrete other"[6] is being avoided. The illegal alien, for instance, who works in a sweatshop or the migrant who has difficulties communicating in our language and has this "strange" appearance—they hardly serve for cosmopolitan identifications or enthusiastic appraisals of the "new hybrid aborigine of the global village."

Nor does Fereshta Ludin, a teacher in Germany, who became "famous" some years ago because of her refusal not to wear the chador while teaching classes in school make the list. The conflict went to court, which ruled against Ludin's insistence on wearing the chador. But that incident affirmed the chador as a symbol of cultural distinction and as a sign of resistance to cultural assimilation, consumption and homogenization.

While the Melitta-coffee-man paradigmatically shows a romantically harmonized way of dealing with "the other" the chador-or-Ludin-trial represents the contrast-paradigm: the highly ambivalent attitude affiliated with "the other:" migrants are in many countries of Europe to a great extent overlooked. This leads—paradoxically—to an increased visibility once these migrants disturb the smooth flow of public administration. So wearing the chador does not per se create a problem—rather: it is something that is being "expected" from women whose families originate from Turkey or Afghanistan. This "picture" is not new. But irritations and conflicts arise when these women suddenly claim their political right to be "integrated" in Western societies, and to be treated as politically mature and self-representing citizens. The chador wearing—very often academically sound, and emancipated—women don't fit into the anticipated picture; rather they create a "third space"[7] which is followed by confusion and anxiety.[8] This anxiety is reproduced and furthered by the media: a picture of a chador-wearing woman on TV or in the Newspaper—intentionally or not—instantly evokes certain, most often negative stereotypes.[9]

The point I want to make here is not to decide on the questions of whether the chador is a religious or a political symbol, a sign of emancipation or a sign of oppression of women, a symbol of faith or a symbol of fundamentalism. These and similar questions are being discussed, assessed, and judged. But it is precisely this discussion, and the fact that courts in

---

5 Baumann, *Postmodernity*.
6 Benhabib, "Concrete Other," 38–60.
7 Bhabha, *Location of Culture*.
8 Terkessidis, "Globale Kultur."
9 Schiffer, "Symbolcharakter."

Germany or France are being authorized to judge a "different" or "strange" cultural symbol, that shows that the redefinition of the relationship with "the other" is imperative. Like the multiculti-hybrid enthusiasm, the assessment of "the other" and the process of judging other cultural symbols bear signs of the age-old eurocentric relationship with "the other." What is happening here is the prolonging of the historic monologue of the West on "the other," the follow up of the continuous subsuming of "the other," which is an act of epistemic violence that, by the construction and use of categories of knowledge, exercises power.[10] While, in former centuries, "the other"—other cultures, religions, societies—have been "discovered" by European explorers and only from then on seemed to be "born"—as childlike, immature, and primitive societies—, today, again, there is a tendency to conceive of "the other" from a European-Western and so-called "enlightened" point of view. This perceives the West as the developed and active pole: the West integrates and harmonizes the differences, brings peace and justice to other parts of the world, minimizes conflicts and proclaims the ideal of civilization.

3. "THE OTHER" AND THE RHETORIC OF MULTICULTURALISM

Even and especially societies that claim to be multicultural define their relationship with "the other" in this typically eurocentric manner. The rhetoric of "multiculturalism" constructs "the other" as part of us, but as a part that ought to be integrated into our society. This process of integration is marked by hegemonic authority. It consists of powerful acts of exclusion and inclusion, and is not at all marked by pure reciprocity or partnership, as we learn from philosophers like Slavoj Žižek from Slovenia. He has stated that the contemporary understanding of multiculturalism only "tolerates the other"...

> ... as long as he is not the *real* other, but the aseptic other of the premodern ecological wisdom or of the fascinating rituals and so forth—when it comes to the real other ... tolerance stops.[11]

This and other critiques of "multiculturalism" do not of course justify violent acts that some might interpret as acts of *resistance* against late-colonial, hegemonic Western monocultures—like, for instance, the assassination of Theo van Gogh in Amsterdam some years ago. Rather, what Žižek and others are calling for is to detect the "repressive tolerance" within the dominant

---

10 See e. g. Harding, *Is Science Multicultural?* 56.
11 Žižek, *Plädoyer*, 75.

ideology of "multiculturalism." This rhetoric of tolerance is meaningless as long as "the other" is excluded from political and economic decisions and therefore repressed and—violently—de-humanized.

I find this way of self-critically analyzing contemporary conflicts with "the other" within Europe far more convincing than for instance Samuel Huntingtons theory of the clash of civilizations or Oriana Fallaci's "The Rage and the Pride," a book that reckons with Islamic fundamentalism and the "invasion of Islam" into Europe that changes Europe into "Eurabia".[12] Many spokesmen of "multiculturalism," as well as Huntington or Fallaci, have in common that they would have us believe, first, that "Western culture" is a unique and pure product, without "the other's" participation, and, second, that our societies and the world as a whole consist of many particular, insular cultures living next to each other—or fighting each other.

Regarding the West, if there is anything characterizing it, it has been precisely the opposite: we are the result of countless cultures, beginning with the Hebrew culture and continuing through almost all the rest: through the Caldeans, the Greeks, the Persian, the Chinese, the Hindus, the Africans, etc. The same is true for almost all other nations. The history of nations is a history of cultural interweaving; it is full of transgressions, exchange processes, and syncretism.[13]

Once, in the eighteenth century, the presumption that cultures are autonomous entities, each having a value and legitimacy in itself, was a very progressive and critical idea. It opposed the hegemonic ideal of the enlightenment to homogenize all cultures and all humankind under the one, most civilized and developed culture of Europe.[14]

The problem with this understanding is not only that it installed "the West" as the powerful center that governed the world, but also that its presumption—that cultures are insular and encapsulated entities—makes it difficult to think about real communication and to find ways to overcome the boundaries that keep self and other apart. Therefore, it is quite a paradox that the concept of multiculturalism, too, rests on this understanding of cultures, as, by this, the only thing that can be achieved might be tolerance, but not communication or transgression. As long as we follow this essentialistic presumption of cultures conflicts between cultures won't be solved because this presumption rather constitutes the source of these conflicts and, thus, furthers separatism.

12 Fallaci, *Rage and the Pride*.

13 Pratt, "Scratches on the Face," 139. Heidemann and de Toro, *New Hybridities*.

14 It was especially Friedrich Wilhelm Herder who argued that cultures are uncomparable entities, each having a value in itself, see: Pagden, "Effacement of Difference."

4. TRANSCULTURALITY OR: THINKING DIFFERENCES DIFFERENTLY

What we need in order to further communication is a new way of perceiving cultural identities and the relationship between "the other" and "the self." The philosopher Wolfgang Welsch[15] and others therefore call for the detection of the "transculturality" of cultures. This perception holds an enormous potential for intercultural, interconfessional, and interreligious encounters:

"Transculturality" assumes that cultures and identities are not static entities separated from each other by irreconcilable differences, but dynamic products of continuous exchange processes. Rather than focussing on separations, transculturality highlights the opportunities of junctions and transgressions between cultures.

Yet "transculturality" does not mean that differences no longer matter. To the contrary! Stressing the distinctiveness of cultural, religious, or confessional identity remains important. Globalisation has, as we can see every day in the news, a universalizing and diversity-oppressing tendency, but it has also given rise to the formation of new local identities and particularism.

So the point the "transcultural perspective" makes is not to undermine the importance of acknowledging and respecting the difference; nor is the political and economic asymmetry to be disguised. Rather, we are invited to think differently about differences.

Diane Ravitch, a critical reviewer of multiculturalism, gives us an example of what is meant by this: She reports on a black runner, a woman, who had expressed that her role model was the Russian dancer Michail Baryschnikov whom she admired, because he was an extraordinary athlete. Now, the thing is: Michail Baryschnikov is not black; he is not a woman; he is not an American; he is not even a runner. Yet he inspires the black woman runner by the way he trains and uses his body. Within the frame of reference of the doctrine of multiculturalism and its separating presumptions the choice of the black woman runner would be merely impossible. Yet it appears naturally and self-evident once the order that constructs irreconcilable boundaries is left behind. What a narrow-mindedness, Ravitch concludes, to believe, that people can only and exclusively gain inspiration from people of the same race or gender.[16]

---

15 Welsch, Wolfgang, "Transculturality."
16 Ravitch, "Multiculturalism," 354.

5. TRANSCULTURAL PERSPECTIVES FOR THE ECUMENICAL MOVEMENT AND THE STRUGGLE FOR JUSTICE AND RECONCILIATION WITH "THE OTHER"

The appeal of the transcultural perspective is to think differently about differences: to perceive them as constructions, which, no doubt, are necessary for the sake of the own identity; yet they are not "given" and therefore they can be transgressed for the sake of real communication.

The Ecumenical movement gives ample evidence of this need for difference, distinctiveness, and identity; but we also find innumerable efforts and answers to the crucial question of how to live out our own distinctive identity and yet deal with the differences in a dynamic, life giving, inspiring, and reconciled way. I would like to close my statement with three unconcluding thoughts on the implications that the cultural studies perspective on otherness, identity, and conflicts might have for the relationship with "the other" within the Ecumenical movement and the joint struggle for reconciliation and justice.

5.1 *The Need to Overcome Static Differences*

Differences and distinctive identities are important, but insistence on difference can lead to narrow-mindedness. There are phenomena within Christian identities that show some parallels to Ravitch's report on the black female runner. "I am Presbyterian during the week and Pentecostal on the weekends," is a pointer to double or multiple confessional or religious belongings, or the Global Christian Forum exemplarily reveal that Christian identity is not fixed or complete, coherent or secure in a never-changing sense. These phenomena correspond to postmodern and Post-Cultural-Turn theories of patchwork-, bricolage-, hobbyist-, crazy-quilt-[17] or, less euphoric, nomadic or flexible-fragmented[18] identities. Stuart Hall, the former director of the Centre for Contemporary Cultural Studies in Birmingham, describes the "postmodern subject" as follows: It is

> conceptualized as having no fixed, essential or permanent identity. Identity becomes a "movable feast" ... The subject assumes different identities at different times, identities which are not unified around a coherent "self." Within us are contradictory identities, pulling in different directions, so that our identifications are continuously being shifted about ... .ß The

---

17 See for "patchwork-identity" and "crazy-quilt-identity": Keupp, "Auf der Suche."
18 See for instance Sennett, *Corrosion of Character*.

fully unified, complete, secure and coherent identity is a fantasy. Instead, as the systems of meaning and cultural representation multiply, we are confronted by a bewildering, fleeting multiplicity of possible identities, any one of which we could identify with—at least temporarily.[19]

Perceptions of a distinctive identity and exclusivistic or monolithic views on, for instance, denominational identities, are thus not adequate any more. Rather, Christian identity is a product of interwoven stories where differences between the confessions matter but where essencialistic concepts of identity and difference lines are also being left behind—sometimes and, most often, on the periphery, in the ecumenical contact zones of the daily life, outside of theological or Church centers and their control and judgement. I think we are just starting to realize how powerful and meaningful the transgression of difference-lines can be in the lives of believers. Here transgressing communication with the "concrete other" takes place—not just tolerance and understanding on a surface level, or gaining knowledge about "the other," which by misjudging "the other" all too often can be a very ethnocentric and violent endeavour.

5.2 Reconciliation Calls for Justice and Transparency about Power-relations

Contemporary cultural studies not only emphasize the transgressional dynamic of cultures and identities but also the detection of political and economic asymmetries. For the credibility of the Ecumenical movement regarding its call for reconciliation, we need a continuous reflection on questions like: Is there something like the Melitta-coffee-syndrome: the exclusion of the "concrete other" for enriching purposes? Who, in the Ecumenical movement, has been or is the one consuming the variety—like a good blend of coffee? And who is being consumed?—Still, economically and politically marginalized Christians feel ecumenically marginalized, too, and ask for a more symmetric relationship. Reconciliation is hard to achieve when the economic-political gap continues to grow larger.

Along with this we need a continuous reflection of an internalized eurocentrism, of an unconscious conceiving of Europe and the West as the active and universalized position. Ecumenical documents like the "Ecumenical considerations for dialogue and relations with people of other

---

19 Hall, "Question of Cultural Identity," 277.

religions" from 2004 appear to still hold this "centric" view when for instance it is stated:

> From a global perspective, we speak as Christians of diverse traditions to the member churches. We hope local churches will study, discuss, and adapt these ecumenical considerations to address their own contexts. In this effort, Christians should seek to go further .... [20]

Signs of the idea of something like a global authority that sets the agenda are still there; we still struggle with power asymmetries.

5.3 *Transcultural Sources in Christian Tradition*

Within the last fifteen years the Pneumatological paradigm and the paradigm of reconciliation have been increasingly emphasized in the Ecumenical movement.[21] These theological shifts seem to assert the awareness of the transcultural character of the Christian faith. The Holy Spirit is a relational, dynamic, life- and experience-centered category. He—or she—points to the pulling down of barriers of communication and to the broadening of the narrow-mindedness that freezes differences and otherness into encapsulated entities. This de-freezing and thawing of those lines of difference that hinder the fullness and dignity of life is an important aspect of reconciliation, a gift Christian churches can share in the struggle for reconciliation, peace, and justice.

BIBLIOGRAPHY

Baumann, Zygmunt. *Postmodernity and its Discontents.* New York: New York University Press, 1997.
Benhabib, Seyla. "The Generalized and the Concrete Other: The Kohlberg-Gilligan Controversy and Feminist Theory." *Praxis International* 6 (1986) 38–60.
Bhabha, Homi. *The Location of Culture.* London: Routledge, 1994.
Bronfen, Elisabeth, and Benjamin Marius, editors. *Hybride Kulturen. Beiträge zur angloamerikanischen Multikulturalitätsdebatte.* Tübingen: Stauffenburg, 1997.
Fallaci, Oriana. *The Rage and the Pride.* New York: Rizzoli, 2002.

---

20 World Council of Churches, *Ecumenical Considerations.*

21. The rediscovery of the Pneumatological dimension of Ecumenical dialogue became explicit in the 7th assembly of the World Council of Churches in Canberra, 1991, on the theme "Come, Holy Spirit, Renew the Whole Creation," followed by the World Mission Conference in Athens, 2005, with the motto "Come, Holy Spirit, Heal and Reconcile" and various Ecumenical publications.

Hall, Stuart. "The Question of Cultural Identity." In *Modernity and its Futures*, edited by Stuart Hall et al. Milton Keynes: Polity/The Open University, 1992.
Harding, Sandra. *Is Science Multicultural? Postcolonialisms, Feminisms, and Epistemologies*. Bloomington, IN: Indiana University Press, 1998.
Heidemann, Frank, and Alfonso de Toro, editors. *New Hybridities: Societies and Cultures in Transition*. New York: Olms, 2006.
Keupp, Heiner. "Auf der Suche nach der verlorenen Identität." In *Verunsicherungen*, edited by Heiner Keupp and Helga Bilden, 47–69. Göttingen: Hogrefe, 1989.
Nederveen Pieterse, Jan. "Der Melange-Effekt." In *Perspektiven der Weltgesellschaft*, edited by Ulrich Beck, 87–124. Frankfurt a. M.: Suhrkamp, 1998.
Pagden, Anthony. "The Effacement of Difference: Colonialism and the Origins of Nationalism in Diderot and Herder." In *After Colonialism: Imperial Histories and Postcolonial Displacements*, edited by Gayan Prakash. Princeton: Princeton University Press, 1995.
Pratt, Mary Louise. "Scratches on the Face of the Country; or, What Mr. Barrow saw in the Land of the Bushmen." In *"Race," Writing and Difference*, edited by Henry Louis Gates. *Critical Inquiry* 12.1 (1985). Chicago: University of Chicago Press 1985.
Ravitch, Diane. "Multiculturalism. E Pluribus Plures." *American Scholar* (1990) 337–54.
Schiffer, Sabine. *Instrumentalisierter Symbolcharakter: Das Kopftuch in den Medien*. No pages. Online: http://www.qantara.de/webcom/show_article.php/_c-548/_nr-27/i.html.
Sennett, Richard. *The Corrosion of Character. The Personal Consequences of Work in the New Capitalism*. New York: Norton, 1998.
Terkessidis, Mark. "Globale Kultur in Deutschland—oder: Wie unterdrückte Frauen und Kriminelle die Hybridität retten." In *Kultur—Medien—Macht. Cultural Studies und Medienanalyse*, edited by Hepp, Andreas and Rainer Winter. Opladen, Wiesbaden: Westdeutscher, 1999.
Welsch, Wolfgang. "Transculturality: The Puzzling Form of Cultures Today." In *Spaces of Culture: City, Nation, World*, edited by Mike Featherstone and Scott Lash. London: Sage, 1999.
World Council of Churches. *Ecumenical Considerations for Dialogue and Relations with People of Other Religions*. Geneva, 2004.
Žižek, Slavoj. *Ein Plädoyer für die Intoleranz*. Wien: Passagen, 2003.

9

Wind, Breeze, Hurricane
On Poetry and Theology—Insights from the Perspective of Brazilian Literature

ROBERTO E. ZWETSCH

"What is this silence that tires not
of dividing itself into other silences?"
—Armindo Trevisan

"There are infinite ways of understanding
that the source of life is God."
—Adélia Prado

INTRODUCTION

Poetry is to theology as breathing to the body. It is the fresh air that renews the blood and the spirituality that provide the foundation of theological thinking. But poetry dis-connects, creates hiatuses, opens spaces, and springs surprises between the cracks of language. Poetry is a specific form of language that enchants and seduces human beings. Without poetry there is no theology. Biblical spirituality is based on it. The Psalms and Jesus' parables are exemplars for this.

The Bible is full of poetry. The poetic language has always been an instrument to translate God's word. Without poetry the biblical witness would be poor. There are many examples, beginning with Genesis, then in the Psalms, Wisdom and the Prophets, to the poetic language of Jesus, and later on in the Christian poetry of all times, especially the erotic poetry of the mystics[1]. Poetry is thus a form of language that is exemplary to communicate the word of God, that is not simply informative speech, but rather *performative*, i.e., a way of saying that makes reality happen. It has more to do with the Hebrew *dabar* than with the Greek *logos*. This is the language of faith, which has the potential to create and transform reality.[2]

The experience of Christian faith is a *sui generis* experience that needs means to feed and express itself. It is a way of living and understanding the world and denotes an experience of divine grace that sustains this world. This experience has been characterized in theology as spirituality. In this article I reflect on Christian spirituality in relation to the lives of the people of God and of theology in Brazil, a wandering spirituality that springs from faith in Jesus Christ. The relevance of the topic is evident in the considerable bibliography that has been available about it, especially since the 1970s.[3] My entry into the spaces of enjoyment of the divine Spirit is Brazilian poetry.

The concept of spirituality is all-encompassing but unpredictable. It is like the wind that blows. In this article, I use a definition by Hermann Brandt. He defined spirituality as the domain of the Spirit, an experience of faith in Christ which embraces the entire life of the believer. It involves a radical experience stirred by the Holy Spirit.[4]

I

We are beings of time and of history. In a creation myth of the Guarany people of Paraguay, it is said that time begins with human beings.[5] But God is before and after time. God's reality does not fit into the casing of time. Yet,

---

1. See Westhelle, "Festa, o lúdico e o erótico," 12–28.
2. Bingemer, "Deus: experiência," 239.
3. See among others Gutiérrez. *Beber no próprio poço*. Casaldáliga and Vigil, *Espiritualidade*. Boff and Betto, *Mística e espiritualidade*.
4. See Brandt, *Espiritualidade*, 43s.
5. See Zwetsch, "Una hermosa flor al borde del camino," 249–60.

this God surprises us because God did not want to remain in eternity. God became human and entered time, living among us. God became a historically situated human being, dated and vulnerable as any one of us. God is with us in Jesus of Nazareth, son of Mary, carpenter, layman, and teacher of law and life.

The Christian community lives from this experience of faith and renews itself repeatedly amid the Brazilian people, often down-and-out and limping, pitiless and yet tender, contradictory as any other humankind. What spirituality motivates or challenges them today?

The methodology here is little known in theological schools and it is truly regrettable. There is nothing more beautiful, profound and inspiring than poetic language. Armindo Trevisan, a poet and art critic, wrote a major essay about the poetic language of the Gospel. He says that a poem is *seminal* language, because it is never completed without the intrinsic collaboration of its readers.

The poetry of the Gospels is not a historical imposition of its Jewish status; Christ chose to express himself in a particular manner, the poetic manner "[. . .] Poetry is a dimension of the incarnation [. . .] it is a providential instrument chosen by God to incite human beings to the greater metaphor of Grace, which conducts them [. . .] to another dimension of life and being."[6]

Trevisan says more. When holding to the *poetic* reading of the Gospel, a reader, even a non-believer, may stumble into an encounter that will mark them definitively. If poetry is pretending, as Fernando Pessoa wrote, in the poetry of Jesus then "pretense is no longer creation, idolatrous in a sense, but is transformed into a live creation, just as the image and likeness of God, modeled in clay, would be no more than a simulacrum, without the divine breath that animates them. Evangelical pretense is thus a playful modality that makes the human heart a partner in its adventure." On accepting this challenge, it is possible for one to encounter the *un-expected*, the *un-suspected*, the *ineffable*, the *unspeakable*. The encounter with Christ will always be an overflowing of life. Therefore, Trevisan states: "Only a poetic reading . . . can make the gospel remain a contemporary of History, not exhausting it along the chronic (or anachronistic) molds of a time, but following it in its indefectible radioactivity."[7]

Let us begin with a poem by Adélia Prado, a poetess from Minas Gerais, who created a revolution in Brazilian contemporary poetry with her Christian erotic poems:

6. Trevisan, *Poesia na bíblia*, 175.
7. Trevisan, *A poesia na bíblia*, 182.

Parameter[8]
God is more beautiful than I.
And God is not young.
That is indeed a consolation.

What a poem! Short and precise, transparent, humorous, encouraging words by a woman freed from the imposition of apparent beauty. It is poetry that liberates young people and mature people, people like us, worried about the mirror and about what will become of our lives.

II

We live in a vertiginous time that is characterized by various and stupefying speeds. Airplanes fly faster than sound. The world wide web of computers allows information to circulate immediately through the world, without any borders. The speed is such that we feel dizzy. Someone who is at the margins of this process appears to be outside history, they do not exist!

The system that now rules the world is highly selective and those who don't adapt and adopt is inconsequential to the market and is a mere number in statistics. As a country, Brazil is hurrying desperately to become part of the global circuit, defending globalization and trying to maintain the face of a poor country struggling to overcome poverty at the same time. But all it does is adapt its economic policies to the world system. How can one join the fight against poverty while co-opting to the world system? How can one overcome the ideological view of this world system to affirm a human world beyond numbers? The struggle for a healthy human society with hope is a challenge. And, without the fresh water of poetry, how can one meet this challenge?

III

The scar[9]
Theologians are mistaken
when they describe God in their treatises.
Wait for me and I will be pointed out
as the one who did something irreparable..
God will be reborn to save me.
Kill me, Jonathan, with your knife,

8. Prado, *Poesia reunida*, 382.
9. Ibid., 392.

> deliver me from the captivity of time.
> ...
> I love time because I love this hell,
> this painful love that needs the body,
> the protection of God to tell itself
> in this afternoon infested by pedestrians.
> Having a body is like writing poems,
> stepping on the edge of abysses, I love you.
> ...

True spirituality, one that is complete and full is that which knows how to bring together body, time and eternity with the bond of love. That is why one must affirm that a Christian spirituality that drowns the body, that denies the passion of living, is not from God.

Christian spirituality is embodied with a passion for living. It knows how to bring eternity together with everyday life, walking through the streets, feeling the heat and cold, dizzy with knowing that one is an incomplete and joyous being. It is a radical cry for the divine fullness of life in body, soul, and spirit. Life is sacred and a marvelous gift. The words, "Kill me, Jonathan, with your knife, I love you," is subversive. Jonathan is Jesus in Adélia Prado's poetry. Christian spirituality is visceral, committed to life and death, to the saving of human dignity.

IV

As beings of history, we are a walking contradiction, tender and hateful, in solidarity and indifferent, lovers and full of jealousy. We say one thing but do another. We are in favor of peace but weave traps for war. We need to accept who we are if we are to understand what forgiveness is!

> *Second didactic poem*[10]
> We are still solving the matters
> of Rome,
> we are Rome
> and old Egypt and Nineveh and Babylon . . .
> And,
> Despite the laboratory games,
> we are still generated in the same way.
> Nothing is born from air.
> The gods themselves,
> as diverse as they are,

---

10. Quintana, *Apontamentos*, 81.

are,
depending on when, on time, on the occasion,
the fancy dresses successively worn and
taken off
by the only and true God.
A divine masquerade? No!
He is not the least guilty for the couturiers.
Behind the disguises
—amid all and everything—
the naked God
smiles complacently,
He smiles, above all,
at the poet who plays the tambourine,
the lyre,
the flute
the deep violoncello
while
at the foot of all crosses
soldiers roll the dice
for the destinies of Rome and the world.

Mario Quintana's words are ironic. The destinies of the world and of humankind are as a rule decided by the powerful with a roll of the dice and soldiers, not forgetting the role of the computers and sophisticated means of instant information. Illusions apart, this uncertain future is decided at the foot of all crosses. The cross is not only a sign of the past, it is fixed in our time, with us— victims and victimizers—at its foot as part of the tragedy. But it is also the plural cross, since it is the crosses that now mark bodies, places, and eras. And Christ identifies with them.

The one who saves us is the naked God, who subtly uses disguises to come close to us. God is gentle to the poor and the poets, but God also knows to say: "Woe unto you that are rich! for ye have received your consolation" (Luke 6:24ff).

V

I return to the poems of Adélia Prado, because she reminds me that the "Naked God" is a present body that challenges us to look at the *other*, it is a body that questions, a sweaty body, marked by suffering. I then bring up a poem that expresses an experience in the Roman Catholic tradition, very popular in Brazil, but that radicalizes the presence-absence of the body of God. Christian spirituality cannot be confounded with morality and decency. It expresses a relationship with the living God and this is its honor and tragedy. Has anyone seen God? Or can anyone speak of God with true knowledge? (1 John 4:12; Romans 11:33–36).

The spirituality that comes from the experience of the cross and the crosses of our time must be corporally transparent, merciful, and love the vulnerable people who need care and advocacy. That is so because it is, itself, the fruit of weakness, of anguish and pain. For this reason, the authentic Christian spirituality has become a singing and living spirituality, of hope that arises out of solidarity.

> *Feast of the body of God*[11]
> Like a ripe tumor
> poetry pulsates painfully
> announcing passion:
> "O crux ave, spes unica
> O passiones tempore."
> Jesus has a pair of buttocks!
> More than Yahweh on the mountain
> this revelation prostrates me.
> O mystery, mystery
> suspended on the cross
> the human body of God.
> . . .
> In this consists the crime,
> taking a photograph of a woman coming
> and saying: behold the face of sin.
> For centuries and centuries,
> the demons insisted
> on blinding us with this lie.
> And your body on the cross, suspended.
> And your body on the cross, unclothed:
> look at me.
> I adore you, o my savior
> who passionately reveals to me
> the innocence of flesh.
> Exposing you as a fruit
> on this tree of execration
> what you say is love,
> love of the body, love.

How can one see love in a tortured, naked body? Only someone who has overcome the burden of appearances and allowed themselves to be

---

11. Prado, *Poesia reunida*, 279.

engulfed by love. Only someone who loves the naked and the exposed can understand them, love them and be transformed by them. Such person can uncover the lie that devalues the body and turn it into merchandise of human trafficking and thus save the body and the entire being from damnation and despondency.

When Jesus was brought to the cross of death, Pilate did not find any crime in him and washed his hands. On Golgotha, watched from afar by some of his astonished disciples, and friends, both men and women, Jesus cried: "My God, my God, why have you forsaken me?" repeating Psalm 22. However, in this cry we find the most radical confidence (Psalm 22:3). God changed the end of this story, acting in the name of God and the State, with the unusual events on Easter Sunday. It is this humanly unlikely surprise that sustains the community of disciples of Jesus worldwide. Everything else is human tradition.

Christian spirituality can only be critical spirituality, since it is born from the cross and its ignominy. On its reverse side, it is the spirituality of hope and of the life that is worth living. It is born from a radical crisis. Christian faith learns how to live from this crisis. Whenever we become accommodated to the *status quo*, we ultimately disfigure the event on the cross. We domesticate it when we place flowers and perfumes on it.

The crisis is a constitutive part of Christian spirituality. Every time we reduce faith to human dimensions, we quiet the Spirit of resurrection and manipulate God. Christian spirituality does not fear crises. It fears laziness, shamelessness, insensitivity toward the suffering of others, mercilessness, and omission. Christian spirituality is patient, stubborn, resolute in its pursuit of justice and peace. It indeed requires the *courage to be*.

VI

The living God[12]
God is not in heaven. God is
at the bottom of the well
where they let him fall.
– Cain, what did you do to your God?!
His bloodied nails vainly scratch
the slippery walls.
God is in hell . . .
We must lend Him all our strength
all our courage

12. Quintana, *Apontamentos*, 64.

> to at least bring him to the surface of the earth.
> And then seat him at our table
> and give him some of our bread and our wine,
> and not let him be lost again.
> Be lost again . . . even if it be in heaven!

Matthew 25:31–46 has become a classical key in the theology of liberation. In this parable, Jesus uses the great judgment to describe a form of presence that goes for his absence amidst people who believe in him. This means that although we do not see him physically, he comes close to us and questions us. He, eschatologically, is very close to us but we don't give him credit.

This is because he is in hell, and we do not usually approach hell because hell is where the *others* are. We prefer the safety of the heaven of our places in the society, be it middle-class or upper middle class. We don't know the hell where God is. That is why it is difficult to invite God to have supper with us and share with God the bread and wine of the Supper. What have we made of the Lord's Supper?

In the poem, sharing the bread and wine is the moment to commune with God as liberating presence of God. We feast sharing goods and food because of the joy of this discovery. As it happened with the disciples on the way to Emmaus (Luke 24), God is in the middle of the table shared in an experience of hospitality as an antidote to all known and unknown hells.

Christian spirituality is manifested in sharing and in relationships and never accepts injustice. It takes risks for the crucial transformations that are vital to our planet. For this reason Christian spirituality is ecumenical and ecological. All, everyone, without any discriminations, receive the Life-giving Spirit, who maintains life and intercedes for us before God (Romans 8:26).

Christian spirituality is a way of life, an experience that convinces us of God's love. As loved beings, we live by grace that comes from the forgiveness of God as liberated people freed to liberate others. That is why we have reasons to dance before the Creator, on the streets and in the temples.

This spirituality encourages us in the discipleship of the Crucified one. Against the trivialization of life and the exacerbation of the individualism, it teaches us to live the freedom of the children of God. And this experience is gratuitous and loving. "For freedom Christ set us free" (Galatians 5:1). This freedom is the foundation for the faith active through love. There are many ways to experience it. It may be the encounter with harsh realities, the revelation in a poem or the love for a friend or a greater cause. It may be experienced in the encounter with voiceless and defenseless people, in hearing a sermon or a song. It may even be loneliness in an instant of pain and weakness. However it always occurs as an experience of the encounter with the Word of the Living God in the power of the Spirit revealed by the letter. In this encounter we are doubly defeated, but paradoxically come out victorious. As in the fight of Jacob with the angel of God in the ford of Jabbok (Genesis 32:22ff.)!

We lose in this fight with God. But this loss, to the contrary of the law of human life, saves us because it marks us for life. And the mark is the freedom to live in the grace and through the grace of God. Paul says: "The Lord is Spirit, and where the Spirit of the Lord is, there is freedom" (2 Corinthians 3:17). The characteristic of this Christian freedom is service. We are free in the service that creates spaces and experiences of freedom. Service is a mark of Christian community life.

The service that is born from Christian spirituality is what we would today express as citizenship. Citizen is the person who breaks with their own interest and takes on the challenge of cooperation. They cooperate for the good of their city, of their people, for freedom to be a reality in it. Citizenship and democracy are concepts that we need to debate in our days.

VII

Dom Pedro Casaldáliga, Bishop Emeritus of São Félix do Araguaia in the north of Mato Grosso state, is also a poet. He dedicates this poem to his mother:

> *The new name*[13]
> Cry and silence and scream
> it is the word that now fills
> the mouth and the spirit.
> That I had never yet
> managed to understand, mother:
> free-dom!
> . . .
> If you baptize me again, some day,
> with the water of the sobs and the memory,
> with the fire of death and of Glory . . .
> tell God and the world
> that you gave me
> the name
> of Peter Freedom!

13. Casaldáliga, *Antologia retirante*, 189.

POEISIS

Dom Pedro wrote this poem when he was under house arrest, surrounded by the security forces of the Brazilian dictatorship in the 1970s, because he dared to challenge the owners of huge landholdings in Mato Grosso, defending rural workers who were in semi-slavery in many farms. Dom Pedro and other friends were considered subversives, dangerous, who were threatened and almost expelled from Brazil.

But there is more to this poem. Only a person who lived on the frontiers of institutionality, who defended the right of the poor and a dignified life for helpless women, can understand what it means to fear for one's own freedom. This was also experience of Martin Luther King Jr. in the US! Christian spirituality gives courage on the path of the search for freedom.

VIII

Summing up, we are beings of time and history. And God is before and after time. But God entered history. This divine presence among us reveals the system of the world, the many dominations of it. And it also reveals our own contradictions, the scars which mark our bodies and desires. God is born to save life as it is: contradictory, but marvelous. What a profound mystery!

Christian spirituality is an experience of those who know the freedom for which Christ liberated us. This freedom becomes creative service to exert our citizenship with maturity. Christian spirituality obtains its strength from permanent prayer. It takes place in the vertigo of time, wherever what Tillich called "ultimate concern" is manifested.[14] Poetry is one of the most beautiful and instigating ways of expressing these encounters.[15]

BIBLIOGRAPHY

Bingemer, Maria Clara Lucchetti. "Deus: experiência originante e originada: O texto materno-teologal de Adélia Prado." In De Mori et al., *Aragem do sagrado. Deus na literatura contemporânea*. São Paulo: Loyola, 2011.
Boff, Leonardo, and Frei Betto. *Mística e espiritualidade*. Rio de Janeiro: Rocco, 1994.
Brandt, Hermann. *Espiritualidade—vivência da graça*. 2nd ed. São Leopoldo: Sinodal, EST, 2006.
Casaldáliga, Pedro. *Antologia retirante*. Rio de Janeiro: Civilização Brasileira, 1978.
Casaldáliga, Pedro, and José Maria Vigil. *Espiritualidade da libertação*. São Paulo: Vozes, 1993.

---

14. Tillich, *Theology of Culture*, 42.

15. My profound gratitude goes to Dr. Luís Marcos Sander for translating this text into English.

Gutiérrez, Gustavo. *Beber no próprio poço: itinerário espiritual de um povo*. Petrópolis: Vozes, 1984.
Prado, Adelia. *Poesia reunida*. São Paulo: Arx, 1991.
Quintana, Mario. *Apontamentos de história sobrenatural*. Rio de Janeiro: Globo, 1987.
Tillich, Paul. *Theology of Culture*. Edited by Robert C. Kimball. New York: Oxford University Press, 1959.
Trevisan, Armindo. *A poesia na bíblia*. Porto Alegre: Uniprom, 2001.
Westhelle, Vítor. "A festa, o lúdico e o erótico na religião: perspectiva teológica." *Estudos da Religião*. 29 (2005) 12–28.
Zwetsch, Roberto E. "Una hermosa flor al borde del camino. A propósito del Génesis de los Mbyá-Guaraní del Paraguay." *Estudos Teológicos* 51 (2011) 249–60.

10

Remembrance
A Living Bridge

MARY PHILIP (JOY)

> *Shimbalaiê...*[1]
> the line, the melody I once heard
> an evening amidst sipping beer
> and breaking open pistachios
> *naale...*[2]
> the hope I once heard in the word
> an inimical night amidst injustice
> and hostile intolerance
> a touch...
> the imprint of the care I once felt
> an early morn amidst falling snow
> and the cold wind.
> A song, one word, a touch

1 A song by Maria Gadú, the Brazilian singer and composer. I am referring to the occasion when Caetano Veloso, one of the famous singer/composers of Brazilain music, sings Shimbalaiê for Maria Gadu.

2. A Malayalam word in the novel *God of Small Things* by Arundhati Roy meaning "tomorrow."

> of love, hope, care
> its memory built a living bridge
> on which I walk
> and
> for others to walk on . . .

Some years ago during one of our many conversations Vítor Westhelle[3] said: "Life is not what one has lived, but what one remembers, and how one remembers in order to tell it."[4] He was quoting the epigraph to Gabriel García Márquez's, *Vivir para contarla*. Life lived in, with, and under memories as a living bridge. While we can put away unpleasant memories, even repress them, it is impossible to forget them. Remembering, as Clarice Lispector says, is "like an open wound."[5] Well, while an open wound is an unimpeded invitation to infections, it is at the same time a door to renewed strength, not to mention new possibilities.[6] So, on the one hand it might lead to death and on the other to new life, resurrection, so to speak. To put it in theological terms it is an eschatological experience. Or in simple terms, it is the hope for a/ the future. To explain: a wound, an injury, breaks open something that was in place. To be precise, it ruptures a margin that was held intact. It creates a division into an inside and an outside leading to the problem/possibility of crossing over. But crossing over is a risky business. Barriers or boundaries or margins are put in place for a purpose—to keep things/people/places apart, to maintain balance. However, I am not sure it serves the purpose. As per the norm or rule, crossing a set boundary can only lead to problems. But there is another way of looking at this. Crossing over can lead to a new and exhilarating experience. And here I cannot but quote my mentor.

Back in the fall of 2002, in my CT III class, while teaching Eschatology, he said, "margins are the threshold to eschatological experiences." At that time my response was "yeah right!" But now I am a believer. Coming back to Lispector's analogy of remembering as an open wound, how can we understand this? When we remember, we are making ourselves vulnerable

---

3. Vítor Westhelle was my doctoral adviser, my mentor, and now I work with him.

4. "La vida no es la que uno vivió, sino la que un recuerda y como la recuerda para contarla." Epigraph to: Gabriel García Márquez, *Vivir para contarla* .

5. Lispector, *Selected Crônicas*, 182.

6. A wound creates a break in my skin, which is the margin/boundary of my body. When this margin, skin, is intact, all is fine, but when infringed, the inside/outside division is no longer there and I become susceptible to viruses and germs threatening from the outside. But, when attacked by germs from outside, the body produces or activates antibodies, which in turn fight the toxins or the germs and restore the bodily functions. Forces that were recessive or subdued or nonoperational are activated and even created anew. Thus I could end up with renewed strength. At the same time I could succumb to the infection with fatal results.

to events of the past, painful or otherwise, on which, hopefully, a scab had already formed—the people, the places or the events, dis-membered and put away as past and closed. By remembering we are re-membering that and those which we had dis-membered; we are bringing them back to the present. The scab is peeled away, and the wound starts bleeding as the tear glands weep. But as I mentioned earlier,[7] memories can lead either to a renewed life or to debilitation.[8] There is thus an eschatological component to the phenomenon of memory/remembrance.

Memory, remembrance, rememory,[9] however you want to name it, they have something in common. It brings to presence something that was absent. It is a revelation, an unveiling of something that was hidden/forgotten. In the same vein, to remember is to re-member. And here I introduce the word, *saudades*, a Portuguese word, which means a sense of longing and hope that arises out of memory. In the text that follows I use these words interchangeably and try to connect the act of remembrance to a living bridge.

WHAT IS REMEMBRANCE?

Remembrance is not recalling. It is not the recounting of a multiplication table I studied in second grade. It is an awakening, the experience that puts our memory to work. When I remember I awaken from my slumber. It is the rooster that crows the beginning of a new day. It is when a memory transforms you. In theological terms, remembrance is the experience that brings about a metanoia, a transformation. It takes you to a place of acquiescence and resistance at the same time, a space of assembling and disassembling, a place of movement that rouses you and inspires you to move, to act. This kind of memory is redemptive or messianic.[10] To use the Jewish philosopher Walter Benjamin's words, it is *Eingedenken*. It is an act of memory that reinterprets the past and revitalizes the present so as to bring about redemption.[11] Remembrances are chips of messianic time through which the messiah might enter[12] and therein lie their eschatological significance. *Eingedenken* is memory that is mindful, sensitive or in other words, empathetic. This empathetic nature has fundamental theological significance as it

---

7. See note 6 above.
8. Renewed life comes out of a reconciliation with the past that enables one to move forward. Debilitation results when the engagement with the past ends in conflict.
9. Rememory is a word that Toni Morrison uses in her novel, *Beloved*.
10. Benjamin, *Illuminations*, 254.
11. Wilding, *Concept of Remembrance*, 7.
12. Benjamin, *Illuminations*, 264.

calls for anamnetic solidarity with the past, with the dead, with the victims of injustice as the struggle continues in the present. It is a memory that makes present. These memories that pour in from the past[13] bring about a presencing of that which was kept away; they become channels of communication, for without communication life is not possible.

REMEMBERING TO RE-MEMBER

Remembrance creates a fissure so that there is a disruption in one's thinking or there is a cognitive dissonance. It wakes us up from stupor and propels us to cast a questioning glance at the present. Is this how things are supposed to be? Should I be doing something to change the situation? Remembrance goads us into action. The words of institution "do this in remembrance of me" point to this characteristic of remembering. This is how I see it: it is not just about eating that bread which is the real presence of the broken body of Jesus. While remembering that Jesus broke his body and gave his life so that we may have life and have it in full, we are summoned to remember the broken bodies around us, to break open our self-contained lives, to move out of our comfort zones and take the risk of crossing boundaries, to reach out to the other so that the other can also have life in its fullness. Remembering is thus an act of re-membering. It symbolizes the restoration of the broken whole. It re-members that which was lost. "Do this in remembrance of me" is an exhortation for restoration/reestablishing of the relationship between God and the world she created.

REMEMBRANCE: A LABOR OF LOVE[14]

How can remembrance be a labor of love? The story of the women in the gospel of Luke is exemplary. On that Good Friday, when there was nothing good, the women had witnessed the gruesome death of their beloved Jesus. They stood at the foot of the cross when everyone else left. They went to see the place where he was buried and on their way back home brought spices to anoint his body on the third day. But what they did the next day is what is pertinent. They kept the Shabbat. And Shabbat is about remembrance. These women would not forget their loved one. They would not let the past be closed; suffering and injustice would not have the last word. Instead the

---

13. Pouring in from the past is how Vítor describes remembrance.

14. This is a reading of Vítor Westhelle where he refers to remembrance as the practice of resurrection.

women remembered. They may have talked about Jesus' childhood when he was an imp playing tricks on his sisters or stealing baklawa's from his mother's hiding place; they may have talked about the miracles he did and maybe even of his stupidity to take on the religious authorities. Whatever it may have been, they did not let go of the past. They remembered. Theirs was a labor of love. In the words of Søren Kierkegaard, "the work of love in remembering one who is dead is a work of the most unselfish love."[15] This brings me to the famous correspondence between Walter Benjamin and Max Horkheimer in 1937. To Horkheimer's comment that "Past injustice has occurred and is closed. The slain are truly slain . . .,"[16] Benjamin retorts,

> The corrective to this sort of thinking may be found in the consideration that history is not simply a science but also and not least a form of remembrance. What science has "determined," remembrance can modify. Such mindfulness can make the incomplete (happiness) into something complete, and the complete (suffering) into something incomplete. That is theology; but in remembrance we have an experience that forbids us to conceive of history as fundamentally atheological, . . .[17]

Yes, the past cannot be closed. We need to remember, and remembrance can be and is transformative, for no gesture of love is ever lost.[18] The women did the unthinkable; they did not let the past be closed, they remembered, and guided by their memories they went to anoint the dead body that could not give them anything in return. And what were they greeted with? Resurrection!

I am not denying the flip side of keeping the past open, but the point here is to remember it so that it brings about a transformation that enables one to move on to new life. This act of remembrance is not something that freezes one up; it rather frees us. It brings about a change where injustice is no longer meted out but justice; it leads captives to freedom. There is an inversion in the order. The power of remembrance is such that it impels one to take risks, to go to places and people we would not otherwise.

REMEMORY AS PRESENCING

Rememory, the word that is most used in *Beloved*, is about acceptance of what happened in the past and incorporating the effect of that acceptance

---

15. Kirekegaard, *Works of Love*, 320.
16. Benjamin, *Arcades*, 471.
17. Ibid.
18. Westhelle, *Word in Words*, 99.

in the present so as to move forward. Thus it is one's engagement of what is past with what is present leading to the realization of one's identity so as to have a future. One understands oneself through rememory. And this rememory is not just a verb, an action or a happening. It is also a noun denoting a place, person, or thing.

> ... Some things go. Pass on. Some things just stay. I used to think it was my re-memory. You know. Some things you forget. Other things you never do. But it's not. Places, places are still there. If a house burns down, it's gone, but the picture of it—stays, and not just in my re-memory, but out there, in the world. What I remember is a picture floating around outside my head. I mean, even if I don't think it, even if I die, the picture of what I did, or knew, or saw is still out there. Right in the place where it happened.[19]

Regardless of whether I remember or not, that place or person or that imprint is still out there. The force that brings about rememory is independent of the person who remembers. It is a memory that makes present. When bodies come together, when one's skin touches another's skin, it leaves an imprint, not the visible mark of an unforgettable passion, but an invisible and yet an unerasable mark, a presence. And then, out of the blue, a voice, a smell, a sensation triggers that presence, involuntarily, as in a dream. That is memory that cannot be forced but is involuntary. No six-digit date written anywhere can trigger it. It just happens, and when it does, it is simply beautiful (or devastating). What happened or did not happen assumes a spatiality that structures one's identity, an identity that is enabling and not inhibiting. Memory/Rememory/Remembrance therefore needs to be both, a verb and a noun, a "verboun." That is what makes it choratic in nature.

REMEMBERING AS A CHORATIC EVENT

Memories are *choratic* in nature. *Chora* is the term used by Derrida to denote a space in between spaces, a place that is neither in nor out, a place that is between and betwixt. They are spaces of estrangement and intimacy; spaces of danger and possibilities; spaces of transition and therefore spaces of trial.[20] *Eingedenken* takes one to these *choratic* spaces. It is an eschatological place, a place of hope. Remembrance is where hope awaits. Something takes place when we remember. Hope pertains through and in memory. As

---

19. Morrison, *Beloved*, 36.
20. Westhelle, *Eschatology*, 100.

in a bridge, it creates a pathway for us to walk on. The hope that is borne of remembering is more than an envisaged occurrence.²¹ Remembering is both commemorative and anticipatory.²² It redeems the potential for change buried in the past. It is an awareness of the entombed resistance leading to a commitment to bearing witness to what has happened in the past, specifically to atrocities, and more importantly to an attentiveness against their unchecked progress toward the present.²³

If one were to forget the past or, to use the words of Horkheimer, to render the past closed, then all we see is a pile of debris as elucidated in the Paul Klee painting Angelus Novus.²⁴ But if we were to remember, we are retrieving or trying to "retrieve repressed moments of resistance from the past"²⁵ that are stored in the present, be it in a story, a building, or our own bodies. In the act of remembering, a countermemory emerges which interacts, often aggressively, with the public memory which in turn acts as a catalyst towards a change to things as they stand. *Eingedenken* searches out the forgotten remnants of the past, not to restore them, but to measure their after-effect in the present.²⁶ *Eingedenken* "'loosens' up the past, thereby retrieving the repressed potential for resistance to oppression."²⁷ The past is no longer closed off from the present but becomes a living bridge.

It is a memory that is shared. It is a collective memory, examples for which are the horrors of the caste system (that still exists in India) and slavery. Even those who have not shared in the experience reap its benefits/horrors. Remembrance thus becomes a channel of communication, a power of resistance, of hope. The act of remembrance becomes a living bridge. Bridges are structures that are built over a hurdle that otherwise cannot be traversed. They provide a passageway across/over the hurdle.

21. A. Benjamin, *Present Hope*, 119.
22. Remmler, *Waking the Dead*, 32.
23. Ibid., 32.

24. Angelus Novus is the Angel of History. The painting "shows an angel looking as though he is about to move away from something he is fixedly contemplating. His eyes are staring, his mouth is open, his wings are spread. This is how one pictures the angel of history. His face is turned toward the past. Where we perceive a chain of events, he sees one single catastrophe that keeps piling ruin upon ruin and hurls it in front of his feet. The angel would like to stay, awaken the dead, and make whole what has been smashed. But a storm is blowing from Paradise; it has got caught in his wings with such violence that the angel can no longer close them. The storm irresistibly propels him into the future to which his back is turned, while the pile of debris before him grows skyward. This storm is what we call progress." Benjamin, *Illuminations*, 257.

25. Ibid., 8.
26. Ibid., 6.
27. Ibid., 19.

Mary Philip (Joy) — *Remembrance*

LIVING BRIDGES

Cherrapunji, in Meghalaya, a northeast state of India, is considered the wettest place on earth. It has the record of highest rainfall in the world, and during monsoon season and for that matter for a good part of the year, villages are quarantined by the rising water and overflowing rivers. Communication is completely cut off. Children cannot go to school, and adults cannot conduct their day-to-day business and meet their livelihood. But then the people of Meghalaya found an ingenious solution to their problem. They grow bridges out of what is part of their living, habitation—fig trees.

Strangler figs and Rubber figs are very common in Meghalaya. Strangler figs are epiphytes—plants that grows on another plant, most often a tree. The host provides the plant a space for it to anchor itself. Seeds of strangler figs are deposited by birds and squirrels on to the branches and stems of the larger trees that grow in the forests. It takes a while for the roots to come out, but once they do there is a spurt of growth and they send their roots all around the tree and downwards to the ground. They grow so heavily on the host tree that the host tree is strangled and what is left is this enmeshed mass of roots. Rubber figs, on the other hand, are large trees belonging to the banyan group. They grow up to forty meters and have a stout trunk of about three meters in diameter. What is peculiar about them is that they grow aerial roots to anchor it into the soil and support its heavy branches.

The local people, the Khasis, have developed a natural way of guiding the roots of either the strangler fig or the rubber fig. The trunks of the betel nut tree are sliced in the middle and hollowed out to form a guidance route. The slender growing fig roots are placed in these trunks which are then guided in the desired direction, over a stream or a river, allowing them to take root only when they reach the opposite bank. Though the natural tendency is for the roots to spread out, they are prevented from doing so by the betel nut tree trunk within which they are enclosed, and thus they grow straight out. This is a long process and when they reach the other end of the river they are allowed to take root in the soil. It takes twenty to thirty years before the bridge becomes functional and then over time the bridge grows and strengthens. Thus by coaxing and directing the secondary roots, strong living bridges are grown/built to cross streams and rivers. Once set firmly in place and functional, rocks are placed to improve the footpaths.

Growing a living bridge, however, is no simple matter. It is a project that cannot be completed in one's life time. Therefore one generation teaches the art to the next, and to the next, and it is thus passed on. Some of these bridges are over one hundred feet long and can even support the weight of fifty or more people at a time. These bridges form the daily commuter route for the Khasis, and some are believed to be over five hundred years old. These bridges serve as paths for crossing over, going across flooded rivers. More importantly they are a means of communication, a legacy, an inheritance that is passed on so that the community is re-membered and not dismembered. These living bridges are what allow for life to happen, to live life.

CODA: WHY AND HOW SHOULD WE REMEMBER?

All of us are keepers of memories that have transformative power as well the power of distortion. The question, however, is, do they make for living bridges? And, why am I talking about remembrance, memory, *saudades* in this volume celebrating the contributions of a theologian who is my mentor and dear friend? I do so because I cannot think of a better way to accolade Vítor; he lives what he told me years ago using the words of Gabriel Garcia Marquez: "Life is not what one has lived, but what one remembers, and how one remembers in order to tell it."

Memories ought to create living bridges. The roots/memories are there and they keep growing. All we need to do is cut our betel trees, place the roots in there, cajole and caution, entice and entreat them to form a pathway, a bridge that keeps on growing and living so that not only we can walk on and over them, but the generations that follow us as well.

Memory is the inner aspect of all critical consciousness that can and should lead to an unveiling of things that lay interred. The act of remembrance stimulates the knowing content of the imagination and thus becomes the vehicle of liberation.[28] Remembrance also brings about justice, though not all remembrances do that. We cannot and should not forget injustices of the past. We owe that to the generations that went before us and that will come after us. We have to remember to re-member that which is lost. Remembering in some ways reproduces reality, especially that of the past and this is indeed important. But what is more important from the perspective of transformation is when remembering is re-creating present reality imaginatively. It is remembering disparate fragments of the past together and creating a new pattern/design with the aid of present experiences that will in turn envision a hopeful future.[29]

So, coming back to Vítor's favorite quote, how do we choose to remember our lives, our history? Why should we remember? Will the memory of a song that you listened to one evening, a word that you heard one night, a touch that you felt one morning—are they going to be a living bridge, channel of communication for generations to come? Do we coax our memories to build bridges? Will they help traverse the hurdles in front of us and those that we relegated to the past? Are our memories the site of hope, where there is *saudades*—a homesickness for a future? Does our remembrance bring about justice? Do we remember to re-member those who are forgotten? We remember together as a community, as a church, as a nation. If we

---

28. Metz, *Faith in* History, 193
29. Phan, *Journey at the Margins*, 114.

remember and tend to the roots, making them stronger, and if we complete the bridge, it just might become part of the commuter route of the network of living bridges connecting us all.

In a sermon preached on September 2008, Vítor said, "we need to be awake for the sake of those who have gone to sleep . . . and when we are gathered in this act of remembrance Jesus will crash the party bringing along with him all those who must be remembered and even those we might not care to remember." Remembrance has, what Benjamin calls, weak messianic power,[30] the power to liberate and transform. The function of remembrance is to "brush history against the grain," to rummage through the debris of the past looking for the cast-off, the discarded, and that which is in danger of being lost—so that they crash the party. "Do this in remembrance of me" thus is not a ritualistic prayer. It is an act of hope that heralds a new dawn, a new day.

Vítor Westhelle is a theologian par excellence for whom remembrance is a living bridge of hope and love and life that keeps on living.

BIBLIOGRAPHY

Benjamin, Andrew. *Present Hope: Philosophy, Architecture, Judaism*. London: Routledge, 1997.
Benjamin, Walter. *The Arcades Project*. Translated by Howard Eiland and Kevin McLaughlin. Cambridge: Harvard University Press, 2000.
———. *Illuminations: Essays and Reflections*. Translated by Harry Zohn. New York: Schocken, 1968.
Kirekegaard, Søren. *Works of Love*. New York: Harper & Row, 1962.
Lispector, Clarice. *Selected Cronicas*. Translated by Giovanni Pontiero. New York: New Directions, 1984.
Márquez, Gabriel, García. *Vivir para contarla*. Neuva York: Knopf, 2002.
Metz, Johann, Baptist. *Faith in History and Society*. New York: Seabury, 1980.
Morrison, Toni. *Beloved*. New York: Plume, 1988.
Phan, Peter, and Jung Young Lee. *Journey at the Margins: Toward an Autobiographical Theology in American-Asian Perspective*. Collegeville, MN: Liturgical, 1999.
Remmler, Karen. *Waking the Dead: Correspondences between Walter Benjamin's Concept of Remembrance and Ingeborg Bachmann's Ways of Dying*. Riverside, CA: Ariadne, 1996.
Roy, Arundhati. *The God of Small Things*. New York: Harper Perennial, 1998.
Westhelle, Vítor. *Eschatology and Space: The Lost Dimension in Theology Past and Present*. New York: Palgrave Macmillan, 2012.
———. *Word in words: Musings of the Gospel*. Tiruvalla: CSS Books, 2009.
Wilding, Adrian. "The Concept of Remembrance in Walter Benjamin." PhD diss., University of Warwick, UK, June 1996.

30. Benjamin, *Illuminations*, 257.

11

Theology as Tapestry Weaving

From a "Lutheran Core" through Mediating Devices—and Back

LUÍS H. DREHER

"DOING THEOLOGY IS AKIN to weaving a tapestry..."[1] In the immediate context of this quote a mention to "context" is made while the hope is expressed that talk thereof ought not to be ever "trite." The underlying idea is that contexts are to be taken seriously when—or because—they go to the heart of matter(s). And they often do. They are not void; they rebel to being talked into the mere object of an "applied" theology. Not only that: they may even produce the inversion—and/or the desire for subversion—of what is adamantly taken as the "same" and the "proper."

Accordingly, "latitudes are no platitudes," at least as an *a priori* rule, and especially as they relate and add their peculiar spice to multifarious debates. This is certainly the case here. This is what the now roughly 30-year-old

1. Westhelle, *Eschatology and Space*, 91; also: "Wrappings of the Divine," 368–80.

theological work done and offered to us all by Vítor Westhelle amounts to. Questioning static arrangements and highlighting dynamic derangements is what the man and his work have been busy with. Yes, this is Vítor's own *nec-otium* in the almost forgotten sense, and only thus pristine, if anything could ever be so. In any case, I am sure there will be more of the good stuff being brewed and waiting for us to see long after his 60th birthday.

Well, here I am really unable to hide my interest in this work, which in the last six to seven years has shown the first mature and well-rounded (enough) fruits on theological *loci*. These results in book form are apparently as loose as loci can be, but they display a general motif. It is given by the 2006 one on God/"fundamental" theology, followed by (more) *prolegomena*, a book on the Church, and a novel Eschatology which even in a first reading leads one to conclude that it has not so obvious and yet important links with the first book, its nature and understanding of the tasks of theology.[2]

Be it as it may, my interest is certainly not triggered by strategic reasons. Neither is it of a purely theoretical kind, as would befit a dispassionate academician. Though a life-long student of his, I quickly learned that all of Vítor's doings with the (W)word are meant *at the same time* for our fruition—hence eliciting interest *as* desire, thereby subverting one of the neat distinctions he so competently brings to the fore. As I use to say: Vítor is my favorite theological mentor among those who are not only remembered, but also living, and fully at that. And here I should add a first extended comment, obviously allowing myself some freedom as I indulge in biographical digressions, as if excused by the very nature of this volume.

In this vein, I must confess that Vítor's total impression on my own itinerary since we both got late to a meeting in Cascavel, Brazil, in a cold July in 1986—and of all I would hardly have a credible tale to tell about the reasons for being so late—is definitely of the kind of a "dangerous-saving memory." For back then I was totally, and even more than today, unsure about quite a bunch of things. More outwardly, things like whether I should really become a theologian, not to mention a pastor. Well, I must say that at least I gave it a try later on, and Vítor played no small role in it.

But let me get back into track: although I do not consider myself to be (so far) really well-read theologically (and philosophically), my best hunch is that perhaps only old Luther could match this kind of overall impression on me. Perhaps a certain Hegel, for many other favorite chips of mine, including a small pack of theologians, are too sober for the task at hand.[3]

---

2. I refer, in this order, to my understanding of the general plan coming out of Vítor's singly authored books viz. monographs: Westhelle, *Scandalous God*, 2006; *After Heresy*, 2010; *Church Event*, 2010; and *Eschatology and Space*, 2012.

3. And Nietzsche was, and Heidegger and many of the French are now, too

Now the "Lutheran core" I will touch upon later, but not expand on, is precisely of the "dangerous-saving" kind I associate with Vítor's work and total impression on people like me. Of this kind is also the man's style, like the one of that other systematic theologian (admittedly, of sorts). And this core shows forth not in spite of, but in the very midst of Vítor's illuminating building and testing of typologies, and of his patient but tremendous ability for rigorous analysis and synthesis as dazzling as it is insightful. As far as I am concerned, Vítor dares and manages to bring together Hölderlin's and Benjamin's deepest yearnings. It is not by chance that these names—and their issues—are frequent, and their diverse casts of mind so well synthesized, in some of Vítor's own pages.

Yet another interlude: as a cinephile—and a dabbler at that—now recalling a must-see for any then *both* naive liberation theologian *and* fan of Ennio Morricone (*The Mission*, 1986), I cite yet another bit of evidence for the "dangerous-saving" core and kind I have in mind. It is found in the *both* painted gray-in-gray *and* apocalyptic sounding, (would-be) closing words of some Pope's envoy. He there said the following: "For as always, Your Holiness, the spirit of the dead will survive in the memory of the living."

Now isn't this similar enough to that same "dangerous-saving" core to life and its corresponding style I just talked about? Of course now nuanced, and undoubtedly made much more concrete, or "contextual," if you like it? Contextual because surrounded by a Latin American ambience from times past and regions present. A liminal and hybrid ambience not too far from the land conflicts in West Paraná, where the theologian became a pastor and enticed another, younger and more skeptical, generation. A core to life similar to old Christian expectations, although different because imagined (i.e. desired) and cast in artistic representation by a Northern fascination with the still potential Paradise beneath the Equator. A paradise which even Christians—in the movie Jesuits, to be more specific—could somehow take part in?!

Indeed, apocalyptic words and representations[4] abound in unexpected places. For Vítor they are, so-to-speak, "fine-tuned" to proleptic lived-experiences represented[5] or "advocated," perhaps unwillingly, in the hegemonic language of the stranger and strategist. Presupposed is, of course, the idea that God speaks and acts in hidden ways which we cannot control and dualistically separate. The dualism, insofar as it occurs, is up to

---

inebriating for my own taste to ever be thrown on the table.

4. "Vorstellung"; for "Darstellung" (by others), Westhelle, *Eschatology and Space*, 109.

5. "Vertretung" = "proxy"; ibidem.

POEISIS

God Himself, or else due to our finite and sinful perspective. God is so free that She does not need, from Her own perspective incompletely transparent to us—but to a point open to equitable "interpretation"—to act always in dual ways.[6]

Hence whatever those lived-experiences may amount to, they may bring the *fascinans* and *tremendum* to the very core of life as it emerges among daily practices/productions by individuals *in* community/society *with a view* to community nurtured by difficult hope and freedom.[7] Significant experiences do this even by "dissimulation," which is the possible tactic for not taking seriously and "as-ordered" a factually inverted world.[8] As such, they are irreducible to any single event of a merely transcendent, quasi "supernatural" kind that, isolated, would empty of a divine breath the remaining space and time.

No gnosis or gnosticism—and I follow Vítor in a very broad use of the word—even of a soft type, is allowed here. If needs be, a lasting ban on "knowledge" takes place even at the uncontrollable cost of unleashing the saving danger of incarnation/cross, this incipient margin of gift/death. Both pairs take place on the boundaries, out of bounds. A hidden but not "invisible" God brings forth loving and lovely products in the midst of human horizontal dealings. God is hidden in what is visible or out of eyeshot, not in the range of all-too-human strategic vision, and thus removed from any relentless Platonic diction. God may be, as Luther well knew, selectively ubiquitous, just impossible to definitely pinpoint and nail down. But in any case given to equitable—not only fair—interpretation in the light of God's promises, however transcendent in a not merely natural, "anthropological," way.

Transcendence is here important, in spite of the affirmation of an immanence and realism proper to God only,[9] and thus, as far as Christian

---

6 Westhelle, "Luther and Liberation," 55: " ... there is no metaphysical necessity that requires God to act in two independent and different ways (spiritual salvation and earthly preservation)."

7. Here R. Otto's transcendental and psychological basis for religious experience is not denied, but expanded as the "logical subject"—to use an expression found in Dilthey—is not bound to an individualistic perspective. The reference to "community" comes from a construal of Luther's two regiments based on F. Tönnies distinction; cf. Westhelle, *Eschatology and Space*, 113ff.

8. A mention to "Verstellung" would be in place here—based as it is on an avowedly external, "transcendent" reading of Hegel, *Phenomenology of Spirit*, 376–77, § 621. Cf. Westhelle, *After Heresy*, passim, on the issues of dissimulation, camouflage, and mimicry.

9. And not to historical or dialectical materialism as defining "worldviews"—see the dialogue on "theology" between Horkheimer and Benjamin, alluded to by Westhelle,

theology is concerned, "antignostic." But this antignosticism does not fall, in turn, into the trap of going so far as to assimilating God to something like a "sacred space." We can thus talk of the "signs of the places"[10] while at the same time averting their cooptation into traditional or emerging harmonic, organic, or holistic paradigms.[11] For if the place is truly the margin, it is also the site of conflict where the decisive word may appear in the ongoing struggle for "adding some space to what is proper."[12]

But space and time are, notwithstanding human (contextual) fights for power, the forms filled by God's free action.[13] They are not, epistemologically speaking, the means of mere receptivity, the mere domain for construing aseptic and positivist "scientific" objectivity. Or else, quasi-religiously speaking, a stock of new idols for "anthropological" proxy worship ensuing after the successful objectification of some kind of civil religion. Neither are they, gnostically and in a more serious "religious" manner, ways of escape for otherworldly salvation. For this kind of "transcendental aesthetic" of pure forms really begs to be subverted: first and foremost in view of the God's sovereign-good spontaneous activity, but then also as the horizontal activity of free humans before other humans and other nature comes to the fore in strategic and tactic ways.

Now, if the decisive dangerous-saving word of the Gospel (cross and salvation through undivided inner/outer time/space) comes lightening

---

Eschatology and Space, 126.

10. Westhelle, *Eschatology and Space*, xi.

11. In the specific case of Latin American, at least in the case of Brazil, some recent trends both in theology and the (religious) social sciences seem to be adapting and moving still farther into forms of theological "integralism." But now they become much more "practical," i.e., closely knit to denominational agendas fighting for (vital) space—in a clear abuse of the proper theological use of the category. Or else integralism is pursued on the basis a "pseudotheology of culture" forgetful, even if cordially and as advocacy/"proxy," of differences in spite of—or because of, in a perhaps stronger reading—the received Iberian motto *ex uno plures*. Such a "theology" does this as it attempts to retrieve something like a "civil religion" on the basis of "cultural" hegemonic models, and thus away from the original more—or only ideally more—"latitudinal" perspective. Given the fact that most Latin American liberation theologies depend on an organic paradigm, be it political or religious, where "everything has its place"; this is not really a complete surprise. (For the passages on which I base this extended remark, cf. Westhelle, *Eschatology and Space*, 10, 83, 109; and for what I see here as the (easy) distortion of the *ex uno plures* principle I draw upon a paper unfortunately only available, to my knowledge, in Brazilian Portuguese: Westhelle, "Entre Américas: convergências e divergências teológicas.")

12. Westhelle, *Eschatology and Space*, 121.

13 At the very least inwardly so, in "remembrance" of a dangerous-saving redemption as restoration of "the materiality of the damaged life of past victims." See Westhelle, *Eschatology and Space*, 126, here following W. Benjamin.

through as normative and is thus transcendental in some way—not to be confused with a really gnostic spark—then someone like Foucault is only half-right. In this sense, his own views on parrhesiastic freedom are as good for theology in an *ad hoc* sense as Aristotle's classification of the human (cognitive) capacities.[14] For in quite the same way as *poiesis* is not primarily human, at least for the (Lutheran) theologian there remains a contingent and yet grounded freedom for others. "Contingent," though, first and foremost because it is given and received. It is an overarching positive freedom found so much harder to explain in the last quarter of a century or so—since questions changed so much in a sort of bacchanalian revel of alternating disjunctions. It is a freedom which is not only power, but just because, by the same token, it does not (utterly) depend on the mere and hoped-for soberness of human communicative praxis. For it pops up elsewhere: "Tangential spaces are the end of the freedom of power and the beginning of the power of freedom."[15]

In other words, but changing subjects again: whatever possible universality there is, it does not come in abstract otherness, or only at The End. It begins now as it becomes determinate, particular. It even allows us to name concrete sins[16], from the margins themselves or in forms of authentic advocacy. Christ's ubiquitousness is eschatologically present as it takes place, being open to equitable interpretation. This is why the good news arriving in any marginal place, even before the Gospel *qua* universal promise is preached, is determinately/dangerously saving. They amount to the news that *parousia* is fortunately "present" —in alternative/alternating time-space continuums, to be recognized and appropriated by Christian discourse. A major challenge indeed; but also a renewed possibility after the so-called end of (modern) history and all the discrediting of presence aided by (abstract) negative theologies whose twin usually appears as some form of "mystical" nostalgia.

Hence the uneasiness caused by this presence. It comes from the Hallelujah Saturday, among the displaced after bitter absence, as if in embodied sparks at that very limen. Vítor is here talking about a saving presence as much hard to find from a center as it is prone to dislodge from power stances: either by persuasion or, if needs be, in the hour(s) of trial and judgment. Such is the very presence of God in and around the cross. And precisely this is what allows us to identify what was earlier adumbrated as the "Lutheran core," dangerously internalized (*er-innert*), though now unavoidably

---

14. Westhelle, *Scandalous God*, 85ff., 126ff.
15. Westhelle, *Eschatology and Space*, 20.
16. Westhelle, "Luther and Liberation."

armored with new mediating devices. As if saving the honor of (other) names. As if flattering a grace-ful(l) tactical nominalism through weaving weak syntheses while carving before our senses exquisite dishes betwixt and between typological analyses.

In any case, as in Luther—the systematician of sorts—signaling a presence to be sought for as long as and only as many threads are interwoven. Only as they are taken account of, eschewing in clever ways the threats of fear on the grounds of solid hope, but alert to emerging, minor, fragile hope.

All of this implies that to talk about God is to talk about humans, allowing into our theological purview humanity's unbelievable, partly unbelieving, richness and poverty. The latter phrasing sure sounds like Pascal's here. But the intention is more concrete, and the metaphysics of individual inwardness makes room for (God's) more determinate and temporal/spatial (own) metaphysics which theology still can't really figure out beyond equitable interpretations. At the same time, human variety, and thus multiplicity, both interferes with and bounces back at a personal unity who at least disclosed itself as not fixed, not immutable, except for an immutability of (good) will. And if so, then capable of self-transgression and dealing with all, but especially other humans, by a loving, movable will which makes room and adds space at the margins. (Needless to say this is not, neither does it want to be, a technical theodicy—much less for quasi-apologetic purposes, as one might conclude from possible new construals of the intellectual heritage between Luther and Kant.)

This wholesome unity through difference remains the master type, the only *figura* properly speaking to both surround and serve as a realistic model for our doings and sufferings. A unity of the kind Auerbach so keenly detected in a different, literary key. A unity receding into a background of saving-dangerous relations: alluring, yes, though frightful enough for any speculative interest which would dare to fathom it, or any merely rational morality which would curtail it. But, in any event, powerful enough to take hold in its disclosures of human imagination and limited freedom for the sake of The Good, against all odds and appearances.

As a matter of fact, the very dynamics of interweaving, taking into account, going out of oneself without completely loosing oneself[17]—keeping

---

17 Tillich, *Main Works*, 417–18. I remind the reader that Vítor's relation with Tillich does not seem to me, on the whole, to be only polemical. One way I could indirectly express this is by sharing a point he hinted at several years ago in a private conversation, namely, that to his mind "Tillich was as much or more a Hegelian than a Schellingian"! As far as I can see, another great theologian, Fr. D. E. Schleiermacher, has not been, thus far, so spared. And even if I could, I would not be able to expand on the possible reasons here due to space restrictions.

(living) "identity," a word so despised in today's academia crusade against "essentialism"—is life itself, both in its divine and (truly) human shape. For only God herself could lead the *imago* back to its undreamed-of future, a future already dormant at the root of so many dangerous-saving reminiscences. This again is part and parcel of the "Lutheran core" shining forth through the dualities and differences of earthly life. Perhaps a core only on the watch, but certainly making room to be somewhen, somewhere the transparent object of pure doxology, the very matter of glory.

In the case of a Christian theologian all the proper distinctions are to be kept, of course. There is no place for *unio mystica* or romantic nostalgia. But such a realism is never to be turned into an excuse not to dare and wander somewhat, "theorizing," as it were, "from below." In place(s), which is where we still all are: in the surroundings of the cross and the empty tomb, during a somewhat lingering Hallelujah Saturday which stands for our believing —and, hopefully and more precisely, faithful existence.

For Vítor—I entreat myself to believe—theology remains both the search for and enunciation of some universality after the still-developing critique of modernity and all its revisions, including major Christian ones especially, but not only, as impacted by idealism and romanticism. This universality is concrete, plural, dialectic, ambivalent, dynamic—and increasingly harder to figure out.

Of course a both needed and actual decentering of modernity and even Western-Northern Christianity, at the level of both theory generally and theology specifically, has been prompted by the emancipatory social, cultural and political tides now moving from the South and the East. But this process must not mean the simple, in a sense still "metaphysical"—in the sense of "dualistic"—inversion of a world which, from the perspective of the hidden or not-so-hidden God experienced and equitably interpreted at the margins, is caught unawares as the paroxysmally inverted world[18].

The main point, however, comes to the fore as we are reminded that if that universality is ever to be found, then only by virtue of the right disposition. Which one? Basically not a disposition virtuous as such, but more like the whole self now becoming latitude by grace. Theology as done in good faith. Theology as a free and generous activity, as lived-experience(s) that conjoin(s) and synthesize(s) both legitimate differences and human (cognitive) capacities. An activity that takes place "from below," as already pointed out, always in already filled and fragmented spaces, simultaneously making room before/to the O/other/s. A disposition targeted at the margins and their possible visibility.

18. Westhelle, *After Heresy*, 37–38.

Targeted, eventually, also at some "theory" there, but then not despising praxis and especially poiesis. Instead, a form of theory responsive to that primal deed done and daily preserved, and the fulfilling of both time and space with its products. All of them undivided in-and-for-themselves, and also *for us*: but then, in the epistemic sense of the double meaning intended here, still in a *chiaroscuro*. A disposition to be found mainly as long as the limits, edges, the real or apparent dead ends, are reckoned with. Not calculated, predicted or instilled with mute idols, but reckoned with in the given time-space continuum of filled, even if for us incurably variegated and perspectival, lived-experience.[19] A continuum, finally, that is not void but already filled and thick with freely given meaning, creative *poiesis*. In fact so thick as not to be simply describable, while at the same time always already wrapping up a deeper reality as it hidden core (and agenda!). A reality only to be etched in the now and then visible margins of breaking, strategically unplanned novelty.

BIBLIOGRAPHY

Hegel, Georg W. F. *Phenomenology of Spirit*. Translated by Arnold V. Miller. Oxford: Clarendon, 1977.

Tillich, Paul. "Philosophical Background of my Theology (1960)." In *Main Works, vol. 1: Philosophical Writings*, edited by Carl H. Ratschow, 411–20. New York: de Gruyter, 1989.

Westhelle, Vítor. *After Heresy: Colonial Practices and Post-Colonial Theologies*. Eugene, Oregon: Cascade, 2010.

———. *The Church Event: Call and Challenge of a Church Protestant*. Minneapolis: Fortress, 2010.

———. "Entre Américas: convergências e divergências teológicas." In *Teologia e ciências da religião: a caminho da maioridade acadêmica no Brasil*, edited by Eduardo R. da Cruz and Geraldo de Mori, 25–42. São Paulo: Paulinas; Belo Horizonte: PUC Minas, 2011. Online: www.vitorw.com/wp-content/uploads/2010/07/Entre-Americas.pdf.

———. *Eschatology and Space: The Lost Dimension in Theology Past and Present*. New York: Palgrave Macmillan, 2012.

———. "Luther and Liberation." *Dialog: A Journal of Theology* 25 (1986) 51–58.

———. *The Scandalous God: The Use and Abuse of the Cross*. Minneapolis: Fortress, 2006.

———. "Wrappings of the Divine: Location and Vocation in Theological Perspective." *Currents in Theology and Mission* 31 (2004) 368–80.

---

19. I here borrow from Dilthey, but only by parting company with both received interpretive options that have attributed to him first psychologism (subjectivism) and later historicism (objectivism).

12

Knowledge Transfigured by Love

Theological Perspectives of Vítor Westhelle's Thought

KATHLEN LUANA DE OLIVEIRA

There are people whose lives fascinate us. There are people who pronounce enchanted words. In rare moments, there are people who rise and do not succumb to the harshness of theological words, bringing to life words solidified by tradition, turning them into poetry. Vítor Westhelle is one of these people; he is a word-charmer, a "boy who got a bird-like look":

> The boy got a bird-like look —
> Contracted a view of origins
> So that he saw things
> likewise
> the birds see
> all unnamed things.

> Water was not the word water yet.
> Stone was not the word stone yet.
> [...]
> The words were free from grammars and
> they could be in any position.
> So that the boy could inaugurate.
> He could give to the stones a flower-like attitude
> And if he wanted to fit into a bee,
> he only needed to open the word bee and go inside
> of it
> as if it were a childhood language.[1]

A boy with a bird-like look, who has the ability to open the words, has no fear of any word, even the ones considered "bad," moralized or hardened by a hegemonic tradition, words like sin, subversion, body,[2] erotic, playful.[3] Westhelle goes to the origins,[4] he goes inside the words[5] and sees something that was already there but was not yet told, something that could not be seen until then.

> Unlike the sciences, there is in theology an irreducible and inescapable residue that makes optical consistency an unattainable principle. . . . Ultimately, it is a matter of faith and not sight. . . . the scientific inadequacy of theology must be examined in light of what it brings to the knowledge, which is not understood or exhausted in the visualization and systematization. The appeal to the imagination and the experience is not only a prerequisite for the theological task, but it is what lies at its core, sustaining and vitalizing the narrative it produces. This is the embodied knowledge which theology depends on, although simultaneously it wants to hide this knowledge in the illusory attempt to achieve an optical consistency.[6]

---

1. "... O menino pegou um olhar de pássaro — / Contraiu visão fontana./ Por forma que ele enxergava as coisas / por igual como os pássaros enxergam. / As coisas todas inominadas. / Água não era ainda a palavra água. / Pedra não era ainda a palavra pedra. / . . . / As palavras eram livres de gramáticas e / podiam ficar em qualquer posição. / Por forma que o menino podia inaugurar. / Podia das às pedras costumes de flor. / . . . / E, se quisesse caber em uma abelha, era / só abrir a palavra abelha e entrar dentro / dela. / Como se fosse infância da língua." Manuel de Barros, *Poemas Rupestres*, 11.
2. Westhelle, "Santa Frida," 157–64.
3. Westhelle, "A Festa," 12–28.
4. Westhelle, "The Word," 167–78.
5. Westhelle, "Communication," 1–27.
6. Westhelle, "Outros saberes," 274.

With a bird-like look dedicated to the task of thinking and to the endless pursuit of understanding, Westhelle is surrounded by an unlimited curiosity. Hence there is no metaphysics that remains untouched; there is nothing that cannot be studied. However, in each study and research, Westhelle places the world, the struggles for justice, equality, freedom against (neo)colonialism,[7] oppression, exploitation.

> This raising of consciousness (*conscientização*) represents a transition from colonialism to postcolonialism. Colonialism or a colonial situation is characterized by two main features. The first feature is called hegemony, the capability of a dominant group to exercise power over the subjected or subaltern group without the need of overt use of force (even if its availability is used as a deterrent). Hegemony is distinguished from tyranny by the fact that it presupposes the tacit assent given by the subaltern group to this exercise of power. This accounts for the presence of power but the absence of the need for the dominant hegemonic culture to use overt force to exercise and maintain control; this is granted by tacit assent. In other words, in a colonial situation the subaltern group simply accepts their situation as a given, the way things are. The second feature of colonialism is then the submissive acceptance by the subaltern group of the representation or identity that is projected upon them by the dominant group. Again, the subaltern group accepts these representations of themselves as matters of fact.
>
> By contrast, a postcolonial situation arises when these two conditions no longer apply, that is, when the subaltern group no longer assents to hegemonic rule by the dominant group and when the subaltern group no longer accepts the imposed representation of who they are by the dominant group. When these new conditions prevail, the oppressed have succeeded in breaking with hegemony and are already engaged in shaping a new world. Nevertheless, it is often the case that the difference between interest and desire remains as a residue from colonial imposition reproducing itself in the postcolonial world as indelible marks inherited from the colonial times.
>
> However, before this consciousness blossoms fully there is a transitional stage in which resistance is exercised and is often taken by the dominant group to be mere subservience, but it is in fact an indication of the resilience of the people. . . .[8]

---

7. Westhelle, *After Heresy*.
8. Westhelle, "No Sin," 104–5.

With a bird-like look dedicated to hearing and praying,[9] Westhelle understands that not everything fits into the limits of reason.[10] The miracles of life, the uncertainties of death, the anxieties and doubts which emerge along the way, are part of his theological investigations. And even where the words do not reach, there is space for contemplation, for marveling at the beauty of the world and the beauty of faith. This marveling, understood by the Greek as *thaumadzein*, emerges from the life and words of Westhelle as an opening to the possibilities, to the novelty, to the events.

The work of Westhelle shows itself as an artwork. By art, it is possible to transform the perception of reality, which is not just a reflection of what it is, but also what it could be, evoking desires and aspirations. Art is not a mere reproduction/representation of life through technique, reproduced in series, but it has something unique that unsettles, fidgets, cherishes, and takes your breath away. Accordingly, whenever the other senses turn to an artwork, a new interpretation can happen, a new discovery may reveal itself. Artwork is alive, it has life; is not automatic, it emerges from a process of spontaneity and freedom and, at the same time, it involves a lot of work; it is the result of a hard and necessary work. In their work, the artist is committed to life; they place themselves in the work, set the world through them and their work.[11]

Westhelle's artwork is permeated by an authentic theology. There is always something to be uncovered with deep and solid critiques, but also with intense Christological,[12] eschatological,[13] and ecclesiastical[14] perspectives. In Westhelle's work we can find a theology with body—a theology that happens among us, between people. In this way, there is confronting of idols and demons. According to Westhelle, the church is the locus for the discernment of spirit in which communion happens.

> ... this feature of the church, of the solidarity of the shaken, the solidarity of those who are moved, pertains to immanence and not to a transcendent reality magically descending upon us. The community that gathers in this spirit is the body of Christ insofar as this body has become thoroughly flesh (*logos ensarkos*) and still is among us totally in the finitude of embodiment.[15]

9. Westhelle, *Word in Words*.
10. Westhelle, "Desabusando," 19–30.
11. Heidegger, "A origem," 5–97; Heidegger, "Para quê poetas?" 307–97.
12. Westhelle, *Scandalous God*.
13. Westhelle, "The Times," 411–24.
14. Westhelle, *Church Event*.
15. Westhelle, "Idols," 14.

World-experiences also cross Westhelle's work, from elucidating in his thinking a plurality of knowledge, which yearn for a better world. Critically and authentically, each reader is invited to walk into the streets and talk with the interlocutors that Westhelle encounters in several places of the world. His theology is full of spices and flavors, always directed to a God who is present in our communion, in our living together.

> . . . It is in this explicit syncretic dialectic of fragmentation and reintegration—and not in the opposition between immanence and transcendence—that the traditional relationship between grace and nature will be cast. Rejecting the question about the world, theology (as much as literature in Latin America) is concerned with bringing to sight the other-worldliness of this world and its inner fantastic, marvelous, and terrifying aspects, realized when "otherness" is found in the depths of this world. Hence, the "other" world, sociologically invisible according to the patterns of the official inscriptions, is ontologically very much present in what lies hidden from sight. The effort of bringing into visibility the fragmented mythical pieces also implies, therefore, the syncretic effort of weaving the together.[16]

Westhelle's exposé is a mélange of anxieties and questions of the present time, and doubts about referentiality, representations, and language. The search for a relevant way of narrating the history of God's people is a commitment in Westhelle's thought. His theology is born and flourishes between narratives and poetry.

> This is the ultimate denial of the business, it is idleness. This is the gift that cannot even be expressed, meant, and cannot be *represented*. However, the interesting nuance to this parable (as in the Parable of the Sower in the synoptic Gospels, Mark 4 and others) is that there is an explanation. There's a speech. But it is a speech about silence. It is a speech on the impossibility of representation bordering the canonical knowledge. It is peculiar to the theological speech that inhabits the gaps of existing episteme. There also inhabit gods.[17]

In that way, thinking theology means to face reality, to face life without being satisfied with the gaps, without being satisfied with the common uses already given to the theology. Westhelle thus realizes the limitations of theological knowledge, the limitations of postmodern thought. Questions on the

---

16. Westhelle and Götz, "In Quest," 21.
17. Westhelle, "Desabusando," 29–30. Author's translation.

theological relevance in modernity[18] are made due to the "incredulity to the metanarratives."[19] Such incredulity does not limit metanarratives; it questions their universal validity and their historical verifiability. In this sense, according to Westhelle, modernity has focused on the incisive critique on religious representations, erasing the "historical proofs" from Christianity. Thus, "each one of these 'proofs' became a substrate that founded the theological enterprise as a positive Science; that is: we had a religion founded on positive data from unquestionable historical convictions."[20] And, in the face of claims of human autonomy, "the age of reason imploded the Gothic cathedral of religious positivism or of historical Christendom, there was no significant doubt raised against the foundation stones of the Christian edifice until then."[21]

By introducing the limitations of the task of thinking, Westhelle asseverates that with the surge of the sciences, rationality criteria are created.[22] It set limits to what could be legitimately registered;[23] it demands a legitimate knowledge that must be exhausted on visualization and on systematization. In view of what can be known, defined, binaries were created, placing the knowledge only on what can be seen. Other knowledge is rendered as false and illusionary. "By delimiting and reducing the experience to the field of immutable mobiles, science or modern rationality created a paradox: while trying to understand the external object to its speech, ... they invented this object intending it to be as more present in concept as more absent in reality."[24] Thus, down came the accusations on theology and religion and they came fast and rolling: illusion, deceit, naiveté, opium ideology.

Anyway, although Westhelle clearly presents all the rational traps that might lead to demise, neither theology/religion nor we, theologians, are dead, at least, not yet. After all, the purpose stated by modernity also open doors to new beginnings; they create paths to the questioning of universal and also considered timeless knowledge. The plurality of voices, smells, spices, experiences fights increasingly for space. It is in this sense that the dialogue between Westhelle and Foucault, for example, emerges as a struggle against domestications, domination and standardizations. Therefore, as

---

18. The Latin American theology points in this direction: the limitations of the modelo f modernity, the view of the center and the boundaries. Dussel, "Sistema." 47.

19. Lyotard, *The Postmodern*, 1984, XXIV.

20. Westhelle, "Modernidade, Mito," 13.

21. Idem. Author's translation.

22. Westhelle, "Outros saberes," 259–60.

23. Ibid., 260.

24. Ibid., 268.

Arendt would say, the announced ends in modernity are significant changes to the thought, to the understanding. Declaring an end to God does not mean God's end, but it does mean a change in the ways of conceiving God. "These 'modern' deaths of God, metaphysics, philosophy and, by implication, of positivism, can be major events . . ." because different ways of thinking are evidenced, even if marginally.[25]

The brilliant critiques of Westhelle are not just externally directed, that is, to a framework outside of theology, but also to the theology itself, especially when there is the insistence of fitting into the perspective of scientific paradigms of seeing. It does not mean just to reproduce metaphysical heritage and, at the same time, it does not mean to abandon the metaphysical heritage. What is pertinent is to understand the human limitation, that not everything can be fully understood. Arendt points to this when she says, "Kant himself believed that the need to think beyond the limitations of knowledge was only awakened by the old metaphysical questions of God, freedom, immortality, and that he had 'found it necessary to deny knowledge to make room for faith' [. . .]."[26] Thus, as proposed by Westhelle, it is necessary to "disabuse the God of the gaps," and not to fall into traps that "[. . .] by avoiding a metaphysical or even positivist discourse, seem to surrender to the most frequent critiques which theology has been submitted in modernity."[27] Religion becomes, in fact, "[. . .] a illusory representation entered in the middle of an agonizing situation with the purpose of dominating and disciplining in large scale. This argument presupposes and maintains that there is an inverse ratio between meaning of human existence and the idea of the transcendent."[28] Thus, religion is seen uniquely by essentialist approaches and/or functionalist ones. Therefore, it is essential, according to Westhelle, to see the epistemological bonds to which theological knowledge has submitted.

> Between religion and science, in relation to their objects, there is a difference in Derrida's meaning of the term (*différance*), which describes the "infinitesimal displacement" of difference itself, is not very different from the other, but the same is not identical itself. And it is in this "difference" that we host theology as a marginal discourse bordering areas of scientific knowledge. It has nothing to do to the rejection of the scientific knowledge on behalf of another ruled knowledge. This is what happens with

---

25. Arendt, *Responsabilidade*, 2004, 230.
26. Ibid., 231.
27. Westhelle, "Outros saberes," 268.
28. Ibid., 269.

every strain of religious fundamentalism, which in this sense is to science what an operating system of a computer is to another (for example, Microsoft and Apple). They do not share the same platform, but they assume the same binary system of logic gates that is the foundation of all modern digital computers. What I mean is something different that escapes from the standards of any platform, if we follow this analogy. Perhaps one approach would be to compare a modern computer to a *yupana*, a kind of Incan abacus, still used at the time of the conquest, whose operating logic is still not rebuilt for sure.[29]

There is something irreducible in theology after all, its truths and hopes do not end with the imminent end of earthly things. In this sense, in the work of Westhelle, we are invited to regain the ability to marvel at what is given; we are asked to reflect on experiences, facing inherited fears and hegemonic thoughts. Therefore, theology does not fit into the mold of modern science, recognizes something irreducible, not fully exhaustible, and yet not devoid of meaning. Referring to George Bataille, Westhelle reaffirms that "the only way to define the world is to reduce it to our measurements and then, with a laugh, discover that it is beyond our measurements."[30]

Thus, for Westhelle, the poet, the artist, knowledge opens windows to something bigger. Even while seeking understanding, the activity of investigating gives place to what theology has to say and cannot be put into words, what goes beyond knowledge. The words of Rubem Alves, may be the best summary of Westhelle's theological thought: "knowledge transfigured by love." Westhelle's theology has its basis in the mystery of the scandal of God on the cross. The emphasis of his theology lies not in knowing but in wondering, in the love, in the communion. Westhelle realizes that, in faith, there is the "courage to love based on the belief, there is freedom to love based on the liberating promise of love."[31]

It is in this sense that theology in the work of Westhelle can be read as "knowledge transfigured by love."[32] In many ways, there is a prophetic characteristic in Westhelle's thought regarding reality: denounce where there is no love and announce where love is needed. Moreover, his theology is committed to that love which implies that a transfigured knowledge is knowledge at the disposal of love and not the knowledge aimed towards progress and evolution or knowledge confined to academies and harsh and

---

29. Westhelle, "Desabusando," 22–23.
30. Bataille, *Impossible*, 1991, 99.
31. Ebeling, *O pensamento*, 1988, 213.
32. Alves, "Teologia," 32.

cold institutions. It is knowledge committed outside its common boundaries. In other words, as a knowledge transfigured by love, the accent does not lie in the knowing, "because it is not by knowledge that bodies are resurrected but by love... That's where the gesture begins, not in the knowing."[33] Westhelle's theology is born from experiences that come out of utterances, shared words, focused on the Word that animates the body and gives it new life. It is a love that cannot be confused with ideology. It has a commitment, because love is not an activity of loneliness; love is love in the presence of other people in this world.

> Look to the present
> Hear the cries of those who suffer
> Hear, from the past, the cries of the Great Victim
> Mix them
> Turn them into a poem
> Eat it, as if it were a sacrament...[34]

Theology in Westhelle's thought addresses events that are not reducible to concepts, it is a speech that makes possible to marvel at an ever new world; it approximates of the events of life. Meanings and experiences that are best articulated by art, poetry, myth, mystique abound in the paths explored and visualized by Westhelle. In Westhelle's thought, we find theological perspectives that indicate the existence of many ways of understanding the world and the place of humans in the world. His theological perspectives highlight plurality that warns us not to forget that the world is not limited to our measures. It is a theology that consists of a knowledge transfigured by the love that is born from a bird-like look, a look that sees beauty in life events.

BIBLIOGRAPHY

Alves, Rubem. Teologia. *Tempo e Presença*. Rio de Janeiro, n. 206, (1986) 32.
Arendt, Hannah. *Responsabilidade e Julgamento*. São Paulo: Cia das Letras, 2004.
Barros, Manuel de. *Poemas Rupestres*. Rio de Janeiro: Record, 2007.
Bataille, George. *The Impossible*. San Francisco: City Lights, 1991.
Dussel, Enrique. "Sistema-mundo, dominação e exclusão: apontamentos sobre a história do fenômeno religioso no processo de globalização da América Latina." In: *História da Igreja na América Latina e no Caribe 1945–1995: o debate metodológico*. Edited by Eduardo Hoornaert, 39–79. Petrópolis: Vozes; São Paulo: CEHILA, 1995.
Ebeling, Gerhard. *O pensamento de Lutero*. São Leopoldo: Sinodal, 1988.

33. Ibid.
34. Ibid..

Heidegger, Martin. "A origem da obra de arte." In *Caminhos de Floresta*. (Holzwege) 5–94. Lisboa: Fundação Calouste Gulbenkian, 2002.

———. "Para quê poetas?" In *Caminhos de Floresta*. (Holzwege). 307–367. Lisboa: Fundação Calouste Gulbenkian, 2002.

Lyotard, Jean-Fançois. *The Postmodern Condition*: A Report on Knowledge. Minneapolis: University of Minnesota Press, 1984.

Westhelle, Vítor. "A Festa, o Lúdico e o Erótico na Religião: Perspectiva Teológica." *Estudos de Religião* 19/28 (July 2005), 12–28.

———. *After Heresy: Colonial Practices and Postcolonial Theologies*. Eugene, OR: Cascade, 2010.

———. *The Church Event: Call and Challenge of a Church Protestant*. Minneapolis: Fortress, 2009.

———. "Communication and the Transgression of Language in Luther." *Lutheran Quarterly* 17/1 (2003) 1–27.

———. "Desabusando o Deus das Lacunas." In *Deuses e Ciências na América Latina*, edited by Valério Guilherme Schaper et al., 19–30. São Leopoldo; Oikos/EST, 2011.

———. "Idols and Demons: On Discerning the Spirits." *Dialog* 41/1, (2002) 9–15.

———. "Modernidade, Mito e Religião: Crítica e Reconstrução das Representações Religiosas." *Numen* 3/1 (2000) 11–38.

———. "No sin South of the Equator? Ideological. origins of the subversion." In *Religião, Política, Poder e Cultura na América Latina*, edited by Kathlen Luana de Oliveira et al. 101–10. São Leopoldo: EST, 2012. Online: http://www.est.edu.br/downloads/pdfs/biblioteca/livros-digitais/LV-RPPC_na_ALC.pdf

———. "Outros Saberes: Teologia e Ciência na Modernidade." *Estudos Teológicos* 35.3 (1995) 258–78.

———. "Santa Frida com Aura e Aroma," In *[Re]Leituras de Frida Kahlo: por uma ética estética da diversidade machucada*, edited by Edla Eggert, 157–64. Santa Cruz do Sul: EDUNISC, 2008.

———. *The Scandalous God: The Use and Abuse of the Cross*. Minneapolis: Fortress Press, 2007.

———. "The Times of God and the Ends of the World: Church and Eschatology in the Lutheran Communion," In *Between Vision and Reality: Lutheran Churches in Transition*, edited by Wolfgang Greive, 411–24. Geneva: LWF/DTS, 2001.

———. "The Word and the Mask: Revisiting the Two-Kingdoms Doctrine" In *The Gift of Grace: The Future of Lutheran Theology*, edited by Niels Henrik Gregersen, Bo Holm, Ted Peters, and Peter Widman, 167–78. Minneapolis: Fortress, 2005.

———. *Word in Words: Musings of the Gospel*. Tiruvalla: Christava Sahitya Smithy, 2009.

Westhelle, Vítor, and Hanna Betina Götz. "In Quest of a Myth: Latin American Literature and Theology." *Journal of Hispanic/Latino Theology* 3/1 (1995) 5–22.

PRAXIS

13

Our Global Diversity—God's Amazing Grace!

MUSIMBI KANYORO

CELEBRATING DIVERSITY

Vítor Westhelle and I share some things in comon. At Lutheran World Federation events we often provided diversity as Lutherans from Brazil and Kenya.

Oh yes, diversity at Lutheran Theological events matters. But it does not take long to actually discover that we have a lot in common and sometimes, the difference is just in the name. For example, did you know that *churrasco* in Brazil is *nyama Choma* in Kenya? Difference or diversity does not define us. What defines us is our common humanity as God's own creation. That is how I celebrate Vítor. He brought another world of geography, gender, theology and *churrasco* close to me and it was good. It was very good.

The writers of the biblical story of creation in Genesis describe a world of diversity. Each time as God creates life of every kind, there is the refrain: "And God saw that it was good [Gen. 1:25]." At the end of the story God even saw that it was *very* good! But, as we know, differences become part of the problem of sin as the story moves on toward building the towers of Babel.

Diversities are not problems to be solved and controlled by dominant groups. Rather they are important ways of assuring that God's gift of diversity in all creation will continue. Because of God's gift of diversity, new voices can be heard and languages and cultures are able to flourish. Such a message is doubly important for us today as it has always been throughout time.

The story of Pentecost in Acts 2:1–21 has often been understood as a sign of the reversal of Babel as nations are brought together and united in the outpouring of Christ's Spirit and the birth of the church. If difference and diversity are gifts, which help us to prevent domination, we stand to celebrate it as God's amazing gift to humanity.

The work of the Spirit is designed to foster understanding and ultimate reconciliation. God makes unity in difference possible by the gift of the Spirit enabling people of all nations to understand one another, no matter what language is spoken. Acts 2:6 says that "... each one heard them speaking in the native language of each." It does not say that they no longer had their own languages and customs but that they could understand one another. This is a different kind of world than the one envisioned by the builders at Babel. Here the unity comes, not through building a tower of domination or uniformity, but through communication.

God's gift of understanding across difference is expressed in the outpouring of the Spirit, which transforms the lives of people and their communities. Accordingly, the Spirit does not so much create the structures and procedures, but rather it breaks open structures that confine and separate people so that they can welcome difference and the challenges and opportunity for new understanding that they bring.

In our chaotic culture of frightening differences, many yearn for hope and meaning in their lives and in their relationships with one another. The gap is too great between communities struggling to survive and those who make decisions that govern the world's economics. Yet the effects on our world—droughts, floods, hunger, and illnesses tell us that as long as we live on one planet, we are obliged to build reconciling bridges or else the common future is in danger. Our Christian discipleship is about proclaiming the visions of God and inviting the world around us into values of God's kingdom.

We can only do that by modelling after the example of Jesus. Perhaps we could borrow a page from the Jesus manifesto which we often cite and recite from Luke 4: 16–19. According to Jesus, the Spirit of God inspired the creative and yet controversial actions he took to give hope to those he met, regardless of the consequences. According to Jesus, the concern of the Spirit of God was to speak for the poor, for the victims of cruelty and systematic injustices, for prisoners, the disabled, the sick and those locked out of any meaningful participation in society by bars of ignorance. The concern of the God of Jesus was particularly for people in whom all hope had been crushed—who felt consigned to long days and even longer nights of quiet desperation and despair. According to Jesus, the concern of the Spirit was to motivate people to share the good news with these forgotten ones. The commitment of the Spirit was to motivate people to have a passionate compassion—to be prepared to struggle in solidarity for the release from all personal, social and political forces that would debilitate them if left and abandoned on their own. The goal of the compassion is to set them free to realize their potential, to be fully human and fully alive, as members of the human community, persons of dignity, persons who can claim the ownership of abundant life.

How do we live and act in sympathy with this God of Jesus? This is a hard question when we move from the theory of teaching theology into the practice of living in communities where there are many practical needs. The essence of being a Christian is to live and act in sympathy with God's Spirit as Jesus did. This implies that we have to be known for keeping the company of beggars, thieves, prostitutes, tax collectors and those who think, act and look like these groups even when they bear different names. This is a tall order.

I have often wondered how to literally obey some of these things that I believe in. When I am back in spaces with limited resources, I find beggers and I catch myself realizing how difficult it is to follow Jesus. In following Jesus we are reminded again and again to emulate his life. Personally, I feel it is easier to retreat to the abstract and let things remain as a thought or an idea than face the reality and do something about it, such as compassion for others, exercising the principle of justice and fairness for all people, not just to some. We are called to think of others, not just us. Justice is not about and for "just us." Justice is universal and it is not limited by religion, culture, gender, race, geography or *churrasco*!

God is asking us to join the dance of celebration not by mere words but by how we live each day so that we can truly be known for being the disciples of Jesus. What might this mean in real life transitions such as moving from one place to another? I have three suggestions.

First we must prepare for every new move because it is hard to mitigate the shock of transition. From my experience as I work and travel extensively throughout the World, economic difference within and between countries and communities is the most difficult reality to adjust to. The space bwtween poverty and plenty is emotionally and morally disturbing. It is a negative symbol of diversity and this often keeps me awake day and night.

Poor people are not a random cross section of population, because poverty does not come randomly. They are mostly likey to be poor, a minority, person of color, lower caste, indigenous, woman or young, old and jobless. Poor people lack opportunities to realize their potential. They lack power, influence, voice, and they are extremely vulnerable to sickness, violence and disasters. People who are poor live in a toxic environment, have low-quality education, and are feared by others. They stand accused of denigrating the values by which decent people live while claiming rights to benefits they have not worked for. The life of the poor is painted as the hot bed of moral laxity, crime, violence and sexual abuse. Poor people are often branded as dishonest, lazy, addicted to welfare, capable of fraud, and substance abusers. Hence, criminality, hooliganism, theft, mugging, robbery, pick pocketing, and misuses of guns are all named as vices of the poor. Often the poor and rich are separated by high electric fences, dogs, laws and of course "stuff."

This makes the realities of poverty less visible to the privileged who see their role only as advocates for policies to victimize and punish poor. The cost of eradicating poverty was once estimated at a mere 1 percent of global income, which at that time was about eighty billion.[1] Today we look at coutries that are acclaimed to be succeeding but the gap between the poor and the rich is ever widening. This is one of the major shocks that those of us who live between the margins of poverty and plenty marvel at. It is the shock of transition from University teaching to local pastoral work. Preparing to mitigate this shock is a task that is often not sufficiently addressed.

The *second* suggestion is for us all to learn to have conversation with our own privilege as persons or nations. Do we define who we are by what we have? Do people with less seem to us as dangerously different so that we live in perpetual fear of their attacking and taking things from us? We live in a world which defines success by the state of the economy. An economic system, which promotes only the market, fails to recognize people and other forms of creation. An economy that is mindful of people will always put a face to every priority and decision. Some of this self examination has the potential of birthing and nurturing empathy with people in situations of need and want.

Third, we all need to be bold and refuse to be prisoners of "FEAR" and claim the promise of hope. Hope is a fragile quality that is quickly destroyed by feelings of powerlessness or self-doubt. Hope is the refusal to accept a

---

1. Human Development Report 1997, UNDP.

desperate reading of reality and the belief that reality can be changed for the better. Hope therefore is resistance. It actively resists the void of hopelessness by working for alternatives and living in faith. Thus hope is not merely an intellectual frame of mind. Hope is to be lived out. To hope for justice and peace is to work for elimination of injustice and to be a peacemaker. To hope for democracy means to practice being democratic in our personal relationships. To hope for wholeness means to face our own lack of wholeness with courage and to be prepared to go through the pain of self-examination, which leads to change.

I have drawn some hope in the peoples movements that gather at the World Social Forum, which attracts more than 20,000 people every year. Porto Alegre in Brazil is its traditional home but it has also met in New Delhi, India, Nairobi, Kenya etc. The World Social Forum gather diversity in one place and affords the privilege of living in the limits of fear and hope. There one sees people living with HIV and AIDS, gay and lesbian people, stateless people, indigenous people, refugees, women and youth rallying together in their personal and collective struggles and they give us a glimpse of what might be the real meaning of keeping company with the marginalized. More than anything the World Social Summit is about building bridges and creating an understanding of diversity and how to manage it. The World Social Forum is not a place to agree on ideologies or fix broken things, but rather a space to create synergies on particular issues. It is the place for learning, accepting differences creating partnerships for common good. The inclusive hospitality of the World Social Forum speaks words of hope to people by allowing courage, wisdom and resistance to hold hands and celebrate the power of collective risk taking.

In conclusion let me share some ways in which my hope has been sustained. For nearly two decades, I have been working globally with women on every continent. I am filled with hope and energized by the visions of women across the globe working together to meet global challenges. The lives and stories of women convince me that we have reason for hope. Women have broken the silence on their oppression and violence, they have achieved education and they continue to struggle for better access to health care, economic stability, environmental security, and human rights for themselves and their communities and families. Women have created shifts in the societal attitudes to women, claimed their space in leadership and decision making and through their determination they have changed the very nature of human society including religious dogma. Women have accomplished this critical agenda using a variety of creative methods, organizing for solidarity and mutual support, all in the belief that it is possible to make the difference. Women have done this with limited resources, while continuing to work as mothers, grandmothers, aunts, daughters, career women, public servants, educators, etc. Women have spent many years building trust, which is the most important social capital for managing diversity.

The women's movement is the largest organised peoples' movement in the world. Women in their search for affirmation have often underlined the principles of equality, participation and reciprocity. Words such as partnership, community, and togetherness are key to women's conversations. As women talked to one another, we began to discover that our individual experiences of discrimination, triviality, abuse and distortion were not unique to particular women but were indeed universal to women everywhere and in every generation. We found a common ground in hearing the collective story of women's experiences articulated in different contexts and times and yet speaking to the same issues.

In the process of listening to each other's stories, we have discovered common themes and trends, but we have also been uncomfortably confronted with differences and sharp distinctions. Our experiences are similar but they are not homogeneous. We are shaped by very different geographical, historical and social contexts. The credibility of women's story is continually challenged by how we acknowledge and manage these differences without being trapped into helplessness, powerlessness, apathy and isolation.

Women's actions are about falling into passion with principles that lead to compassion. Principles are not substitutes to passion. Principles don't move us like passions do, but principles can guide our passions and groom them into compassion. Such principles help us to implement justice, fairness and to be consistent so that we do not become ambiguous in the way that we act. By working with women, I have leaned that our ultimate task for healing our world is to inspire hope and to dance and celebrate the gift of diversity.

14

Psalm 90
God behind God

WALTER ALTMANN

Lord, you have been our dwelling-place in all generations. Before the mountains were brought forth, or ever you had formed the earth and the world, from everlasting to everlasting you are God. You turn us back to dust, and say, "Turn back, you mortals." For a thousand years in your sight are like yesterday when it is past, or like a watch in the night. You sweep them away; they are like a dream, like grass that is renewed in the morning; in the morning it flourishes and is renewed; in the evening it fades and withers. For we are consumed by your anger; by your wrath we are overwhelmed. You have set our iniquities before you, our secret sins in the light of your countenance. For all our days pass away under your wrath; our years come to an end like a sigh. The days of our life are seventy years, or perhaps eighty, if we are strong; even then their span is only toil and trouble; they are soon gone, and we fly away. Who considers the power of your anger? Your wrath is as great as the fear that is due to you. So teach us to count our days that we may gain a wise heart. Turn, O Lord! How long? Have compassion on your servants!

PRAXIS

> Satisfy us in the morning with your steadfast love, so that we may rejoice and be glad all our days. Make us glad for as many days as you have afflicted us, and for as many years as we have seen evil. Let your work be manifest to your servants, and your glorious power to their children. Let the favor of the Lord our God be upon us, and prosper for us the work of our hands. O prosper the work of our hands!

In the process of reflecting about the meaning of Psalm 90, the following statement of Aniceto, a native Brazilian, a chief of the Xavante people, caught my attention: "The Whites have already stolen our land. Now they don't want to let us have heaven."[1] This prompted me to understand this psalm by way of contrasting it with Aniceto's affirmation, allowing this psalm to break through long established ideas and thought patterns. Thus, Aniceto's uncompromising word and the tragic experience that underlines it constitute the stimulus and the perspective in the reading of Psalm 90. In order to better understand the sentence, we would have to keep in mind that in Portuguese the word "terra" means both "land" and "earth," and the word "céu" designates both "sky" and "heaven." Therefore the sentence reads: "The Whites have already stolen our land/the earth. Now they don't want to let us have the sky/heaven."

1. HEAVEN AND EARTH

Aniceto's word reflects the experience of rupture between heaven/sky and earth/land. We know that this rupture was caused by Western technological and scientific progress, which turned nature into a mere object of human action and manipulation. We know that the indigenous cultures did not make such a division. On the contrary, the native community lives in consonance with nature, conscious of integrating with it a cycle of life, from "generation to generation" or "from everlasting to everlasting," as our psalm suggests (v. 1).

Certainly, our psalmist does make a clear distinction between God, on one side, and nature and humanity on the other. Much before anything else, there was God, again "from everlasting to everlasting." However, I consider as mistaken those interpretations that transform this distance, as well as the idea that God is prior and higher than anything else, into a "principle of antagonism": "An infinite qualitative difference between God and human being" might have been a valid affirmation for Karl Barth over the ruins of

---

1. "O Branco já rouba a nossa Terra. Agora não quer deixar a gente ter o céu." *Apud Tempo e Presença* 153 (1979/9) 7.

World War I, but it is not useful as an affirmation pertinent to the essence of life and nature.

Our psalm makes it clear that God's distance must be seen together with God's proximity, in harmony with everything else that exists, nature and, as a part of it, humanity: God turns the human being "back to dust" and, again, back to life (v. 3). The rain falls and passes away; the grass grows and dries. But Got is "our dwelling," "our refuge" (v. 1), in whom we can trust.

Where then does that rupture between heaven and earth, of which Chief Aniceto spoke, come from? In order to get closer to answering this question, let us deal with:

2. "ALL OUR DAYS" (V. 9)

The psalmist reflects on the basis of his/her life experience. He/she—well, it could have been a she, couldn't it? So let's assume that possibility—she experiences life as limited. Human life is limited, very limited, when compared with mountains and the earth. It is extremely limited and transitory, when compared with God. For God, a thousand years are like the day that has passed. What are then the 70 years or even the 80, which to our eyes are so admirable (v. 10)? Modern astronomic and biological knowledge would radicalize the proportions considerably. Be as it may be, the psalmist reckoned with 70 to 80 years. In Latin America, until today, the higher figure is the average experience only of the Cubans! For the majority of Latin Americans, to reach 70 years is admirable.

Yet, the transitoriness of life becomes really a threat only when seen in light of God's wrath (v. 9). "Who considers the power of your anger? Your wrath is as great as the fear that is due you" (v. 11). And yet, the psalmist knows: God's wrath is not a part of God's "nature." It is, as Luther characterized it, God's "strange work." For the psalmist recognizes it: behind God's wrath, there is our guilt. What meaning might a word like guilt, apparently old-fashioned, have for us civilized and modern human beings, so proud of our scientific and technical achievements? The experience and the wisdom of the psalmist, however, admit: everything hidden will come forward to light, "our secret sins in the light of your countenance" (v. 8).

Let us recall once more Aniceto's affirmation. From his point of view and based on his experience, all that our progress achieved receives one simple name: "Robbery." "The Whites have already stolen our land." Even more: it is a systematized robbery, for "now they don't want to let us have the heaven!" Why is it that the life expectancy of so many people around the world goes just barely beyond 50 years of age, and in many regions remains below 40? Everything hidden will come forward to light! Here are the structures of robbery and appropriation of goods and resources of our planet; here are the systems of exploitation and extermination. How could human being and nature, heaven and earth, creation and God, be in harmony? Everything has been transformed in "toil and trouble" (v. 10).

Therefore, in taking our third step, it is important that we be aware of the necessity of attaining:

3. "A WISE HEART" (V. 12)

The psalmist dares to shout to God. Even more; she exhorts God to change radically. Just as she does not accept a distant God, in the sense of one who is absent and indifferent, she does not resign herself in experiencing God's wrath, even considering it as "just." She shouts to God: "Turn, O Lord!" In this passage we find the customary biblical term for conversion, which means to turn around (v. 13). The psalmist appeals to the "God behind God," to God's love against God's wrath. Evidently, this clamor is already part of what the psalmist understands by "a wise heart." A "wise heart" does not have anything to do with fatalism. It acknowledges reality, does not nurture illusions, but does not fall into resignation either. She, the psalmist, shows unconformity even with God. "Turn around!" The situation cannot remain as it is.

Precisely this would be the "robbery of heaven," to which Chief Aniceto called our attention: not that we would reckon with a God of vengeance, but precisely with a God that would resign Godself with evil, destruction, injustice, and death. The psalmist realizes: This conformist god would not be God; it would be an idol, even if it would present itself with the name of the true God. For it belongs to the nature and to the strategy of the idol to present itself as God. For example, the idol called riches presents itself as "god" against brotherly and sisterly communion and against the spirit of sharing resources; the idol of "whiteness" presents itself as "god" over against the native peoples. Turn, O Lord!

Such a "wise heart" brings about human "conversion," as well. First of all, it is a conversion of understanding, that is, of perspective. It gives us wisdom "to count our days" (v. 12). This does not mean only the knowledge that we are transitory and that we must die. Luther's translation of the verse also implies the same meaning: "Teach us to remember that we must die." The majority of the commentaries have a similar understanding. Wisdom, thus, does not restrict itself to the limits of our life, but includes equally the possibilities of our life, even if limited. If it were not this way, it would make no sense for the psalmist to have spoken earlier about our guilt nor later on about our works. "To count the days" means, therefore, also to recognize the opportunities, the possibilities, the challenges, the appropriate moments.

Thus the psalmist asks for quite another perspective to face life: a perspective of joy and gladness each morning (v. 14), as many days of joy as there are of tribulation, as many of hope as there are of disgrace. This is precisely the perspective not of the powerful ones, who are condemned to remain unsatisfied—because they are insatiable!—but the perspective of the little ones, who cannot but see the world with new eyes, with a "wise heart."

From here let us take the following step:

4. "THE WORK OF OUR HANDS" (V. 17)

There are those who do not know what to do with verses 13 to 17 of the psalm. They think that it is a separate psalm, and not of the same import as the preceding one. There is a lament that Psalm 90 does not bring to a close in verse 12. On the one hand this interpretation does not sit well with the new perspective that allows the psalmist to see reality with hope and joy. On the other hand they also cannot admit that our psalmist is concrete or materialist.

A "wise heart," that is acceptable. To accept that we are going to die, to admit our guilt—that is all factual and even necessary. However, that we should *do* something seems to mess up everything thoroughly again, or so they think. And, furthermore, the psalm concludes with a materialistic ideal—"the work of our hands"—such a socialist idea, if I allow myself to say so! It is so praxis related, so fanatic! In this case, wouldn't it be better to renounce again to that "wise heart." To admit to such a temptation, however, would be something meagerly pious. It is better, therefore, to disqualify verses 13 to 17 or, even better, to ignore them tacitly.

Our psalmist, however, reached a different type of wisdom. Not cleverness, but wisdom. She discovered that a new understanding goes hand in hand with a new work. "Heart" and "hands" necessitate themselves mutually. There aren't anymore works of destruction, of disruption of nature and extermination of indigenous populations, for example, to erect a civilization of cars, of iron structures and of technological weapons. But, on the contrary, *works* in which our children, the future generations, can see the "glorious power of God" (v. 16). Let us remember once more Chief Aniceto. Our faith and our theology must be human and ecologically responsible.

Similarly, our faith and theology must express an egalitarian and fraternal dimension in the relations between men and women.[2]

We conclude our reflection returning to our departure point, now in new depth. We take our fifth and final step:

5. NEW HEAVENS AND A NEW EARTH.

This is a deep Christian hope: "In accordance with God's promise, we await for new heavens and a new earth, where righteousness is at home" (2 Pet 3:13). Let us keep in mind that in the original language, as well as in modern languages other than English, the same word is used for righteousness and justice. Therefore we could also say that "in accordance with his promise, we await for new heavens and a new earth, where just relations are at home." I remember now those other representatives of Native Brazilians, as the Chiefs Raoni and Payacán, who years ago, in their lifelong struggle for justice, attempted to exercise pressure upon international financial institutions and to sensitize world public opinion, traveling to the United States and Western Europe, in order that the Amazon region and their inhabitants might be preserved efficaciously, not only the Amazonian bay, but nature and their inhabitants everywhere, as well. Aniceto spoke about the robbery of land and sky, earth and heaven. Raoni and Payacán wanted to rescue the perspective of unity and concreteness of heaven and earth. They didn't fall pray to resignation, but searched for a new understanding (a "wise heart") and a new work (the "work of our hands").

They denounced the dreadful development projects that threatened to victimize peoples around the globe. They did so in Brazil, but they also went to the matrix of their historical exploitation and to the center where ultimate decisions about their fate were made: to the then so-called First World (or affluent countries). No addressee, in the North and the South, can be forgotten. How long, how long, o God? Turn! Have mercy on us! Strengthen us every morning! Make us glad again! Give us a wise heart! O prosper the work of our hands!

---

2. For example, the well-renowned German theologian Artur Weiser still exposed the idea that in this psalm "the problem of God and humanity is focused with masculine courageous integrity and examined unto its depths with inexorable seriousness of faith" (*wird das Problem Gott und Mensch mit männlich mutiger Wahrhaftigkeit angefaßt und in erbittlichem Glaubensernst bis in seine Tiefen verfolgt*)! (*Die Psalmen*, 7th ed., ATD 14/15, [Göttingen: Vandenhoeck & Ruprecht, 1966] 405).

BIBLIOGRAPHY

Tempo e Presença 153 (1979/9) 7.

Altmann, Walter. "Salmo 90: Deus atrás de Deus." In *Palavra a seu tempo : Prédicas, alocuções e estudos bíblicos*. São Leopoldo: Oikos; São Bento do Sul: União Cristã, 2010.

15

Experience and Its Claim to Universality

The Nature of Experience[1]

REINHARD HÜTTER

EXPERIENCE IS ARGUABLY ONE of the most difficult topics for the philosopher and the theologian to tackle. For experience is exceedingly elusive, manifold, and simultaneously common. Experience embraces two polar extremes: on the one hand, in its biographical particularity, experience is virtually ineffable. Yet on the other hand, insofar as it is a function of human nature, experience has universal formal characteristics. It is because of the simultaneity of these two polar extremes of every human experience that all experience is analogically related, to the effect that experience can be communicated and hence shared such that by way of the operation of analogical imagination and the capacity of empathy I can receive the experience of others and assimilate it to a certain degree. Hence, Terentius could rightly claim, *Homo sum: nihil humanum mihi alienum est*: "I am human, so nothing human is strange to me."

---

1. A more extensive version of this contribution can be found in *Communio* 37.2 (2010) 186–208.

Because experience is, however, such an elusive reality and because we live after the so-called linguistic turn, I'd like to get a preliminary handle on the fundamental constituents of experience by paying attention to the grammar of experience. In ordinary English, "experience" is found in primarily three grammatical functions: first, as a transitive verb: "Have you ever experienced a sunrise in the summer at 4:00 a.m. on the top of a mountain?"; second, in an intransitive sense with the verb "to have": "I always look forward to having a new experience!"; and finally as an adjective qualifying some agent or practitioner: "She is an experienced teacher" or as a noun without any article to articulate the same: "She has experience as a teacher." The verbal and adjectival uses will help us to get a handle on the formal characteristics of experience.

The transitive verb—"to experience something"—registers the incessant influx of reality on our senses and our intellect, with differing intensity insofar as the focus of our intentionality selects segments relevant to the particular end we happen to pursue. Any particular aspect of this influx of reality can be singled out by the focus of our mind's intentionality. When this focus of our intentionality is sustained for longer and becomes reflexive, we tend to speak of "having an experience." There are, however, four indispensable prerequisites to "having" an experience: (1) agent intentionality focused on some end (normally this end is not a specific experience one wants to have, but it also can be just some specific experience one indeed wants to have), (2) some set of experiences stored in memory that allow some kind of "background" to the new—or the same—experience I have (they have to be at least experiences shared by others), (3) a self-reflective awareness that allows a narration of the experience in the overall matrix of my story. An essential ingredient of the latter is (4) a complex set of judgments I make in the course of assessing and thereby having the experience. Only as constituted by these judgments can I narrate the experience as my experience. When one or more of these four aspects are missing, we might still experience incessantly something, because, after all, we are alive. In such a case, however, I have not had an experience.

It is only in light of the accumulation of having had many experiences relevant to specific practices (widely conceived) that we apply the adjective "experienced" to a person as a practitioner: an experienced teacher or architect, an experienced sailor or conductor, an experienced judge, confessor, or bishop. Significantly, we do not tend to talk about an experienced saint—in the sense of "experienced in sainthood"—for sainthood transcends each and every practice of which we could become experienced practitioners.

Experiencing, having experiences, an experienced practitioner—experience in three linguistic registers, the third presupposing the second, the second presupposing the first; the first coming to fruition in the second, the second coming to fruition in the third.

With these three linguistic registers in the back of our mind, we can take the next step and consider the nature of experience in light of the *conditio humana* in general. For it seems to be undeniable that the nature of experience is configured by the same characteristics that are constitutive of the human condition: contingency, temporality, and teleology.

There is, first, the fundamental *contingency* of the reality in which I find myself: biological, historical, cultural-linguistic, social, and religious. Experience is both made possible by any of these factors, and therefore also dependent upon them. Because experience, however, is primordially configured by the ten categories or predicamentals and because human embodiment, linguisticality, and transcendentality is a universally shared condition, the particularity resulting from the constant variations among these factors can never result in an absolute incommensurability.

There is, second, *temporality*: experience means being conditioned by the irreversible arrow of time, not only in a physical but also in an existential sense. I live in the indivisible flow of past, present, and future, and there is no experience that is not configured in this threefold way. There is also a "finis" or "end" toward which my life is moving, an irreversible finality of which death is an integral component. This finality is like the mathematical value in front of the bracket inside of which each experience is made and by which each experience is qualified.

The consideration of this irreversible "finis" already touches upon the third characteristic: *finality* or *teleology*: Experience in the second and third register (and arguably also in the first) is linguistically configured such that as remembered experience it becomes part of a narrative that is governed by some end. (In that a human life reflects the structure of human agency that in turn reflects the structure of an intellect: the final end is first in perception and last in realization.) Experiences in the first register that cannot be integrated into the narrative of one's life and thus integrated as remembered experience (in the second register) are failed candidates of experience, that which we nowadays call "traumatic."

It is in this threefold configuration of experience (contingency, temporality, finality) that we experience, have experiences, and become experienced in this or that regard. The narrative structure that I invoked earlier, however, implies more than human nature in its threefold configuration of contingency, temporality, and finality or teleology. For we must consider here the difference between nature and person, the difference between the configuration of a substance (first perfection) and the operation of the person in virtue of the substance (second perfection). In short, in moving from the first to the second to the third linguistic register, a qualitative perfection of experience is connoted that does not depend on the structure of human nature, but rather on the operation of the human person.

Pertaining to operation we must first consider the end, the *telos*. Experience in the second and third linguistic registers is a function of the overarching end toward which an agent is directed. For this end, most truly the supernatural end explicitly desired by way of grace, but unavoidably some version of the proximate natural end, will constitute the overarching framework in and the kinds of judgments by way of which experiences are made or had and in which one becomes an experienced practitioner of this or that sort.

There is, second, *virtue*. The experience of a virtuous person is different from the one who lacks the habituation in the cardinal virtues, let alone the infusion with the theological virtues. More importantly, the virtuous person makes inevitably other experiences than the incontinent or the vicious person does. While in the first register of experience the general influx of reality is arguable roughly the same for all, the virtuous person arrests the attention at different points than the incontinent or the vicious person does, and if at the same point, then in a different way and within a different context of stored experiences. Hence, in the second register, the virtuous person has different experiences from the vicious person; which means that not all experiences are communicable along the incremental gradation of a simple structural analogy. Rather, this structural analogy is qualified by a non-symmetric analogy of perfection. While the saint can understand the experience of a villain, the villain cannot understand the kind of experiences a saint makes.

Let us now turn to the second register in some more detail. For "having an experience" has a certain internal dynamic structure. An experience can be had only in light of some previous experience and insofar as it opens up to further experiences. (All antecedent experiences—before we begin to have our own—are analogically received by way of shared stories, be these stories from our grandparents, parents, or stories we read as children.) If one of these components is lacking, we might experience this or that, but we are not able to have an experience. It is not only the developed reflective apparatus of the intellect alone, but the memory of experiences (be they our own or analogically received experiences) and the openness to new experiences that are absolutely constitutive of "having an experience." This is one of the reasons why the young, even if they are bright, are not necessarily able to "make an experience" and why the old, as soon as they cease to be open to new experiences, cease to have any experiences. Indeed, ceasing to have new experiences is identical with having become old. It is at this point that we can specify that "having an experience" is only possible in the horizon of "having a new experience." It might not turn out to be a new one, I might have had this experience before, but I only had it—again—because I was open to having a new experience. And for the latter, the openness to having new experiences, to obtain, indeed, to flourish, one needs to develop the virtue of magnanimity or natural hope.

When we consider the openness to having new experiences as the condition for the possibility of having any experience, then the *status viatoris* of the human being comes into full relief: contingency, temporality, finality: a creature equipped and ordained for a fulfillment that essentially transcends humanity's nature and capacity of operation. Because of this equipment and ordination, the *viator* is essentially open for the whole of reality, especially also the reality of transcendence in general and the reality of the essentially supernatural in particular.

When we consider the *viator*'s openness to the whole of reality, we need to consider two specific virtues that are indispensable to sustain this openness for the whole of reality in the order of human operation: *humility* and *magnanimity*. And here I finally cannot delay any longer the long overdue explicit reference to Thomas Aquinas. We have all our experiences as essentially embodied and timed beings. Hence we need to attend to the question of how our bodies are involved in our experiences. The way they are, Thomas would suggest, is first and foremost by way of the passions. Passions are instinctive drives, or in Thomas's terminology, "acts of the sensitive appetite" that originate in the body and pertain to the soul *per accidens*, that is, insofar as the soul is united with the body. The passion of hope is most essential for human life, for, as Thomas states, "hope is a movement of the appetitive power ensuing from the apprehension of a future good, difficult but possible to obtain; namely, a stretching forth of the appetite to such a good."[2]

The strength of the movement of this appetitive power is proportionate to our present capacities, as well as to the nature of the good we aim to attain. Such hope is common and indeed indispensable to the human condition. Hope moves us constantly toward all kinds of arduous goods not yet attained. In light of the realization by the human mind that a desirable good, difficult to obtain, is in principle in reach and with persistence and effort of will can be attained, hope moves us toward this good. Hence by way of the anticipation of the good and the subsequent determination of the will toward it, as well as the appetitive movement toward it, our mind

---

2. *Summa Theologiae* (*ST*) I–II, q. 40, a. 2: "[S]pes est motus appetitivae virtutis consequens apprehensionem boni futuri ardui possibilis adipisci, scilicet extensio appetitus in huiusmodi obiectum."

already participates in the good to be attained, whence arises confidence and a certain pleasure.³ Such an ordinary hope arises solely from our specific capacities, skills, faculties, as well as experiences, and is consequently also limited by them.⁴

The virtues correlative to the passion of hope are humility and magnanimity. Remember, the object of the passion of hope is "a future good, difficult but possible to obtain," and the passion of hope "a movement of the appetitive power," "a stretching forth of the appetite to such a good."⁵ Thomas characterizes this appetite as "irascible" (in contradistinction to a "concupiscible appetite"), because the former is directed to all kinds of goods that are hard to obtain and the obtaining of which might involve the overcoming of difficult obstacles. For the irascible appetite to be rightly governed by reason, namely, to be aiming at attaining the just mean, it must be informed by two specific moral virtues. Humility (rooted in the cardinal virtue of temperance) moderates the passion of hope and thus assists it in acting in conformity with the dictates of reason. Magnanimity (rooted in the cardinal virtue of courage) strengthens the passion of hope and directs attention to the subject of the moral act by aiming at the accomplishment of great deeds, as well as at the requisite honors that accompany the attainment of greatness.⁶ Because of the central and sustaining role that magnanimity plays in governing the passion of hope, some interpreters of Aquinas have understood, with good reason, the natural virtue of magnanimity as the natural virtue of hope.⁷

---

3. Pertaining to the confidence to which such hope gives rise, see *ST* I–II, q. 40, a. 2, ad 2: "When a man desires a thing and reckons that he can get it, he believes that he will get it; and from this belief which proceeds in the cognitive power, the ensuing movement in the appetite is called confidence." "[I]llud quod homo desiderat, et aestimat se posse adipisci, credit se adepturum: et ex tali fide in cognitiva praecedente, motus sequens in appetitu fiducia nominatur." Pertaining to the pleasure such hope gives, see *ST* I–II, q. 32, a. 3: "[Q]uia maior est coniunctio secundum rem quam secundum similitudinem, quae est coniunctio cognitionis; itemque maior est coniunctio rei in actu quam in potentia: ideo maxima est delectatio quae fit per sensum, qui requirit praesentiam rei sensibilis. Secundum autem gradum tenet delectatio spei, in qua non solum est delectabilis coniunctio secundum apprehensionem, set etiam secundum facultatem vel potestatem adipiscendi bonum quod delectat. Tertium autem gradum tenet delectatio memoriae, quae habet solam coniunctionem apprehensionis." In contradistinction to the passion of hope, which gives rise to pleasure, the theological virtue of hope gives rise to joy—"rejoicing in hope" (Rom 12:12).

4. *ST* I–II, q. 40, a. 5.

5. *ST* I–II, q. 40, a. 2.

6. *ST* II–II, q. 129, a. 1.

7. See Gauthier, *Magnanimité*, esp. 295–371. The text of Aquinas most centrally in support of understanding magnanimity as the natural virtue of hope is *In Sent*. III, d.

PRAXIS

Now, every experience is had in light of some end (and the experience itself might be in some specific cases such an end). Simultaneously, the capacity of "having an experience" and the perfectibility of this capacity are entailed in the structure of human nature. Because every end is a desired good to which the passion of hope is directed, the perfection of "having experiences" requires the virtue of humility as well as the virtue of magnanimity or natural virtue of hope. For it is by way of humility that we become increasingly attentive to the dictates of reason and hence increasingly attentive to having some experiences instead of others. And it is by way of magnanimity, the aiming at the accomplishments of great deeds, that we stretch out to making new experiences of certain kinds and do not settle with some fixed acquired store of experiences. On the way of becoming an experienced practitioner of some practice, the development of the virtues of humility and magnanimity are indispensable.[8]

At the conclusion of these reflections on "Experience and Its Claim to Universality" I would like to add a brief post-script on the "experience" of saints.

Only a source categorically different from human philosophical wisdom can be a reliable guide toward even an inchoate insight into this matter. Such guidance is available from a single source only and only by way of a gratuitous and inchoate participation in that source, that is by way of divine faith. By way of divine faith we come to understand that God sent his only begotten Son to take on our *status viatoris* by taking on human nature in order that Christ Himself might be the way, the truth, and the life by way of Whom we may reach the end that divine faith makes us desire most, the ultimate end attained in the *status comprehensoris*.[9] By incorporating us into Himself, we already receive a share in his own divine life under the condition of the *status viatoris*, which entails our free cooperation and the possibility of turning away from this divine life. It is by way of the supernatural, infused virtues of faith, hope, and charity that we come to participate in the divine life. "The greatest of them all is charity" (1 Cor 13:13),

---

26, q. 2, a. 2, ad 4: "Sed tamen magnanimitas non est idem quod spes virtus; quia est circa arduum quod consistit in rebus humanis, non circa arduum quod est deus; *unde non est virtus theologica, sed moralis, participans aliquid a spe*" (my emphasis).

8. Now we can also understand why a practice is more than a set of skills. For to become experienced in a set of skills requires only the accumulation of a certain technical versatility. But the acquiring and exercise of skills do not entail the making of any experiences in the proper sense of "making experiences."

9. John G. Arintero, O.P., describes the whole of the Christian life, comprising the *status viatoris* as well as the *status comprehensoris*, in the briefest and most beautiful Johannine terms: "The Son of God came into the world to incorporate us into Himself and to make us live by Him as He Himself lives by the Father" (*Mystical Evolution*, 1).

because charity, when it perfectly informs all other virtues, makes the *viator* adhere to God *as already possessed*. Charity is nothing but the prelude to and most perfect anticipatory participation in the blessed life, in the *status comprehensoris*.[10] When we receive the gift of sanctifying grace, that is, the principle of participation in the divine life, the theological virtues fortify and perfect humility and magnanimity by ordering them to the ultimate end of the *status viatoris*.

Now it appears to me that, should we ever be on the look-out for exemplifications of such inchoate participation in the divine life, we do well to attend to the lives of the saints. Faith, hope, and charity, as supernaturally infused dispositions, are the direct effect of sanctifying grace, that is, the principle of the divine life in the Christian. Saints are those who cooperate most intensely and heroically with this principle of the divine life and hence repeatedly merit an increase in charity.[11] And this is the reason why the saints remain always essentially young: they remain always open to making new experiences in an ever expanding horizon of divine charity, infused by sanctifying grace. Thus, the saints show us most fully what it means to be the kind of persons whose "experience with experience" teaches them to receive every new experience as a gift of God's loving providence, which in turn keeps them open in the most profound, intensive as well as extensive, way to the whole of reality and that means first and foremost to the Giver of all reality. In that, the saints are exemplary *viatores*. For their "experience with experience" is shaped by a constant deepening of faith (the contemplation of the mystery of God's triune life of love), hope (the anticipatory embrace of the divine life in the life of unceasing prayer), and charity (the union with the love and hence life of God).

It becomes obvious now in which way we can never speak of a saint as "experienced" and in which way we indeed must speak of the saint as "experienced," indeed as the most experienced of all *viatores*. For what constitutes sainthood, the ever intensified embrace of and heroic cooperation with sanctifying grace does not per se constitute any distinct practice or set of practices (though it clearly is sustained by contemplation and prayer). Consequently, the saint's experiences qua saint cannot be integrated into the framework of such a distinct practice or set of practices. Hence a univocal increase in the experience of sainthood (Christian perfection thus being

---

10. The *viator*'s first pursuit engendered by the increase of charity is the detachment from sin, the *viator*'s second pursuit is the persistent struggle for the progress in good, and the *viator*'s third pursuit is "to aim chiefly at union with and enjoyment of God: this belongs to the perfect who *desire to be dissolved and to be with Christ*" (ST II–II, q. 24, a. 9).

11. *ST* I–II, q. 114, a. 8.

identical with becoming experienced in sainthood) is per se impossible. In the case of the saint (who, it is important to recall, is in this nothing but simply the exemplar of every Christian), every experience is received as a gift of God and referred back to God in gratitude and thus integrated in a narrative the beginning and end of which is God and the center of which is the life, death, and resurrection of Christ. Because the end of this narrative is not anymore the saint's own end, but her or his end in Christ, the saint will abandon any self-deceptive attempt at owning his or her experiences (second linguistic register). The typical modern version of such a form of self-deceptive ownership would be the "autobiography"—authorship as the achievement of one's self by oneself. Saints do not write autobiographies—and Augustine's *Confessions* is not an autobiography but precisely the doxological disowning and suspension of a biography.[12] The same is true for what some might wrongly consider as the "autobiographies" of St. Teresa of Avila and of St. Therese of Lisieux.

While the saint can never be "experienced" in sainthood, the saint is arguably the most experienced *viator* there is. Because the saint ever more heroically embraces the inchoate participation in the life of God which is charity (a participation given to every baptized Christian), the saint has a connatural awareness of the difference between the life of divine charity and the depth of misery and sin in which humanity is entangled. Hence the saint is the only person who without falling into prideful pretension or into clever cynicism, can utter Terence's dictum, *Homo sum: nihil humanum mihi alienum est.* "Nothing that is human is alien to me." If we want to inform ourselves with ever greater accuracy about "experience and its claim to universality" we do well by entering the school of the saints and we do even better by praying God to make us saints, too. By thus radically opening ourselves to the surpassing, the ultimate liminal experience, our experience will never ever again be the same. For the ultimate experience, even if only inchoately had by way of the theological virtue of charity, does not destroy but perfect our expectations, even the wildest. *Quoniam caritas ex Deo est; et omnis qui diligit, ex Deo natus est et cognoscit Deum* (1 John 4:7).

---

12. "The thirteen books of my *Confessions*, which praise the just and good God in all my evil and good ways, and stir up towards him the mind and feelings of men. As far as I am concerned, they had this effect on me when I wrote them, and they still do when I read them. What others think is their own business: I know at least that many of the brethren have enjoyed them and still do" ("*Confessionum* mearum libri tredecim, et de malis et de bonis meis Deum laudant iustum et bonum, atque in eum excitant humanum intellectum et affectum. Interim quod ad me attinet, hoc in me egerunt cum scriberentur et agunt cum leguntur. Quid de illis alii sentiant, ipsi viderint; multis tamen fratribus eos multum placuisse et placere scio.") (Augustine, *Retractions*, II. 6, 1).

BIBLIOGRAPHY

Aquinas, Thomas. *Summa theologica*: Complete English Edition in Five Volumes. Vol. 4. Translated by Fathers of the English Dominican Province. Westminster, MD: Christian Classics, 1981.

Arintero, John G. *The Mystical Evolution in the Development and Vitality of the Church*, vol. 1. Translated by Jordan Aumann. St. Louis/London: Herder, 1949

Augustine of Hippo. *The Fathers of the Church: St. Augustine, Retractions*. Translated by Sister M. Inez Bogan, R.S.M. Washington: Catholic University of America, 1968.

Gauthier, R.A., O.P. *Magnanimité: L'idéal de la grandeur dans la philosophie païenne et dans la théologie chrétienne*. Paris: J. Vrin, 1951.

16

Classrooms and *Choratic* Spaces
A Meditation on Seminary Teaching

KATHLEEN D. BILLMAN

> *Choratic spaces are places of transition and therefore of trial. They are margins in which possibilities can be born but where the tragic, the terrible, lurks, and annihilation impends. This is why in these spaces hope and despair are so closely associated and why they are religious spaces par excellence, where fascination and terror meet. . . .*[1]

IN 2006 VÍTOR WESTHELLE and I designed and offered a course called "Fostering Narratives of Hope"—one of the course options for senior students to fulfill the senior interdisciplinary seminar requirement in the LSTC MDiv curriculum. Participating in that course has been one of the most important experiences I have had as a seminary professor, primarily because I have so often felt that we were standing on holy ground with students who have shared that classroom with us. I carry precious memories of being deeply moved by the vulnerability risked by so many students over the years. There have been many moments when I felt we were not just

---

1. Westhelle, *Eschatology and Space*, 101–2.

discussing the mystery of the relationship between despair and hope, cross and resurrection, but rather *experiencing* something of that transformative mystery.

Now that Vítor is teaching half the academic year in Brazil and half the academic year in Chicago, I may not experience again in the near future the joy of teaching this course with the colleague who first imagined it with me several years ago and in whose company I have learned so much. Thus, in remembrance and gratitude, this contribution to *Churrasco* is a meditation on the implications of Vítor's discussion of *chora* and *choractic* spaces for the vocation of a seminary teacher. The classroom "space" to which I will be referring is what is described these days as a "traditional" classroom to distinguish it from online/virtual classrooms. Respecting the limits of space, my remarks here are limited to the places in which people dwell *together in physical space* for a period of time as embodied teachers/learners. The slash mark between teachers/learners is intended to convey the conviction that the designated "teachers" are continually taught by their students, as well as the hope that students both learn from and relish teaching their teachers.

These reflections are offered with some trepidation. For one thing, if there is anything I have learned from Vítor (and course evaluations!) it is to be humble about what we claim to understand about what occurs in a space with others; "otherness" is otherness. Also, the holiest moments are the hardest ones to describe (more about that later). But the risk seems worth taking, for at least two reasons. First, several themes in Vítor's theological work—e.g., the eschatological possibility that accompanies encountering the "other," the importance of contextual experiences, and *chora* and *choractic* spaces—have profound implications for teaching and learning, especially in theological schools. Second, after a few iterations of the course, it is both blessing and challenge to attempt words for how dwelling in "space" with seminary students has contributed to how I think about these themes, and I have these students in mind as conversation partners as well as the colleagues who teach and learn with them. The risk to speak, especially when one is quite aware that one is speaking from a very limited perspective, is also the risk to learn.

CHORATIC SPACE

In *The Scandalous God* its author points to the importance of recovering *space* for eschatology,[2] a project fully developed in later works and most recently in *Eschatology and Space: The Lost Dimension in Theology Past and*

2. Westhelle, *Scandalous God*, chapter 9.

Present. This compelling argument, impossible to do justice to in this meditation, is that the *eschaton* is not confined to "last things" and should not be solely captive to theological investigations of time (whether *chronos* or *kairos*), but is something that occurs in space.

> So this is the *eschaton*, the space between the spaces, the margins that demarcate the limits of desire and interest, the house and the street. It is the space between spaces, belonging to neither, yet adjacent to both, which is best expressed by the Greek word *chōra*, which etymologically means "to lie open, to be ready to receive," a space between places or limits.[3]

The descriptions of *chora* found in Vítor's work include recurring themes: the encounter with the world of the other, especially the "other" who is different and excluded from one's own world; adjacency with both a familiar world and a new world but "in-between," belonging to neither; an experience in which the "close association" between despair and hope, paradise and hell, are revealed; the "moment that is not negotiable ... in which death and the gift of life come to self-realization."[4]

What does *chora*—the "space between spaces"—space which by its very nature cannot be planned, administrated, or negotiated—have to do with a course or a classroom? Courses are governed by syllabi, performance expectations, and planned activities, and are shadowed by the awareness that judgments will be made on how well students and faculty perform (Vítor has been known to quip, "We teach for free. They pay us to grade."). Expectations abound that one will teach/learn in ways that increase knowledge, competency, and skill. Assessment is the most frequently heard educational term of recent decades. Riding in the door with assessment's important reminder that the educational activities we do should help us accomplish the purposes we profess are some other unwelcome hitchhikers, such as anxiety and perhaps at times tedium (on how many syllabi do students need to be reminded that a course is designed to contribute to outcome ten of the seminary curriculum?)

Recognizing the impossibility of "managing" *chora*, I expect that many of us who spend our lives teaching and learning in seminary classrooms hope to experience *with* students something like eschatological space. Along with students, we who teach and learn with them recognize that "Little paradises and hells abound. In *every moment of one's life* the vicinity of both—paradise and hell—and the adjacency both have with *everyday life*

---

3. Westhelle, *Eschatology and Space*, 79. See also Westhelle, *Church Event*.
4. Ibid., 124–5.

might be experienced ... and this moment that is not negotiable is the one in which death *and* the gift of life come to self-realization."[5]

One of the biblical references to *chora* is crossing the Jordan.[6] One of my favorite parts of that story is what happens just after the crossing, when Joshua sends representatives from each of the tribes back into the river to retrieve stones from the river and carry them to a camping place (Joshua 4). These stones were to remain as a reminder of the moments of crossing (*chora*), and what God did in that space of terrible danger and deep longing. "Camping at Gilgal" is a phrase I have conjured whenever I want to look back and ask, "What do these stones, these memories, mean?"

We cannot manage or conjure *choratic spaces* as theological educators, but we can reflect on our memories of what may have contributed to "holy ground" experiences in the classroom; to collect a few stones from the river as reminders. What choices made a difference? Space permits "camping at Gilgal" long enough to muse on a few.

A SPACE FOR REMEMBRANCE[7]

Most students who register for Narratives of Hope are seniors returning from a twelve-month internship. The return to school may be anticipated or dreaded, depending on a host of factors, but the phrase "the space between spaces" seems an apt description of the senior year for most LSTC MDiv students. Behind them and still *with* them are countless experiences of pastoral ministry. The months ahead are filled with obligations and testing; the challenge of living with memories of a year ended and questions about what the future will hold. We wanted to offer a place for *remembrance*, in which the students' significant experiences of ministry would constitute one of the primary texts of the course.

What invitation might evoke such remembrance? We invited students to tell a story of hope/despair that they experienced/witnessed in the course of practicing ministry. Acknowledging that there is interpretation and analysis that goes into relating a story, we asked students to describe an experience of hope/despair without explaining why it was chosen or evaluating it.

---

5. Ibid. Emphases mine.
6. Ibid., 99.
7. I am so grateful for the work Mary Philip has done on remembrance and for the collegial conversation that helped me name "space for remembrance" as something I was struggling to articulate in the first draft of this essay. I am also grateful to two recent participants in the course, Sarah Rohde and Nathan Sutton, for reading a draft of the essay and making helpful comments.

In order to illustrate what we were asking (and to model insofar as possible the risk and vulnerability of what we were asking them to do), Vítor and I each shared a story of hope/despair of our own at the beginning of the course.

Strict word counts were given for this assignment—800 words—so that we could offer students roughly equalized time boundaries for telling their stories. We gathered the stories at the beginning of the course, arranged them so that we would hear two or three during each class session, and insofar as possible scheduled them to accompany the readings and topic of each class period that seemed most relevant for the situations presented. Students read their narratives aloud as the entire class listened.

Of all the things I have been asked to explain about the course assignments over the years, I can recall no one who ever asked about the slash mark between hope/despair. With only a few exceptions, the close association between hope and despair resounded through the narratives brought to the course. As a student in the course once observed, "Sometimes despair and hope sit side by side."

The stories of hope/despair told and reflected on over the years have been the heartbeat of the course, and in many ways it has been these narratives that have revealed the "space between spaces." A student describes facing limits of knowledge and confidence, or of utter helplessness in the face of an intractable dilemma, or of shattering personal grief, and the very act of telling testifies to hope's presence. A student tells the story of being changed by an encounter with someone whose life circumstances are completely different from anything in the student's own experience—an encounter that disrupts one way of perceiving life and opens another. A white student and an African American student both bring stories of encounters with the legal system. The juxtaposition of what happens to the characters in the stories is jarring; the systemic inequities of the nation in which these stories take place are suddenly and unsettlingly up close and personal, in the "house," not just in the street.

A SPACE FOR WITNESSING STORIES

Once stories are invited, how are they received? In the exquisite story, *The God of Small Things,* Arundhati Roy's character Rahel observes "with adult hindsight" in reflecting on childhood experience that "It is after all so easy to shatter a story. To break a chain of thought. To ruin a fragment of a dream being carried around carefully like a piece of porcelain. To let it be, to travel with it . . . is much the harder thing to do."[8] What does "traveling with a story" entail? How are vulnerable stories cared for and learned from by both their hearers and their tellers?

Silence. We have discovered that there is always a period of silence after a story is told in class. Sometimes the silence itself is the most profound response, and it is very likely that we have not offered silence a longer presence before the turn to words. It is in that silence that I have experienced most profoundly the power of the traditional classroom: the embodied dwelling together in a space where words sometimes do not come easily; when *bodies* convey something about the impact of a story before there may be words to describe the impact. It is not uncommon to feel more than can be expressed verbally. That is one precious gift of being together in a physical space.

Four kinds of inquiry. In struggling with how to define the role of those who witness the telling of a story, we borrowed four kinds of inquiry from narrative therapist Michael White, who explored the role of *outsider witnesses* in fostering "rich story development . . . the building of thick conclusions about identity, and . . . the endurance and expansion of preferred outcomes in the lives of people who were consulting with us."[9] We asked listeners to first speak about the actual *expressions* that caught their attention or captured their imagination, paying special attention to those expressions (words, phrases, sentiments) that convey what the storyteller seems to value or hold dear. Then we asked them to focus on *images* evoked by the expressions they were drawn to and what those images might reflect about the person's values, purposes, hopes, dreams, commitments. Third, we asked the listeners to share why they were drawn to these expressions—what had *resonance* for their own experience of life and/or ministry (White calls this "embodied interest"—something in one's own history that "lit up and came into memory on account of these expressions").[10] Finally, we asked the listeners to say where listening to this story has taken them with regard to their own understandings of self and ministry—where the story has moved or *transported* them.[11]

Everyone listens as the reflecting team discusses together their responses to these four inquiries. Others in the class who, along with the story

8. Roy, *God of Small Things*, 181.
9. White, *Maps of Narrative Practice* , 184.
10. Ibid., 191.
11. Ibid. See 190–92 for White's fuller description of all four categories of inquiry. I am indebted to Christie Cozad Neuger for first opening up to me the possibilities of using such a method of inquiry in collegial conversation on a colleague's writing as well as use of reflecting teams in the classroom.

teller, have overheard this conversation are invited to share anything that they would like to add, and the storyteller then is invited to "retell the retelling"—to say what reflecting team members' expressions especially caught their attention, evoked images about their own hopes and values, resonated with their own experiences, and moved their perceptions about ministry and possibilities for their pastoral practice and vocation into new horizons.

Return. Although emotion is present and valued, this kind of storytelling and story listening is intended to lead to choice and action. White uses the term "katharsis" (to distinguish it from contemporary understandings of catharsis) to describe what happens in response to witnessing powerful expressions in the stories people tell. Katharsis is not just having an experience of emotional release, but involves being transported to another place in which one might, among other things, "achieve a new perspective on one's life and destiny . . . reconnect with revered values and purposes for one's life . . . make new meanings of experiences of one's life . . . initiate steps in one's life otherwise never considered . . . think beyond what one routinely thinks."[12] The culmination of the storytelling is the return, at the end of the course, to the stories of hope/despair told at the beginning of the course, in which each student now reflects on why *that* story, what its meanings were *then* and what new meanings are seen *now*. What understanding of the "association" of hope and despair can one find in, with, and under the way the story was narrated the first time, and what can one see, looking back, on the identity and values of the narrator—has anything changed? What encounters with texts, presentations, and the stories of *others* open up new horizons of meaning and action?

A SPACE FOR IMAGINATION AND RESPONSIBILITY: POETICS AND POLITICS

> Poets have no advice to give people. They only want people to see differently; to revision life. They are not coercive. They only try to stimulate, surprise, hint, and give nuance, not more. They cannot do more because they are making available a world that does not exist beyond their imagination; but their offer of this imaginative world is necessary to give freedom of action . . . Poets speak porously. They use the kind of language that is not exhausted at first hearing. They leave many things open, ambiguous, still to be discerned after more reflection. They do not pretend to know the future, but offer the present as a shockingly

---

12. Ibid., 195.

> open and ambiguous matter out of which various futures may yet emerge . . . Poets trust other people to continue the image, to finish the thought out of their own experience.[13]

> Hope is not the same thing as thinking that what one ardently desires is *likely* to happen. It is the virtue one needs when grim facts might tempt one to give up on promoting or protecting important goods. In this case the goods are liberty and justice, and the temptation is to assume that they are now essentially out of reach. The temptation, in short, is despair. . . .[14] The democratic imagination wants replenishment on a daily basis.[15]

The above quotations are taken from readings assigned in recent Narratives of Hope classes—the first from a well-known biblical scholar and the second from a religion professor who has written on the future of democracy in the United States. The close association between despair and hope about the future of the "American church" (Brueggemann) and the future of democracy in the United States (Stout), join other course authors in pushing the conversation about hope and despair into civic and global struggles. But deeply personal narratives of hope/despair in ministry also disclose the intimate relationship between individual and corporate life, the pastoral and the political; the vital role of social context in ministry.

There is a close relationship between poetics and politics. Both Brueggemann and Stout, through different means, seek to stimulate imagination. Brueggemann focuses on the poetic sensibilities at work in Jeremiah, Ezekiel, and Deutero-Isaiah to confront the dismantling of a world and point to a world that exists only in the imagination and that will be received as gift of God. Stout asserts that "When despair is the disease one hopes to remedy, anecdotes can be antidotes."[16] He tells the stories of people organizing to make a difference in their communities "to make a reader experience the emotional component of the hope that the tellers of these stories embody in person."[17] But the goal is not the emotion itself. The goal is participation and action.

In Narratives of Hope we practiced in limited and imperfect ways a form of resistance to thin stories, traveling long enough with one another's stories to receive the images and metaphors of hope and despair evoked by

---

13. Brueggemann, *Hopeful Imagination*, 23.
14. Stout, *Blessed Are the Organized*, 283.
15. Ibid., 288.
16. Ibid., 283.
17. Ibid.

them; life portraits of the world that is and the world that can only be imagined. The power of social context to explain and constrain is not finally all that we have. Alternative worlds can still be imagined. The "space between spaces" exists there, too. And when words do not yet exist, the *community* is the holding space for what is already and not yet. "We all struggled to find adequate language for our experiences of hope and despair, and yet I believe hope was felt in the very experience of entrusting the stories to others and letting them dwell in our midst."[18]

Such are the rhythms we tried to encourage in Narratives of Hope: the interplay of theoretical/theological frameworks and the complexities of complex, living personal/community narratives; the interplay between my/our story and the stories of others; the interplay of empathy and analysis; the interplay of poetics and politics. But in none of those attempted rhythms can I say, "It was *there* I can locate *chora* and experience it again." I come full circle to one of the assertions at the heart of *Eschatology and Space*:

> And these are the two opposite and complementary sides of an eschatological event: lament and remembrance, condemnation and justification, grave and grace. The dividing line between these pairs, the threshold, cannot be defined, measured, or theoretically located. In the moment that is done, it is no longer here; it can only be lived through, experienced. Eschatological experiences are vaguely analogous to the behavior of subatomic particles: in the moment it is located and detected, it is no longer there.[19]

Yet sometimes, within such fragile rhythms, with all their awkwardness and imperfect harmonies, something happens that is beyond management, good intentions, or negotiation that makes me eager for the next class and so grateful to be in this seminary classroom space together. It does not finally matter that these experiences elude my powers of description. It matters, rather, that they sustain hope and trust in the One who is at work in the space between spaces, calling us to hopeful action in the world precisely when and where, after our best efforts, we are deeply aware that we cannot manage the outcome, and receive that truth as a gift of grace.

BIBLIOGRAPHY

Brueggemann, Walter. *The Hopeful Imagination: Prophetic Voices in Exile* Philadelphia: Fortress, 1986.

18. Narrative of Hope student.
19. Westhelle, *Eschatology and Space*, 137.

Roy, Arundhati. *The God of Small Things*. New York: Harper Perennial, 1998.
Stout, Jeffrey. *Blessed Are the Organized: Grassroots Democracy in America*. Princeton: Princeton University Press, 2010.
Westhelle, Vítor. *The Church Event: Call and Challenge of a Church Protestant*. Minneapolis: Fortress, 2009.
———. *Eschatology and Space: The Lost Dimension in Theology Past and Present* New York: Palgrave Macmillan, 2012.
———. *The Scandalous God: The Use and Abuse of the Cross*. Minneapolis: Fortress, 2006.
White Michael. *Maps of Narrative Practice*. New York: Norton, 2007.

17

Charting a New Vision
Paul's Copernican Revolution for Our Witness to the Gospel[1]

JOSÉ DAVID RODRÍGUEZ

"Let it be known to you then that this salvation of God has been sent to the Gentiles; they will listen"

ACTS 28:28[2]

---

1. The content of this text is based on a key note lecture I presented at the Multicultural Seminar sponsored by the Evangelical Lutheran Church in America (ELCA) on October 10, 2004 held at the Lutheran School of Theology at Chicago (LSTC) which was never published. The lecture incorporates central concerns of particular interest that have characterized not only my theological thinking throughout my career as a Latino Lutheran teaching theologian, but also an important part of my colleague and "compadre," Dr. Vítor Westhelle's theological legacy. The substance of the original lecture was edited for the purpose of incorporating it in this publication.

2. The Revised Standard Version of the Bible comments that other ancient authorities add verse 29 that reads, "And when he had said these words, the Jews departed, arguing vigorously among themselves."

INTRODUCTION

In October of 1981, the Lutheran Council in the USA, with the financial assistance from what was then called Aid Association for Lutherans, convened a national "Transcultural Seminar," held at the Lutheran School of Theology at Chicago (LSTC). The conference brought together approximately 100 Lutheran leaders active in ministry with people from diverse backgrounds of cultures, races, and languages throughout the United States and its territories. The goal of this event was to explore and collectively make recommendations for developing a new community of faith (a new Lutheran church body) to celebrate and incarnate a church for all peoples.[3]

Our friend and colleague, Dr. Albert "Pete" Pero, now professor emeritus of LSTC, provided the keynote address for this occasion. At that time he challenged both the leadership and constituency of the Lutheran church to lead forward a ministry with a vision established on what he theologically defined as the concept of "self-transcendence."[4]

Yet, in spite of Pete's courageous efforts throughout these years, and the faithful witness of our various communities, today we are confronted with new challenges to meet the goals established thirty-two years ago in witnessing to a church for all people. Since the nature of this text necessarily limits my approach in exploring these numerous challenges, I will focus my attention on two of them that need to provoke our interest and response. The first of these challenges is the key issue of *identity* facing Lutheranism in the United States and all over the world. This concern has been raised more poignantly in a publication edited by Richard Cimino, *Lutherans Today: American Lutheran Identity in the Twenty-First Century*, where some of its authors explore the impact on the current controversy of embracing multiculturalism as a trend that challenges the core of Lutheran identity.

The second and closely related challenge is one of *perspective*. I've been experiencing the gravity of this latter challenge in conversations with Bishop Hansen,[5] members of his special committee on restructure, and representatives of other communities of color of the Evangelical Lutheran Church in America, as we engage in discussions on the Bishop's proposals for reforming and restructuring the ELCA.

---

3. Wu, *Catching a Star*, 15.
4. For a complete version of Dr. Pero's address see *Catching a Star*, 29–52.
5. Presiding Bishop of the ELCA.

PRAXIS

EMBRACING MULTICULTURALISM: A CHALLENGE TO LUTHERAN IDENTITY

In her review of the book edited by Richard Cimino, Susan Wilds McArver argues, that among the key issues present in this timely publication is the one focusing on *Lutheran identity*. For her, questions about Lutheran identity have been raised since the beginnings of the seventeenth century European settlement on the U.S. American continent.[6] The book examines the latest incarnation of that struggle in a period of growing awareness of cultural and religious pluralism. For this author, the greater significance of this issue today lies in the fact that Lutherans have consolidated themselves from smaller ethnic churches into two major and one smaller body (ELCA, Lutheran Church-Missouri Synod [LCMS], and Wisconsin Evangelical Lutheran Synod [WELS]) bringing wide-raging ethnic, theological, and polity differences into closer proximity and a sometimes uneasy coexistence.[7]

For the African-American Lutheran biblical scholar Peter Nash, one of the basic flaws of this publication lies in the fact that the issue of identity, rather than being confined to the perspective of North American Lutheran groups, needs to be placed in a broader international context, where the practical realities of a global world, and the theological shared hope of ecclesial union with at least our worldwide Lutheran communion partners, establishes a more adequate context to explore basic concerns of Lutheran identity.[8]

A more significant problem of the publication is, according to Nash, the ill-considered attack of one of its authors that carelessly lumps together several controversial issues currently debated in the U.S. as an expression

---

6. While I agree with the general point made by this author in her review, I need to clarify that on the specific point she makes regarding the European settlement on the U.S. American continent since the seventeenth century, I am closer to Peter Nash's perspective which claims that the inaccurate use of the term American/America to identify a continent, fails to indicate that the geographical extension of the American continent comprises more than just the country of the United States of America but includes other American countries located in North America (Canada, México), South America (Argentina, Brazil, Colombia, Ecuador, etc.) and the Caribbean (Cuba, Puerto Rico, Haiti, etc.) with more than 25 national Lutheran bodies that the authors of this publication ignore. Nash, "U.S. Lutheranism's State," 28. In addition, a more accurate historical perspective would have to mention the Lutheran colony established by the Welsers in Venezuela during the sixteenth century (1528–1546) as the beginning of the Lutheran European settlement in the American continent. See Bastian, *Historia del Protestantismo*, 46–48.

7. Wilds McArver, "Consolidation and Quarreling," 26.

8. Nash, Ibid.

of what he calls the "ideological" nature of multiculturalism, which leads to the dilution of Lutheran identity.[9]

For all the efforts of other authors in the publication to bring a more balanced appraisal of this debate in their own explorations of the topic, Nash concludes, and I concur with his assessment, that the assumption of confessional identity employed by most of these authors, seems often to be a commitment to a European ethnic perspective in the guise of confessional fidelity.[10]

In my estimation here lies the core of the problem. When we deal with issues concerning our most basic convictions, we are all tempted to be led by the uncritical assumption of a specific perspective, conditioned by the particular ethnic, social, historical, androcentric, and heterosexual context from which it originally emerged, and project it as being normative for all and every occasion. Those who challenge it tend to be regarded, not just as holding a different and viable perspective from which we might also learn, but rather wicked and hateful individuals, led by a malicious attempt to corrupt and destroy our most sacred and revered principles. To avoid this pervasive temptation I suggest we turn our sight to scripture to discover what, for the Puerto Rican theologian Luis N. Rivera Pagán, is the Pauline revolution for our witness to the gospel.

PAUL'S COPERNICAN REVOLUTION FOR OUR WITNESS TO THE GOSPEL

In exploring the historical witness that distinguishes the expansion of Christianity to these lands since the sixteenth century, the Puerto Rican theologian and historical scholar Luis N. Rivera Pagán makes the claim that the future of America "has a history indelibly marked by the efforts of innumerable men and women living the gospel under the protection of divine grace and mercy. Unfortunately, that history is also a procession of bitterness, much of it caused, paradoxically, by those who established themselves as spokespersons of Christianity. From the first encounter between indigenous American communities and European Christians in 1492, that contradiction has marked our history."[11]

Our present time,[12] in which the challenges raised by the slow-paced free market globalization of capitalism and its culture of insensitivity lead to

9. Ibid.
10. Ibid., 29.
11. Rivera-Pagán, "Word Became Flesh," 52.
12. It is noteworthy that following the suggestive phrase coined by the Mexican

a deafness, or to what other scholars have called a "hunger for bread," and a myopia to the "hunger for God" and "humanity," that expresses the very particular spirituality and religious sensitivity of subjugated and despised peoples,[13] the themes of culture, race, gender, ethnicity, and spirituality take on renewed force for those who aspire in their practice of faith, a faithful witness to the incarnation of the Gospel.[14]

To recognize the significance of the claims made throughout history by these subjugated and despised peoples, which includes the polyphony—not always symphonic—of ethnic groups, cultures, spiritualities, languages, and forms of religious expressions, freed of imposed uniformity; seeking a reconceptualizing of the understanding and the practice of faith, in which—thanks to a surprising eruption of the Spirit—the plural dialogue of Pentecost is reenacted and new paths are designed for the inculturation of the Gospel, the author points to what he calls the Pauline revolution.

Pointing to the negative history of the Greek word *ethnos*, which during the golden age of Athenian philosophy acquired a pejorative meaning referring to those beyond the pale of Hellenic language and culture, coming closer semantically to the term *bárbaros* (barbarian) and the characteristic antagonistic distinction found in the Septuagint between *laós* "the people of God," and *éthnê*, "the pagan or Gentile nations," in their proselytism, Hellenic Jews conserved and intensified the practice of requiring converts to adopt the worship and cultural traditions of Israel. Ironically, this practice manifested the paradox that although God was considered creator of all nations *(éthnê)*, this very God had also granted Israel the exclusive distinction of being God's people, leaving Gentile nations relegated to eternal condemnation.[15]

In this context, the last words of Paul in the Acts of the Apostles carry with them a Copernican revolution in the biblical concept of divine providence: "Let it be known to you then that this salvation of God [*tò sôtêrion toû theoû*] has been sent to the Gentiles [*toîs éthnesin]; they will listen*" (Acts 28:28).

God's grace is proclaimed to the *éthnê,* and the ethnic groups. All ethnic groups are given the possibility of becoming integrated into the people of God, leaving aside all forms of discrimination and all prejudicial

---

theologian Elsa Tamez, Rivera-Pagán describes the present time as one suffering a "messianic drought." Ibid., 53.

13. Rivera-Pagán takes this image from Jung Mo Sung's presentation recorded in the same publication under the title, "Hunger for God," 35–42.

14. Ibid.

15. Coenen, et al., *Diccionario,* 438–445.

forms of worship and culture that have tried to claim the privilege of divine providence.

The concepts and missionary practice of Christianity have had, nonetheless, the periodic effect of reconstructing the distinction between God's people and the nations of the world, identifying the first with Western, white, and Northern, and the second with non-Western, dark, and Southern cultures.[16] The multiethnic and pluricultural opening that Paul gives to the Gospel acquires great pertinence in that indigenous communities, Latino, Asian, African American, Arab/Mid Eastern, as well as people from many other ethnic communities demand full respect and dignity for their cultures. As heirs and heiresses of that history, we need to pay special attention to the words with which Paul concludes his radical transformation of the biblical message, "This salvation has been sent to the ethnic groups; they will listen."

This theological perspective does not necessarily assume the negation of one's own traditions, particularly if they may be traced to the Western European lineage. During the sixteenth century and from there forward throughout every other age, men and women of faith have drawn from the bosom of Western Christianity the unmasking Word of the Gospel imparting authentic continuity to the Scripture's prophetic lineage. What Paul's radical claim implies is to leave aside the traditional separation between "civilized people," with their prerogatives and privileges of dominance, and "backward peoples," destined for submission to the free will of the former, what the late Palestinian-American scholar Edward Said has called "the fundamental ontological distinction between the West and the rest of the world."[17] Likewise, this central imperative of the Gospel assumes overcoming—in word and deed, in personal subjectivity and in social objectivity,— the painful current reality identified by Gustavo Gutiérrez when he claims that, "Today indigenous peoples and most of the black population in this continent continue to see their ways of living, values, customs, their right to life and liberty trampled."[18]

As Rivera-Pagán argues in his eloquent and persuasive exploration of this topic, in the relationship between human cultures and Christian faith, all peoples have their own particular contribution, that which marks and distinguishes them as historically unique.[19] This Copernican revolution es-

---

16. In our North American context we could add the categories of gender and sexual orientation to this list.

17. Said, *Culture and* Imperialism, 108.

18. Gutiérrez, *En busca de los pobres*, 276.

19. Rivera-Pagán, "Word Became Flesh," 64–65.

tablished by Paul in biblical hermeneutics is what I call the basic challenge of *perspective* that we continue to face today for our faithful witness to the Gospel.

To summarize the point that I am trying to develop in this text, my effort in exploring the present challenges confronting the ministry and mission of the ELCA relate to the need of developing a new *vision*, a new and different *perspective*, to lead the church forward in its faithful witness to the Gospel.

CHARTING A NEW VISION: THE LEGACY OF GUSTAV WARNECK

In a publication edited by Dr. James K. Echols (former president of the Lutheran School of Theology at Chicago) rendering the text of the 2003 Hein-Fry Lecture Series of the ELCA celebrating both the fortieth anniversary of Dr. Martin Luther King, Jr.'s "I Have a Dream" speech and its implications for the future of this nation, Justo L. González, the distinguished Latino Church History scholar, comments that, while a *dream* tends to shatter when one wakes up to the painful realities of the present world, its real power lays in becoming the collective *vision* of those who, empowered by God's gracious and loving initiative, witness in their practice of faith to this powerful promise of the Gospel.[20]

Valdir Steuernagel, a Brazilian Lutheran scholar who completed his doctoral studies at the Lutheran School of Theology at Chicago, published in an international journal of missions an article establishing a dialogue between Gustav Warneck (whom many consider the father of the modern theory of missions) and those who are at the forefront of missionary activity today, which I find very relevant to assist both the constituency as well as the present leadership of the ELCA, in developing a collective *vision* to respond to the various challenges confronting its present ministry, including the one relating to restructuring.[21]

For Steuernagel, among the many contributions of Warnek stands his claim for a foundational biblical ground in developing an understanding of Christian missions. Quoting numerous biblical references, he argued that the missionary enterprise of the church is driven by God's initiative of love, incarnated in the redeeming work of Jesus Christ for the salvation of all creation, prompted by the power of the Holy Spirit. Another of Warneck's contributions was his claim that we are *all* called both individually

20. González, "Dream," 69–82.
21. Steuernagel, "El despertar misionero," 7–17.

and collectively as the body of Christ in the world to participate in God's mission. For Warneck, this is the central task of the community of believers. Finally, Warneck emphasized the need for developing an adequate understanding of history and our sociological reality for an effective witness in the church's missionary activity.[22]

For Warneck, who died in 1910 (and by the way, who never left Germany during his career as a Lutheran pastor and professor of missions), the developments in human knowledge during the nineteenth and twentieth centuries signaled the promise for the fulfillment of the missionary activity of the church to all corners of the world.

While Warneck's contributions were then, and still now, provocative and persuasive, Steuernagel reminds us that the initiator of the modern theory of missions was so captivated by the progress developed by the rich industrial nations of his time, that he failed to noticed the tragic consequences of the imperialistic developments of these powerful nations over the poor and developing countries in the world.

In spite of Warneck's failure to separate the missionary activity of the church from the neocolonialist liberal project of powerful nations by the turn of the nineteenth century, Steuernagel reminds us that one of Warneck's long-lasting contributions to the theory of missions was his insight and ability to demonstrate that, in most cases, the missionary activity of the church is driven by the *dreams* and *vision* of marginalized and excluded groups within the human community, confronting the dominant sociopolitical and ecclesial powers, in bringing their hopes and aspirations to fulfillment.[23]

It is here where I think that the contributions of Warneck maintain an unwavering continuity with the message of the Gospel, what we earlier called Paul's Copernican revolution in biblical hermeneutics, and the *vision* of the faithful throughout history.

FROM VISION TO STRATEGY: THE PREDICAMENT OF OUR TIME

At the beginning of this text I argued that today we are confronted with new challenges as we continue our efforts in meeting the goals established thirty two years ago, when we gathered at LSTC to explore and collectively develop recommendations for the ministry and mission of a Lutheran church for all peoples. We need to realize once again that for our efforts to be effective, we

22. Warneck, *Outline for a History*, 3–7, 74–85.
23. Steuernagel, "El despertar misionero," 15.

need to move from *vision* to *strategy*, that is, from the stimulating experience of a vision of the future, to the practical implications of charting a path, for that vision to become the leading compass of our present practice of faith.

Our times, like the times of many of the faithful of old, are times of immense transitions, great challenges, and enormous changes. The globalization of the world market economy, the evolving technological revolution, new administrative methods to increase productivity, and the preemptive war against world terrorism have led some economists, sociologists, politicians, and religious leaders to proclaim that the primary factor in the present world situation is certainly the terrible power of the logic of exclusion.[24] Increasing numbers of people in the United States and other countries in the world are excluded from the marketplace. This means that they become excluded not only from the fruits of development, but often from the very conditions that make possible a life of dignity—sometimes from survival itself. In a world caught up in what an increasing number of theologians from developing countries describe the "idolatry of the marketplace," what should be the mission of the Christian Church? What good news should we announce in order to be faithful to the Gospel?

The first step in addressing this predicament is to unmask the sin of idolatry. We must unveil the spirit of idol worship—the worship of work, of human and social actions and relationships undertaken solely for the accumulation of wealth and for the purpose of unlimited consumption. We must establish a simple and irrefutable truth: the economy should exist to serve the lives of all. People should not be impelled to abide in economic laws designed solely for the accumulation of wealth.

A second important step is to realize that the people of the Americas are not only excluded from the marketplace, but are also denied their humanity and religious/spiritual longings. If the good news of the Gospel is to bear fruit in our society, the mission and ministry of the church must engage in a basic theological task: a critique of a theology of retribution, which sanctions and supports a "culture of contentment" and a "theology of prosperity." We need to show that the God of Sara, Abraham, and the prophets of the people of Israel, the God who dwelt with us in the redemptive work of Jesus Christ empowered by the Holy Spirit, is not the cause of suffering and injustice, nor the provider of the minority's wealth. We need to announce that God's name cannot be used in vain to undergird injustice, prejudice and cynicism. This prophetic denouncement is necessary because salvation is a product of God's loving and gracious initiative and not the

---

24. This brief examination of our world predicament follows closely the analysis provided by Jung Mo Sung mentioned earlier (see footnote 11).

consequence of our own merits. And if we are to live in accordance with this loving and gracious initiative of God, we must look with gratitude beyond the logic of the marketplace and recognize the right of all people to a good and dignified life. In other words, we must reclaim the values of solidarity and equality.

In sociological terms, we need to struggle for developing a society in which everyone has a place, a world in which we all learn to respect each other's differences, and the right of everyone to a life of dignity. To be sure, in this society the marketplace will play an important function. But just as surely, it will not be either a sanctified or omnipotent marketplace. There must be state and social mechanisms of control that will complement the mechanisms of the marketplace, so that the basic rights of all people will be respected and ecological systems will be preserved.

A VISION OF THE FUTURE FOR THE PRESENT

In October of 2004 Bishop Hansen invited us to respond to a draft document proposal for the restructuring of the ELCA church-wide organization. In his invitation he stated that the intentional design of the document aimed at incorporating the insights and perspectives of the whole church by means of an interactive style to continue to nourish and facilitate a collective vision throughout the entire process. I have participated in the past and will continue to participate in this initiative. In fact, the significance of being valuable and constitutive partners in such projects for the planning and design of the principles and priorities should guide our common ministry, should remind us once again of this important task ahead of us.

My hope is that our diligent and thoughtful contributions, along with the contributions of those who will also join us in this task, will help us move forward in this journey of faith. As we move forward together in this assignment, let the eloquent words of the hymn *Lift Every Voice and Sing* reminds us to continue to,

> Lift every voice and sing till earth and heaven ring,
> ring with the harmonies of liberty.
> Let our rejoicing rise high as the list'ning skies,
> let it resound loud as the rolling sea.
> Sing a song full of the faith that the dark past has taught us,
> sing a song full of the hope that the present has brought us;
> Facing the rising sun of our new day begun,
> let us march on, till victory is won.

> Stony the road we trod, bitter the chast'ning rod,
> felt in the days when hope unborn had died;
> Yet with a steady beat, have not our weary feet
> come to the place for which our parents sighed?
> We have come over a way that with tears has been watered;
> we have come, treading our path through the blood of the slaughtered.
> Out from the gloomy past, till now we stand at last
> where the white gleam of our bright star is cast.

Today (January, 2013), as we look back at the journey of the ELCA towards a multicultural church body, the percentage of people of color and language other than English in the ELCA has increased to the highest level in its history. The information now available on the ELCA website states that from 2004 to 2007, the increase has been from 3% to a 3.04%.[25] The road trodden has been a rocky one indeed, but let's continue to join our voices in a joyful and hopeful song, marching on till victory is won.

BIBLIOGRAPHY

Bastian, Jean Pierre. *Historia del Protestantismo en América Latina*. México: Casa Unida de Publicaciones, 1990.

Coenen, Lothar, et al. *Diccionario teológico del Nuevo Testamento*, vol. 3. Salamanca: Ediciones Sígueme, 1983.

González, Justo L. "The Dream: A Future for the Present." In *I Have a Dream: Martin Luther King Jr. and the Future of Multicultural America*. Edited by James K. Echols. Minneapolis: Fortress, 2004.

Gutiérrez, Gustavo. *En busca de los pobres de Jesucristo*. Lima: Centro de Estudios y Publicaciones, 1992.

"Lift Every Voice and Sing." *Lutheran Book of Worship*, hymn 562. Philadelphia: Augsburg Fortress, 1979.

Nash, Peter T. "U.S. Lutheranism's State." *Lutheran Partners* 20:5 (September/October 2004) 28.

Pero, Albert. "Self-Transcendence: A Foundational Theological Concept for an Inclusive Church." *Catching a Star: Transcultural Reflections on a Church for All People*. Edited by Richard J. Perry, 15. Minneapolis: Lutheran University Press, 2004.

Rivera-Pagán, Luis N. "The Word Became Flesh: Incarnation, Gospel, and Culture in Latin America." In *Hope and Justice for All in the Americas: Discerning God's Mission*, edited by Oscar L. Bolioli, 52. New York: Friendship Press, 1998.

Said, Edward W. *Culture and Imperialism*. New York: Knopf, 1993.

Steuernagel, Valdir R. "El despertar misionero del Tercer Mundo." *Mission* 6 (June, 1987) 7–17.

25. See: http://www.elca.org/Growing-In-Faith/Ministry/Multicultural-Ministries/Resources/Racial-Makeup.aspx.

Sung, Jung Mo. "Hunger for God, Hunger for Bread, Hunger for Humanity: A Southern Perspective," In *Hope and Justice for All in the Americas: Discerning God's Mission*, edited by Oscar L. Bolioli, 35–42. New York: Friendship Press, 1998.

Warneck, Gustav. *Outline for a History of Christian Missions from the Reformation to the Present*. London: Oliphant, Anderson, & Ferrier, 1906.

Wilds McArver, Susan. "Consolidation and Quarreling." *Lutheran Partners* 20:5 (2004) 26.

Wu, Lily R. "Forward." In *Catching a Star: Transcultural Reflections on a Church for All People*, edited by Richard J. Perry, 15. Minneapolis: Lutheran University Press.

18

(Re)-Claiming *Oikoumenē*?
Ecumenism, Ecology, Empire

BARBARA ROSSING

ONE EVENING IN 2005 over a home cooked Brazilian meal Vítor and I were talking about the Lutheran World Federation and the subject of Ecumenism. He was in the last phase of finishing up the draft of the manuscript of the now acclaimed book, *The Scandalous God: The Use and Abuse of the Cross*. He mentioned that my text in *Walk in the Ways of Wisdom: Essays in Honor of Elisabeth Schüssler Fiorenza* was one of his favorite texts. So on this occasion of celebrating Vítor and his contributions to theological academia and to the ecumenical world at large, I offer a reworked version of that text that now adds a consideration of ecology and eschatology. This essay will investigate the Greek word *oikoumenē* ("world"), asking: Is there a liberating strand of the word *oikoumenē* in the biblical tradition that can be retrieved for life in the *ekklēsia* as democratic assembly today, as we face crises such as the ecological crisis?[1]

---

1 *Oikoumenē* is the feminine passive participle of the verb *oikein*, to dwell or inhabit. Hence its meaning as "the whole inhabited world." The English word "ecumenical" derives from the adjective *oikoumenikos* or "pertaining to the whole world."

Barbara Rossing   *(Re)-Claiming* Oikoumenē?

At first glance the answer would seem to be an obvious "Yes," affirming the promise of *oikoumenē*. The World Council of Churches, whose logo is a ship with the overarching slogan "Oikoumene," has been at the forefront of movements of liberation and eco-justice, promoting democratic visions. For many global and liberationist Christians, involvement in the ecumenical movement has been one of the most progressive dimensions of ecclesial life. Ecumenists and ecological theologians trace their commitments back to the Greek notion of the *oikoumenē* or house (*oikos*) that includes the whole inhabited world, which is expanded to include all creation, not just the human world.[2]

In literature of the Roman era, however, the word *oikoumenē*—from which the English term "ecumenical" derives—carried a more imperial meaning beyond its original geographical meaning. More than "the earth as inhabited area" in a geographical sense, *oikoumenē* came also to mean "the world as administrative unit, the Roman Empire."[3] I will argue that throughout most of the New Testament *oikoumenē* carries this second or political connotation of the Roman empire.

While in contemporary ecumenical discussions it can seem attractive to attempt to re-define *oikoumenē* in a positive sense, we need to recall that in earliest Christian literature *oikoumenē* was primarily a term of empire, rarely used in a liberating context. Indeed, the legacy of *oikoumenē* is so problematic that the question remains whether the term can be reclaimed apart from its kyriarchal and imperialist tendencies.[4] The challenge for any reclaiming of the word *oikoumenē* today—whether for a positive ecumenical vision or an eco-justice vision—must be to repudiate the imperial trajectory of *oikoumenē* and to seek alternative models that embrace ecclesial diversity and democracy.

The word *oikoumenē* is used in the Greek Old Testament and in the New Testament. For the text that follows I will focus on its usage in Septuagint and the book of Revelation, and make suggestions for its current usage in ecumenical and ecological discourse.

---

2. For a vision of *oikoumenē* as including all creation see the essay by General Secretary Konrad Raiser of World Council of Churches, "Ecumenism in Search of a Vision" reprinted in *Ecumenical Movement*, 76.

3. These are the first and second definitions of *oikoumenē* in the third edition of *A Greek-English Lexicon*.

4. The term "kyriarchal" was coined by Elisabeth Schüssler Fiorenza to describe the "social-political system of domination and subordination that is based on the power and rule of the lord/master/father" (*Sharing Her Word*, 190 n. 52).

PRAXIS

OIKOUMENĒ AS THE WORLD CREATED BY GOD: THE SEPTUAGINT

Oikoumenē in the Septuagint is largely positive, encompassing the whole geographical world, both physical and human, that is accountable to God. In the Septuagint, *oikoumenē* is the translation for the Hebrew word *tebel* ("world"), often used in poetic parallelism with "earth" (Hebrew: *eretz*; Greek: *gē*). God is the creator of the *oikoumenē*, the one who "has made the earth (*gē*) . . . who established the world (*oikoumenē*) . . . and has stretched out the heaven" (Jer 10:12, 51:15 [LXX Jer 28:15]). The term *oikoumenē* is especially frequent in the Psalms: "The heavens are yours, the earth is yours, and as for the world (*oikoumenē*) and its fullness, you founded them (Psalm 89:11). The apostle Paul's only usage of the word *oikoumenē* is a quote from Psalm 19 (LXX Psalm 18), where *oikoumenē* is parallel to *gē*: "Their line is gone out through all the earth (*gē*) and their words to the end of the *oikoumenē*" (Rom 10:18).

God lays claim to the whole *oikoumenē*: "The world (*oikoumenē*) is mine" (Psalm 50:12; LXX 49:12); "The earth (*gē*) is the Lord's and all that is in it; the world (*oikoumenē*) and those who dwell in it" (Psalm 24:1).

OIKOUMENĒ AS EMPIRE

By the first century BCE, however, Rome also laid claim to the *oikoumenē*. In propaganda and iconography celebrating Rome's conquests of lands and peoples, *oikoumenē* was claimed not only the ends of the world in a geographical sense but also in a political sense, as the ends of Roman imperial sway.[5]

In his landmark analysis of Rome's and Augustus's "ecumenical and ostentatious claims" Claude Nicolet argues that Rome's empire and its geographical knowledge developed hand in hand, as evidenced in the use of the Greek word *oikoumenē* and the Latin term *orbis terrarum*.[6] Romans were called "lords of the *oikoumenē*" (*kyrioi tēs oikoumenēs*; Plutarch, *Tiberius Gracchus* 9.6), a claim realized and further expanded through military conquests by Pompey, Julius Caesar, and Augustus. In 61 BCE a huge trophy

---

5. For the purposes of this essay I work with a definition of "geographical" as having to do with the *gē* or earth, and "political" as having to do with *polis* or empire. The distinction between the two terms is heuristic, since my point is to show that they are closely related.

6. Nicolet, *Space, Geography and Politics*, 11.

of the conquered *oikoumenē* was carried in triumphal procession in Rome to celebrate Pompey's three military victories over Libya, Europe and Asia:

> He [Pompey] celebrated the triumph in honor of all his wars at once, including in it many trophies beautifully decked out to represent each of his achievements, even the smallest; and after them all came one huge one, decked out in costly fashion and bearing an inscription stating that it was a trophy of the inhabited world (*oikoumenē*).[7]

Ancient authors' usage of the term *oikoumenē* reflects the use of *oikoumenē* for imperial propaganda. Aelius Aristides' "Roman Oration" lauds the harmony and unity that Rome's conquests brought to the whole *oikoumenē*:

> What was said by Homer, "The earth was common to all," you have made a reality, by surveying the whole inhabited world (*oikoumenē*), by bridging the rivers in various ways, by cutting carriage roads through the mountains by filling desert places with post stations, and by civilizing everything with your way of life and good order. . . And now, indeed, there is no need to write a description of the world, nor to enumerate the laws of each people, but you have become universal geographers for all. . . by opening up all the gates of the inhabited world (*oikoumenē*). . . and by organizing the whole inhabited world like a single household" (*syntaxantes hōsper hena oikon hapasan tēn oikoumenēn*). (*Or.* 26. 101–102)

The speech by King Agrippa II in Book 2 of Josephus's *Jewish War* is a poignant example of the imperial context of the term *oikoumenē*. Throughout the whole *oikoumenē* Roman power is undefeated, Agrippa tells his hearers (2.362). Finally Agrippa asks the Judaeans:

What allies then do you expect for this war? Will you recruit them from the uninhabited (*aoiketou*) wilds? For in the habitable world (*oikoumenē*) all are Romans.[8]

OIKOUMENĒ IN THE NEW TESTAMENT

"In the *oikoumenē* all are Romans:" this fact—mourned by Agrippa, celebrated by Aelius Aristides—describes the first century context both geographically and politically, and it must be kept in mind as we investigate

---

7. Dio's *Roman History* 37.21.2
8. Josephus, *Jewish War* 2.388.

the meaning of *oikoumenē* in the New Testament. The word *oikoumenē* is used eight times in Luke-Acts and three times in Revelation, with fewer occurrences in Hebrews, Romans and Matthew. The recent third edition of the *Greek-English Lexicon of the New Testament and Other Early Christian Literature* (BDAG) assigns New Testament references to *oikoumenē* to the geographical definition of the "earth as inhabited area" or to the derivative definition of "inhabitants of the earth." The question, however, is whether BDAG's second or more political definition of *oikoumenē* as "the world as administrative unit, the Roman Empire" is not also the predominant understanding of *oikoumenē* in the New Testament.

References to *oikoumenē* in the book of Revelation exemplify the problem. Revelation uses the phrase "the whole *oikoumenē*" three times, always negatively. However, are these references primarily geographical—that is, relating to the *gē* or earth—in the tradition of the Septuagint and BDAG's first definition, or are they more political, relating to the Roman imperial system? Chilean liberation scholar Pablo Richard argues for the political reading of *oikoumenē* as Rome: "The inhabited world, or *oikoumenē*, is not all the earth, but the world that is organized and controlled by the Roman empire. Everything else is the world of the barbarians."[9]

Revelation's first reference to *oikoumenē* is Rev 3:10, in the letter to the Philadelphians. David Aune translates *oikoumenē* here as "earth," using the same word as he does for translating "*gē*" later in the same verse: "I will preserve you from the time of affliction which will come upon the whole earth (*oikoumenē*) to afflict the inhabitants of the earth (*gē*)."[10] The second reference to *oikoumenē* is Rev 12:9, where *oikoumenē* is the world that has been deceived by Satan, Rome's surrogate: "The great dragon was thrown down . . . that deceiver of the whole *oikoumenē*, he was thrown down into the earth." Revelation's final reference to *oikoumenē* comes just before the anti-Roman chapter 17, in a description of the evil spirits that issue from the mouth of the dragon after the sixth bowl is poured out, "They are demonic spirits, performing signs, who go abroad to the kings of the whole world (*oikoumenē*), to assemble them for battle" (Rev 16:14).

Is Aune correct that *oikoumenē* is synonymous with "the inhabitants of earth" in Revelation? Does Revelation sustain the Septuagint's close parallelism between *oikoumenē* and "earth" (*gē*), with *oikoumenē* having primarily a geographical meaning, as in the Septuagint usage? Or does the term take on a more anti-Roman political cast, as Pablo Richard suggests? Since

---

9. Richard, *Apocalypse*, 61, commenting on Rev 3:10.

10. Aune, *Revelation 1–5*, 228. Aune argues that in Revelation the "whole *oikoumenē*" is synonymous with the "inhabitants of the earth," a phrase used also in Rev 13:3 (239). Charles Talbert likewise translates *oikoumenē* as "earth" in Rev 3:10 (*Apocalypse*, 22).

Revelation contains only these three references to *oikoumenē* compared to its 78 references to "earth," comparisons are difficult. Nonetheless, in my view, we can identify a crucial shift in the relationship between *oikoumenē* and *gē* from the Septuagint to the book of Revelation, and indeed to the whole New Testament. While Aune is correct that there is a parallelism between *oikoumenē* and *gē* in Revelation when the terms are used negatively for judgment, what is missing from Revelation is any positive sense of *oikoumenē*.

Unlike the Septuagint, Revelation never asserts that the *oikoumenē* is created by God. This is a crucial difference from "earth" (*gē*), which does carry a positive sense in Revelation as God's creation and as an active agent of God's salvation.[11] Although the earth suffers judgment and tribulation, Revelation also always underscores that God created the earth (Rev 14:7)—a claim that is absent for *oikoumenē*. Earth plays a saving role in Revelation 12, when earth rescues the woman from the dragon's river. God's saints will reign "on earth" (Rev 5:10), another positive reference. Most importantly, Revelation proclaims that the earth will be renewed in God's future world, as God's dwelling place, when God creates a "new earth" along with a new heaven (Rev 21:1). No such positive renewal is envisioned for the *oikoumenē*.

If Revelation refrains from referring to the *oikoumenē* as created by God it is because for Revelation *oikoumenē* represents the Roman Empire—an empire that must come to an end. In light of the book's overall anti-Roman polemic, the "hour of trial that is coming upon the whole *oikoumenē*" in Rev 3:10 should be read not so much as a general eschatological tribulation that will come upon the earth, but more pointedly as the trial or judgment that God will bring upon *the entire Roman Empire* and on all those who benefit from Rome's injustice.[12]

Moreover, it is striking that Revelation does not attempt to reclaim the *oikoumenē* as belonging to God. *Oikoumenē* is portrayed rather as a realm supported by violence, a realm that has been deceived by Satan (Rev 12:9) and aligned with Rome and its kings for battle against God (Rev 16:14), a realm of future tribulation and judgment (Rev 3:10).

The word *oikoumenē* is used also in the gospels, where it seems to refer much more to the Roman empire than scholars have seen.[13] The Gospel

---

11. For the argument that Earth (*Gē*) plays a positive role in Revelation, see Rossing, "Alas for the Earth!" 183–95.

12. Such a political reading of Rev 3:10 mitigates against an escapist reading by which some have used this verse as proof that they will be "raptured" up from earth before the tribulation. See for example Lindsey, *Rapture*, 119–24.

13. Luke Timothy Johnson is the exception. He translates as "empire" in a number

of Luke situates Jesus' birth alongside Augustus' imperial declaration in Luke 2:1: "In those days a decree went out from Caesar Augustus that the whole *oikoumenē* should be enrolled." Satan tempts Jesus by offering to give him the kingdoms of the *oikoumenē* (Luke 4:5). Both Matthew and Luke use the word *oikoumenē* in references to the end (*telos*) and to the tribulations that will come upon the nations: "And the gospel of the kingdom will be preached in the whole *oikoumenē*, as a testimony to all nations.. and the end will come" (Matt 24:13–14); "There will be distress of nations ... people fainting with fear and with foreboding of what is coming upon the *oikoumenē*" (Luke 21:25). These references to the *oikoumenē* in the context of the "end" should also be read in a more political sense—asserting the end of empire even more than the end of the geographical world or earth.

Thus the New Testament is strikingly silent regarding any depiction of the *oikoumenē* as having been created by God, as part of creation. Unlike the words *kosmos* or *gē*, there is no positive or ecological connotation to the term *oikoumenē*.[14] The New Testament refrains from any reclaiming of the *oikoumenē* for God.

OIKOUMENĒ TODAY: END OF THE WORLD OR END OF EMPIRE?

What are the implications of such a reading of *oikoumenē* for ecclesial life today? Does it matter that *oikoumenē* came to mean the Roman Empire, or that the New Testament uses the term in a largely negative sense? In my view, translating *oikoumenē* as "empire" rather than "world" can have important implications for two important areas of contemporary theology: ecology and ecumenism.

First, in relation to ecological theology, reading of *oikoumenē* as empire has implications for our eschatology—a topic on which Vítor works.[15] The New Testament, and particularly the Apocalypse, is sometimes portrayed as anti-earth or even escapist, since its eschatology seems to be concerned with the end of the world. There is a strong sense of an "end" in eschatological discourses of the New Testament, to be sure. But the question we must ask is: What is it that is coming to an end? In Revelation what is declared to be coming to an end is not the earth itself but primarily the *oikoumenē*

---

of passages in Luke and Acts, although not in Luke 2:1, 4:5, or 21:25. See Johnson *Sacra Pagina*.

14. An exception is Hebrews which uses *oikoumenē* in reference to God's future world to come (Heb 2:5; 6:5). 1 Clement 60:1 refers to the *oikoumenē* as God's creation.

15. Westhelle, *Eschatology and Space*.

or empire. If we translate the *oikoumenē* as "empire" in a verse such as Rev 3:10, for example, then the "hour of trial that is coming upon the whole *oikoumenē*" is not at all a general world-ending tribulation that God inflicts upon the earth, but rather a courtroom scene in which God puts the empire on trial. Such an anti-imperial reading is supported by a crucial verse for an ecological interpretation of Revelation, Rev 11:18, where God declares that the time (*kairos*) has now come "for destroying the destroyers of earth." What must be destroyed is not the earth itself but rather the idolatrous "*destroyers*" of earth—that is, the Roman empire, with its entire predatory economy of domination of the earth.

This crucial distinction between the *end of empire (oikoumenē)* and the *end of the created world (kosmos* or *gē,* earth*)* is one that can serve us ecologically, as we seek to respond to climate change and other aspects of the global environmental crisis today. Viewed in terms of biblical critique of empire, what must come to an end today may well be all the toxic illnesses of "empire" today— our culture's unsustainable practices—but not the earth itself. The New Jerusalem vision of Revelation 21–22 proclaims that there is a hope and a future for God's people on earth beyond the end of *oikoumenē*, beyond the end of empire. We must seek readings of eschatological discourses that help people envision life beyond this empire. God's will is not to destroy the earth but to heal it.

The second area for which this reading of *oikoumenē* as empire can be important is ecumenism. Emperor Constantine convened the first "ecumenical council" of Christians in 325 CE, summoning bishops from the whole *oikoumenē*. The church was now legitimized by the Roman empire, creating an undeniable link between the church's use of the word "ecumenical" and Rome's claims over the *oikoumenē*. Jaroslav Pelikan observes about the imperial context of Nicea and the double meaning of the term "ecumenical":

> That extension of the "apostolic council" to a position of universal authority created the concept of the "ecumenical council," with "ecumenical" here taking the double meaning of "for the general church as a whole" and "imperial in scope and in authority" (*oikoumenē* meaning also, as noted earlier, at least "the Roman Empire").[16]

The first ecumenical council at Nicaea was itself a product of empire. Thus, when the modern ecumenical movement locates its work within this tradition we need to ask whether and how it can appeal to *oikoumenē* without perpetuating an imperial view. As Pelikan notes, from its earliest

---

16. Pelikan, *Excellent Empire*, 26.

ecclesial usage the term "ecumenical" had a dual meaning. The question is whether the two meanings can be sufficiently separated so that the church can avoid being "imperial in scope and in authority" while still working "for the general church as a whole." Or is an ecumenical understanding of the church and *oikoumenē* inevitably imperial, because it pursues globalized unity at the expense of local community?

Interestingly, some of the most vocal critiques of the use of the term *oikoumenē* within the ecumenical movement today are being raised by critics of economic globalization. The World Council of Churches' Harare assembly message includes an appendix on globalization contrasting the global market's "*oikoumenē* of domination" with "the *oikoumenē* of faith and solidarity that motivates and energizes the ecumenical movement."[17] Similarly, a recent Lutheran World Federation document on the global economy condemns globalization's hegemonic view of *oikoumenē* and proposes instead an alternative vision of *oikoumenē* that values plurality and cultural diversity:

> Globalization brings a competing vision of the *Oikoumenē*, the unity of humankind. But the unity of humankind being promoted by globalization is one of exploitation and domination, while the unity envisaged by the *Oikoumenē* is one characterized by solidarity and justice. Our vision of the *Oikoumenē* puts great value in plurality and cultural diversity for mutual enrichment and for affirmation of life experiences as expressed in different traditions.[18]

This is an attractive vision, but one must ask: where, in the biblical or historical tradition, do we find the roots for such a vision of *oikoumenē* that "puts great value in plurality and cultural diversity"? Unlike the term *basileia*, for which the New Testament provides a positive model in Jesus' proclamation of the *basileia* of God, there is no such positive precedent for *oikoumenē* in the New Testament. Not even the Septuagint uses the term *oikoumenē* in the sense of valuing diversity. Moreover, if one goes back to the Septuagint to re-claim a positive strand of the term *oikoumenē*, there is still the problem of the Christian kyriarchal use of the term through history. Christian ecumenical councils historically have embraced hierarchical and centralized models of unity in the *oikoumenē* more along the lines of Aelius

---

17. "Policy Reference Committee II Report 8.4, Appendix II: Globalization," 16; in Kessler, *Together on the Way*.

18. "Engaging Economic," 11. For a critique of economic and structural imbalance in the *oikoumenē* written already in 1984 see Bonino, "Oikumene and Anti-Oikumene," 227–30.

Aristides' description of Roman rule—"organizing the whole *oikoumenē* like a single household"— rather than models of unity that respect plurality and cultural diversity.

Any attempt to reclaim or redefine the word *oikoumenē* for the agenda of ecumenism must begin by repudiating the imperial trajectory of the word, including the church's own imperial legacy. Emperor Constantine convened the first ecumenical council because he did not want to allow difference or dissent in the *oikoumenē*. Imperial Rome imposed its vision of a united *oikoumenē* by means of military conquest. Those who want to reclaim "*oikoumenē*" today must reject such kyriarchal models of unity, and must also be attentive to critical issues that feminist and postcolonial liberation theologians are raising. The "ecumenical" history of the Roman empire reminds us that those at the center will tend to construct a single unified "household" in which those at the margins are silenced for the sake of unity and universality. By contrast, we must seek de-centralized models that stand with those at the "margins of the *oikoumenē*" (Rom 10:18), advocating what Vítor Westhelle calls a "strong case for a weak ecclesiology."[19]

If the image of the *oikoumenē* organized as a "single household" from the center is inevitably imperial, then from what other images can we draw to shape our ecclesial life? As ecumenist Konrad Raiser notes, the image of *koinōnia* is widely embraced within the ecumenical movement today as a New Testament image that can address economic disparities in the *oikoumenē* as well as deepen communion across theological and ethnic diversities.[20] Marlene Perera, a Roman Catholic theologian from Sri Lanka, images the *ekklēsia* in the Asian setting as multiplicity—women, men, children interacting together—rooted in local community:

> I see not one church but a multiplicity of churches that have been baptized by and taken root in the different faces of numerous human communities, manifesting the richness of the face of the immanent God walking with us on this pilgrimage. In this perspective it is the local church in all its richness and weakness which enters into deep communion with other churches, thus manifesting another profound visage of God. Communion is their unity in diversity.[21]

---

19. Westhelle, unpublished manuscript. Translating *ta perata tēs oikoumenēs* in Rom 10:18 as the "margins" of the *oikoumenē* is Westhelle's suggestion.

20. But the discourse of *koinōnia* can at times be used to stifle debate in the name of unity, as in 1 Cor 1:9–10. For this critique, see Rossing, "Models of Koinonia," 65–80.

21. Perera, "New Models and New Praxis," 50–51; reprinted in *Ecumenical Movement*, 248–49.

PRAXIS

Drawing on the ecological paradigm of the diversity of life, Brazilian ecofeminist theologian Ivone Gebara proposes the ecclesial image of "biodiversity."[22] In her view, the wonderful multiplicity of God's created world provides a model for embracing local diversity and pluralism in Christian community and ecclesial life as well. In our world where rampant destruction of both the natural world and human community is accelerating, Gebara calls for renewed religious biodiversity as a way of "weaving qualitative ties among people through small communities":

> To speak of religious and cultural biodiversity is to attempt to give the human community a structure that will once again allow it to live out relationships that are more personal, closer to nature, and in deeper contact with the dreams and hopes of the great variety of human groups . . . To bring biodiversity into theological reflection is to open ourselves up to pluralism in the expressions of Christian experience, and therefore to change our understanding of what "unity" is . . . (B)iodiversity requires a new effort to form small faith communities.[23]

Like Gebara's image of biodiversity, I want to suggest an image for ecclesial diversity and community that is drawn from the realm of nature: the image of a braided stream. Braided streams are rivers of many branches, criss-crossing, weaving together and then dividing again—often found in glacial or mountain settings—making a pattern of ever-shifting water channels. From a distance a braided stream can look like beautiful strands of French-braided hair, with the sun sparkling off each strand. Unlike a tributary stream model, where multiple branches feed into a single main channel, a braided stream divides as often as it joins together, flowing in a very wide channel.

If we apply the braided-stream image to ecclesial life, we can envision a model of unity that does not seek to funnel everyone into one monolithic channel, but instead cherishes the diverse ecclesial strands that criss-cross and divide, braiding together across a wide spectrum. In a braided-stream model of *ekklēsia*, many diverse strands and perspectives will sparkle together as part of God's wide, pluriform, multi-vocal, flowing stream. Whatever ecclesial images, whether *koinōnia* or biodiversity or the braided, stream, models of diversity—rather than imperial models of *oikoumenē*—must shape our ecumenical vision.

---

22. Gebara, *Longing for Running Water*.

23 Ibid., 207–8. See also Rhoads, *Challenge of Diversity* on the analogy of biodiversity to ecclesial and theological diversity.

BIBLIOGRAPHY

Aune, David. "Revelation 1–5." In *Word Biblical Commentary*, vol. 52. Dallas: Word, 1997.

Bonino, Jose Miguez. "Oikumene and Anti-Oikumene." In *The Ecumenical Movement: An Anthology of Key Texts and Voices*. Grand Rapids: Eerdmans, 1997.

Danker, Frederick William, editor. *A Greek-English Lexicon of the New Testament and Other Early Christian Literature*. Chicago: University of Chicago Press, 2000.

Fiorenza, Elisabeth Schussler. *Sharing Her Word: Feminist Biblical Interpretation in Context*. Boston: Beacon, 1998.

Gebara, Ivone. *Longing for Running Water: Ecofeminism and Liberation*. Minneapolis: Fortress, 1999.

Johnson, Luke Timothy. *Sacra Pagina: The Gospel of Luke*. Collegeville, MN: Liturgical, 2006.

———. *Sacra Pagina: The Acts of the Apostles*. Collegeville, MN: Liturgical, 1992.

Josephus, Flavius. *Jewish War*. Translated by J. Thackeray. Cambridge: Harvard University Press, 1928.

Kessler, D., editor. "Policy Reference Committee II Report 8.4, Appendix II: Globalization." In *Together on the Way: The Harare Report*. Geneva: World Council of Churches, 1998.

Lindsey, Hal. *The Rapture*. Bantam, 1983.

Nicolet, Claude. *Space, Geography and Politics in the Early Roman Empire*. Ann Arbor: University of Michigan Press, 1991.

Pablo, Richard. *Apocalypse: A People's Commentary on the Book of Revelation*. Maryknoll: Orbis, 1995.

Pelikan, Jaroslav. *The Excellent Empire: The Fall of Rome and the Triumph of the Church*. San Francisco: Harper and Row, 1987.

Perera, Marlene. "New Models and New Praxis," in *Women's Visions*, edited by Ofelia Ortega. Geneva: WCC, 1995.

Raiser, Konrad. "Ecumenism in Search of a Vision." In *The Ecumenical Movement: An Anthology of Key Texts and Voices*, edited by Michael Kinnamon and Brian E. Cope, 70–77. Grand Rapids: Eerdmans, 1997.

Rossing, Barbara. "'Alas for the Earth!' Lament and Resistance in Revelation 12." In *The Earth Bible*, vol. 5: *The Earth Story in the New Testament*. Edited Norman Habel and Shirley Wurth. Sheffield: Sheffield Academic Press, 2002.

———. "Models of Koinonia in the new Testament and Early Church." In *The Church as Communion*, edited by Heinrich Holze. Geneva: Lutheran World Federation Documentation, 1997.

Talbert, Charles. *The Apocalypse*. Louisville: Westminster John Knox, 1994.

Westhelle, Vítor. *Eschatology and Space: The Lost Dimension in Theology Past and Present*. New York: Palgrave Macmillan, 2012.

A Prayer

DEANNA A. THOMPSON

Our Maker, who art wrapped in nature
Hallowed be thy mask.
Thy *eschata* come;
Thy reversal be done;
In spaces as it is in history.
Give us this day our solidarity;
And forgive us our placelessness,
As we forgive those who ignore the abyss.
Lead us not into ecological destruction,
And deliver us from abuses of the cross.
For thine is the epiphany, and the incarnation, and the hope.
For all people and all places,
Amen.

Vítor Westhelle's Publications

DISSERTATION

Religion and Representation: A Study of Hegel's Critical Theories of Vorstellung *and their Relevance for Hegelianism and Theology*. Ann Arbor: UMI, 1984.

BOOKS

Eschatology and Space: The Lost Dimension in Theology, Past and Present. New York: Palgrave Macmillan, 2012.
Deuses e Ciências na América Latina. Editor with Valério Guilherme Shaper, Kathlen Luana de Oliveira, and Eduardo Gross. São Leopoldo: Oikos/EST, 2012.
After Heresy: Colonial Practices and Postcolonial Theologies. Eugene, OR: Cascade, 2010.
The Church Event: Call and Challenge of a Church Protestant. Minneapolis: Fortress, 2009.
Word in Words: Musings of the Gospel. Tiruvalla: Christava Sahitya Smithy, 2009.
O Deus escandaloso: Usos e Abusos da Cruz. Translated by Geraldo Korndörfer. São Leopoldo: Sinodal, 2008.
The Scandalous God: The Use and Abuse of the Cross. Minneapolis: Fortress, 2007
Evisioning a Lutheran Communion: Perspectives for the Twenty-First Century. Edited with Mark Thomsen. Minneapolis: Kirk, 2002.
Philip Hefner: Created Co-Creator. Editor with Ralph Klein. *Currents in Theology and Mission* 28/3-4 (June/August) 2001. Chicago: Lutheran School of Theology Chicago, 2001.
Voces de Protesta en América Latina. Mexico: CETPJDR/LSTC, 2000.
Justiça social e preservação do ambiente: desafios da luta pela vida. Goiânia, Goiás, Brasil: Comissão Pastoral da Terra; São Paulo: Edições Loyola, 1992.
Luta Pela Terra: Caminho de Fé. With Marcelo de Barros Souza and Ivo Poleto. São Paulo:Loyola, 1990.
Proclamar Libertação. Editor with Nelson Kipp. Vol. XVI. São Leopoldo: Sinodal, 1990.
Proclamar Libertação. Editor with Nelson Kipp. Vol. XV. São Leopoldo: Sinodal, 1989.

Vítor Westhelle's Publications

MULTIMEDIA RESOURCE

DVD: "The Theology of the Cross in Contemporary Society." Three Lectures by Vítor Westhelle, a Study Guide, and the recent publication, *The Scandalous God: The Use and Abuse of the Cross* (Fortress) published by Select Multimedia Resources of the ELCA.

CHAPTERS, ESSAYS, & ARTICLES

Forthcoming

"Bible and Colonialism." New York: Palgrave Macmillan.
"What Aspects of Lutheran Theology Contribute to a Holistic Development Model? Or, Is there Something to be Looked At?" Lutheran World Federation.
"Religion and Society: Contemporary Challenges." Escola Superior de Teologia.
"Class, Sin and Displacement." New York: Palgrave Macmillan.
Luther's *Theologia crucis*. Oxford University Press.
Kreuz *Luther Lexikon*
"Contemporary Society: Profile and Religion." UNISINOS.

Published

2012

"Exploring Effective Context: Luther's Contextual Hermeneutics." In *You Have the Words of Eternal Life: Transformative Readings of the Gospel of John from a Lutheran Perspective, Documentation 57/2012*, edited by Kenneth Mtata, 107–20. Minneapolis: Lutheran University Press.
"Theology of the Cross: A Theology of Revelation and a Lutheran Understanding." *The Lutheran* 25.10 (2012) 18–19.
"Desabusando o deus das lacunas." In *Deuses e Ciências na América Latina*, edited by Valério Guilherme Shaper, Vítor Westhelle, Kathlen Luana de Oliveira, and Eduardo Gross, 19–30. São Leopoldo: Oikos/EST.

2011

"Lutheranism and Culture in the Americas: A Comparative Study." In *Transformations in Luther's Theology: Historical and Contemporary Reflections*, edited by Christine Helmer and Bo Kristian Holm, Arbeiten zur Kirchen- und Theologiegeschichte 32, 229–44. Leipzig: Evangelische Verlagsanstalt..
"Entre Américas: convergências e divergências teológicas." In *Teologia e Ciências da Religião: A caminho da maioridade acadêmica no Brasil*, edited by Eduardo R. da Cruz and Geraldo de Mori, 25–42 São Paulo: Paulinas; Belo Horizonte: PUC Minas.

"Displacing Identities: Hybrid Distinctiveness in Theology and Literature." In *Out of Place: Doing Theology on the Crosscultural Brink*, edited by Jione Havea and Clive Pearson, 42–64. London: Equinox.

2010

"Liberation Theology: II Systematics—Ethics. In *Religion Past & Present*, edited by by Hans Dieter Betz et al., 461. Leiden: Brill.
"Liberation Theology: II Systematics—Dogmatics. In *Religion Past & Present*, edited by by Hans Dieter Betz et al., 460–61. Leiden: Brill.
"Liberation Theology: II Systematics—Fundamental Theology. In *Religion Past & Present*, edited by Hans Dieter Betz et al., 460. Leiden: Brill.
"Liberation: 1 Dogmatics." In *Religion Past & Present*, edited by Hans Dieter Betz et al., 456–57. Leiden: Brill.
"Hybridity and Luther's Reading of Chalcedon." In *Gudstanken aktualitet: Bitrag om teologiens opgave og protestantismens indre spaendinger: Festskrift til Peter Widmann*, edited by Else Marie Wiberg Pedersen and Bo Kristian Holm og Anders-Christian Jacobsen, 233–53. Copenhagen: ANIS.

2009

"Igreja e tradição na vocação ministerial." In *Igreja e ministério: Perspectivas evangélico-luteranas*, edited by Wilhelm Wachholz, 7–15. São Leopoldo: Editora Sinodal.
"Perfis de ministério." In *Igreja e ministério: Perspectivas evangélico-luteranas*, edited by Wilhelm Wachholz, 16–29. São Leopoldo: Editora Sinodal.
"Cruz e ministério como práctica da ressurreição." In *Igreja e ministério: Perspectivas evangélico-luteranas*, edited by Wilhelm Wachholz, 30–37. São Leopoldo: Editora Sinodal.
"Speaking for the Church—Speaking to the Church." In *Transformative Theological Practices*, edited Karen L. Bloomquist, 183–91. Minneapolis: Lutheran University Press.
"Power and Politics: Incursions into Luther's Theology." In *The Global Luther: A Theologian for Modern Times*, edited by Christine Helmer, 284–300. Minneapolis: Fortress.
"Santa Frida with Aura and Aroma: On Frida Kahlo's Kitchen and her Broken column." *Perspectivas* 13 (Fall) 69–82.
"The Barmen Theological Declaration: On Celebrating a Text Out of Context." *Currents in Theology and Mission* 36:2 (April) 137–40.
"Clashes of Confession: The Case of Latin America in a Global Context." *Currents in Theology and Mission* 35.4 (August) 293–300.

Vítor Westhelle's Publications

2008

"Santa Frida com Aura e Aroma." In *[Re]Leituras de Frida Kahlo: por uma ética estética da diversidade machucada*, edited by Edla Eggert, 157–64. Santa Cruz do Sul: EDUNISC.

"Transfiguring Lutheranism: Being Lutheran in New Contexts." In *Identity, Survival, Witness: Reconfiguring Theological Agendas*, edited by Karen L. Bloomquist, 11–23. Geneva: LWF/DTS.

"Traumas e opções: teologia e a crise da modernidade." In *Teologia e Pós-modernidade-Novas Perspectivas em Teologia e Filosofia da Religião*, edited by Jaci Maraschin and Frederico Pieper Pires, 13–35. São Paulo: Fonte Editorial.

"Margins Exposed: Representation, Hybridity and Transfiguration." In *Still at the Margins: Biblical Scholarship Fifteen Years after the Voices from the Margin*, edited by R. S. Sugirtharajah, 69–87. New York: T. & T. Clark.

"Clashes of Confession: The Case of Latin America in a Global Context." *Currents in Theology and Mission* 35.4 (August) 293–300.

"What to Say about Hell: A Symposium." *The Christian Century* 125.11 (June 3) 23–24.

"Mal." In *Dicionário Brasileiro de Teologia*, edited by Fernando Bortolleto Filho, José Carlos de
Souza, Nelson Kilpp. São Paulo: ASTE.

"Baptism of Tears: See through the Eyes of John the Baptist." *The Lutheran* (January) Web exclusive.

2007

"Liberation Theology: A Latitudinal Perspective." *The Oxford Handbook on Eschatology*, edited by Jerry Walls. New York: Oxford University Press, 311–27.

". . . . Because the Dawn has Come." In *Mission with the Marginalized*, edited by Samuel. W. Meshack, 26–28. Tiruvalla: Christava Sahitya Samithi.

"Internationalism and Globalization: The Question of Responsibility." In *Mission with the Marginalized*, edited by Samuel. W. Meshack, 450–55. Tiruvalla: Christava Sahitya Samithi.

"Uses and Abuses of the Cross: The Reformation, Then and Now." *Trinity Seminary Review* 28.2 (Summer/Fall) 83–91.

"Resurrection: The Gift of Shabbat." *The Lutheran* 20.4 (April) 20–22.

2006

"This Gracefully Witty World." In *The Grace of the World that Transforms God: Latin american Dialogues with the 9th Assembly of the WCC,* edited by Nancy Cardoso, Edla Eggert, andAndré S. Musskopf, 80–91. Porto Alegre: Editora Universitária Metodista.

"Mundo em Graça(do)." In *A Graça do Mundo Transforma Deus: Dialogos Latino-Americanos com a IX Assembléia do CMI*, edited by Nancy Cardoso, Edla Eggert, and André S. Musskopf, 80–91. Porto Alegre: Editora Universitária Metodista.

"Are Science and Humanism Suited to Enter the Ancient Quest of Christian Theology? A Response to Lluís Oviedo." *Zygon: Journal of Religion and Science* 41.4 (December) 843–52.

"Exposing Zacchaeus." *The Christian Century* 123.22, (October 31) 27–31.

"Usus Crucis: Use and Abuses of the Cross and the Practice of Resurrection." *Seminary Ridge Review* 8/2) 31–43.

2005

"Revelation 13: Between the Colonial and the Postcolonial, a Reading from Brazil." In *From Every People and Nation: The Book of Revelation in Intercultural Perspective*, edited by David Rhoads, 183–99. Minneapolis: Fortress.

"The Word and the Mask: Revisiting the Two-Kingdoms Doctrine." In *The Gift of Grace: The Future of Lutheran Theology*, edited by Niels Henrik Gregersen, Bo Holm, Ted Peters, and Peter Widman, 167–78. Minneapolis: Fortress.

"Symptoms of the End of Western Hegemony." *Theologies and Cultures* II.2 (November/ December) 31–47.

"Luther on the Authority of Scriptures." *Lutheran Quarterly* 19.4 (Winter) 373–91.

"Igreja e Tradição: Opções e Obstruções Ecumênicas." *Estudos Teológicos* 45.2: 81–89.

"Is There A Universal Theology Of The Oppressed?" *Gurukul Journal of Theological Studies* XVI.1–2, (January and July) 92–108.

"Traumas e Opções: Teologia e a Crise da Modernidade." *Margens* 1.1 (March).

"A Festa, o Lúdico e o Erótico na Religião: Perspectiva Teológica." *Estudos de Religião* 19.28 (July), 12–28.

"Theorie und Praxis, III. Fundamentaltheologisch." *Die Religion in Geschichte und Gegenwart*, 4th ed. Vol. VIII.

2004

"Ecumenics and Economics: Economic Justice and the Unity of the Church." In *El silbo ecuménico del Espíritu: Homenaje a José Míguez Bonino en sus 80 años*, edited by Guillermo Hansen, 157–76. Buenos Aires: ISEDET.

"The Dark Room, the Labyrinth, and the Mirror: On Interpreting Luther's Thought on Justification and Justice." In *By Faith Alone: Essays on Justification in Honor of Gerhard O. Forde*, edited by Joseph A. Burguess and Marc Kolden, 316–31. Grand Rapids: Eerdmans.

"Wrappings of the Divine: Location and Vocation in Theological Perspective." *Currents in Theology and Mission* 31.5 (October) 368–80.

"Towards an Ethics of Knowledge." *Zygon: Journal of Religion and Science* 39.2 (June) 383–88.

"The Church's Crucible: Koinonia and Cultural Transcendence." *Currents in Theology and Mission* 31.3 (June) 211–18.

"Religiöse Sozialisten: II. Lateinamerika." *Die Religion in Geschichte und Gegenwart*, 4th ed. Vol. VII.

"The Poet, the Practitioner, and the Beholder: Thoughts on the Created Co-Creator." *Zygon: Journal of Religion and Science* 39.4:747–54.

2003

"Gottes Zeit und das Ende der Welt: Kirche und Eschaologie in der Lutheran Gemeindschaft." In *Zwischen Vision und Realität: Lutherische Kirchen im Übergang*, edited by Wolfang Grieve, 73–89. Geneva: LWF.
"Multiculturalism, Postcolonialism and the Apocalyptic." In *Theology and the Religions: A Dialogue*, edited by Viggo Mortensen, 3–13. Grand Rapids: Eerdmans.
"Communication and the Transgression of Language in Luther." *Lutheran Quarterly* 17.1 (Spring) 1–27.
"A kommunió felöl értelmezett ekkléziológia es akereszt." *Lelkipásztorl* 78/7: 247–51.

2002

"Schleiermacher frente al pecado." In *Schleiermacher: Reseñas desde América Latina*, edited by Guillermo Hansen, 140–51. Buenos Aires: ISEDET.
"Is Europe Christian? A Challenge to a Viking." In *For All People: Global Theologies in Context* (Essays in Honor of Viggo Mortensen), edited by Else Marie Wiberg Pedersen, Holger Lam, and Peter Lodberg, 75–85. Grand Rapids: Eerdmans.
"A Vision." In *Envisioning a Lutheran Communion: Perspectives for the Twenty-First Century*, edited by Mark Thomsen and Vítor Westhelle, 136–46. Minneapolis: Kirk.
"Ideology." In *Dictionary of the Ecumenical Movement*, 2nd ed. Geneva/Grand Rapids: WCC/Eerdmans.
"Religião e pós-modernidade: O mérito de um equívoco: apocalíptica e pós-colonialismo." In *500 Anos de Brasil e Igreja na América Meridional*, edited by Martin N. Dreher, 166–77. Porto Alegre: EST/CEHILA.
"Crises of Society-Crises of the Church?" *McGilvary Journal of Theology* (November).
"Schleiermacher Defronta-se com o Pecado." *Revista Teológica Londrinense* 3:11–20.
"Idols and Demons: On Discerning the Spirits." *Dialog* 41.1: 9–15.
"On Displacing Words: The Lord's Prayer and the New Definition of Justice." *Word and World* 22.1 (Winter) 27–35.

2001

"Saint, Servant, Prophet: A Theological Reflection on the Church in Asia." In *Between Vision and Reality: Lutheran Churches in Transition*, edited by Wolfgang Greive, 65–76. Geneva: LWF/DTS.
"A Tanzanian Experience: The Vicissitudes of an Elusive Tapestry." With Else Marie Wiberg Pedersen. In *Between Vision and Reality: Lutheran Churches in Transition*, edited by Wolfgang Greive, 89–92. Geneva: LWF/DTS.

"Priest, Preacher, Servant: A Theological Reflection on the Church in Europe." In *Between Vision and Reality: Lutheran Churches in Transition*, edited by Wolfgang Greive 367–74. Geneva: LWF/DTS.

"The Times of God and the Ends of the World: Church and Eschatology in the Lutheran Communion." In *Between Vision and Reality: Lutheran Churches in Transition*, edited by Wolfgang Greive, 411–24. Geneva: LWF/DTS.

"'The Noble Tribe of Truth': Etchings on Myth, Language, and Truth Speaking." In *Grundtvig in International Perspective: Studies in the Creativity of Interaction*, edited by A. M. Alchin, S. A. J. Bradley, N. A. Hjelm, and J. H. Schørring, 87–102. Aarhus: Aarhus University Press.

"A Cookbook for Midas." *Currents in Theology and Mission* 28.3–4 (June/August) 175–76.

"Original Sin Revisited: Schleiermacher's Contribution to the Hefnerian Project." *Currents in Theology and Mission* 28.3–4 (June/August) 385–93.

2000

"Modernidade, Mito e Religião: Crítica e Reconstrução das Representações Religiosas." *Numen: Revista de Estudos e Pesquisa da Religião* 3.1:11–38.

"The Way the World Ends: An Essay on Cross and Eschatology." *Currents in Theology and Mission* 27.2:85–97.

"Theological Shamelessness: A Response to Arthur Peacocke and David A. Palin." *Zygon: Journal of Religion and Science* 35.1:165–72.

"Augsburg Confession VII and the Historic Episcopate." *Dialog* 39.3:222–28.

1998

"Creation Motifs in the Search for a Vital Space: A Latin American Perspective." In *Lift Every Voice: Constructing Christian Theology from the Underside*, edited by Susan Thistlethwaite and Mary Engel 146–58. 2nd ed. Maryknoll, NY: Orbis.

"Crises of Society, Crises of the Church: Toward an Eschatological Reading of the Saeculum." In *Communion, Community and Society: The Relevance of the Church*, edited by Wolfgang Greive, 97–109. Geneva: LWF/DTS.

"Befreiung: I Dogmatisch." In *Religion in Geschichte und Gegenwart*, 4th ed. Vol. I.

"Befreiungstheologie II: Systematisch, 1. Fundamentaltheologisch." In *Die Religion in Geschichte und Gegenwart*, 4th ed. Vol. I.

"Befreiungstheologie II: Systematisch, 2. Dogmatisch." In *Die Religion in Geschichte und Gegenwart*, 4th ed. Vol. I.

"Befreiungstheologie II: Systematisch, 3. Ethisch." In *Die Religion in Geschichte und Gegenwart*, 4th ed. Vol. I.

"O Tamanho do Paraíso: Pressupostos do Conceito de Pecado na Teologia Latino-Americana." *Estudos Teológicos* 38.3: 239–51.

Vítor Westhelle's Publications

1997

With Martin Dreher "Gottfried Brakemeier." In *From Federation to Communion*, edited by J. H. Schørring, P. Kumari and N. A. Hjelm, 477–80. Minneapolis: Fortress. German: *Vom Weltbund zur Gemeinschaft*, 422–25. Hannover: LVH.

"Conquest and Evangelization in Latin America." In *Word Remembered, Word Proclaimed*, edited by Stephen Bevans and Roger Schroeder, 89–107. Nettetal: Steyler.

"Theological Education: Quo Vadis?" *Currents in Theology and Mission* 24.3 (June) 273–85.

"And the Walls Come Tumbling Down: Globalization and Fragmentation in the LWF." *Dialog* 36.1:32–39, 1997.

1996

"Elements for a Typology of Latin American Theologies." In *Prejudice Issues in Third World Theologies*, edited by Andreas Nehring, 84–101. Madras: Gurukul.

"Invisibility and Dissimulation: The Problem of the Other in Latin American Theologies." In *Prejudice Issues in Third World Theologies*, edited by Andreas Nehring, 141–60. Madras: Gurukul.

"Proclamation and Obligation: On the Demonstration of the Spirit and of Power." *Word & World* 16.3:328–39.

"Two Omens and an Oracle: Reflections on the Convocation of Teaching Theologians." *Currents in Theology and Mission* 23.3:185–91.

1995

"Cross, Creation, and Ecology: The Meeting Point Between the Theology of the Cross and Creation Theology in Luther." In *Concern for Creation: Voices on the Theology of Creation*, edited by Viggo Mortensen, 1159–67. Uppsala: Tro & Tanke.

"The Weeping Mask: Ecological Crisis and the View of Nature." In *Creation and the Future of Humanity: LSTC Writings on the Environment*, edited by Jan Harbaugh, Linda Kersten, and David M. Rhoads, 72–78. Chicago: Committee on LSTC as a Green Zone.

"Cross, Creation, and Ecology." In *Creation and the Future of Humanity: LSTC Writings on the Environment*, edited by Jan Harbaugh, Linda Kersten, and David M. Rhoads, 37–40. Chicago: Committee on LSTC as a Green Zone.

"Outros Saberes: Teologia e Ciência na Modernidade." *Estudos Teológicos* 35.3:258–78.

"The End of Christendom and Other Captivities: A Response to Douglas John Hall." *Currents in Theology and Mission* 22.6:441–45.

With Hanna Betina Götz, "Usynlighet og virkelighet." *Norsk Teologisk Tidsskrift* 96.1:20–34.

"Scientific Sight and Embodied Knowledges." *Modern Theology* 11.3 (July) 341–61.

"The Current Crisis in Latin American Theology." *Dialog* 34.1 (Winter) 39–43.

"In Quest of a Myth: Latin American Literature and Theology." With Hanna Betina Götz. *Journal of Hispanic/Latino Theology* 3.1 (August) 5–22.

1994

"Re(li)gion: The Lord of History and the Illusory Space." In *Region and Religion*, edited by Viggo Mortensen, 79-95. Geneva: LWF.

"Cruz, Criação e Ecologia." *Estudos Teológicos* 34.3:291-300.

1993

"Fragmentation, Dissonance, and Truth." In *History of the LWF*, edited by Viggo Mortensen. Geneva: LWF.

1992

"'The Third Bank of the River:' Thoughts on Justification and Justice." In *Justification and Justice*, edited by Viggo Mortensen, 29-36. Geneva: LWF.

"Teologia e Pós-Modernidade." In *Teologia Sob Limite*, edited by Jaci Maraschin, 143-65. São Paulo: ASTE.

"500 Anos de Evangelização: A História Suprimida." In *500 Anos de Invasão—500 anos de Resitência*, edited by Roberto Zwetsch, 45-54. São Paulo: Paulinas.

"Die neue Haut der unsichtabaren Schlange." *Weltmission heute* 12:9-28.

"A Voz que Vem da Natureza." *Caderno de Estudo da CPT* 5:30-43.

"Erobroing og evangelisiring in Latinamerika: tre missionsmodeller og deres faelles forudsaetning." *Mission* 4:3-7.

"Entre Abel e Caim: Comunicação Teológica na América Latina." *Estudos Teológicos* 32.3:264-77.

1991

"A Teologia da Criação e o Desafio Ecológico." In *Francisco e Ecologia: Para que a Vida Prevaleça*, 17-34. Petrópolis: Sinfrajupe.

"Missão e Poder: O Deus Abscôndito e os Poderes Insurgentes." *Estudos Teológicos* 31.2:29-46.

"Una Sancta: A Unidade da Igreja na Divisão Social." *Estudos Teológicos* 31.1:29-46.

"The Weeping Mask: Ecological Crisis and the View of Nature." *Word & World* 11.2:137-46.

1990

"Os Sinais dos Lugares: As Dimensões Esquecidas." In *Peregrinação: Estudos em Homenagem a Joachim Fischer pela Passagem de seu 60° Aniversário*, Martin N. Dreher, ed. (São Leopoldo: Sinodal), 255-268.

"Ways of Justice in a Journey to Peace." In *Peace and Justice: Toward an Ecumenical Peace Ethic*, edited by Götz Planer-Friedrich, 45-62. Geneva: LWF.

Vítor Westhelle's Publications

"Creation Motifs in the Search for a Vital Space: A Latin American Perspective." In *Lift Every Voice: Constructing Christian Theology from the Underside*, edited by Susan Thistlethwaite and Mary Engel, 128–287. San Francisco: Harper & Row.

"Marcos 10. 46–52." Homiletic study in *Proclamar Libertação*, vol. XVI, edited by Nelson Kilpp and Vítor Westhelle, 283–87. São Leopoldo: Sinodal.

"A Cruz, a Teologia e as Rosas: O Significado Soteriológico da Cruz na Teologia." *Estudos Teológicos* 30.3:224–43.

"Thinking about Luther in a Submersed Reality." *Lutherjahrbuch* 57:163–73.

"A Voz que Vem da Natureza." *Estudos Teológicos* 30.1:16–26.

1989

"Theology Challenges Science and the Church." In *The New Faith-Science Debate*, edited John M. Mangum, 23–35. Minneapolis/Geneva: Fortress/WCC.

"But it shall not be so among you." *The Year 2000 and beyond*. Chicago: Evangelical Lutheran Church in America.

"Eine Reise zum Frieden über Wege der Gerechtigkeit." In *Frieden und Gerechtigkeit*, edited by Götz Planer-Friedrich, 51–70. Munich: Chr. Kaiser.

"Apocalipse 15.2–4." Homiletic study in *Proclamar Libertação*, vol. XV, edited by Nelson Kilpp and Vítor Westhelle, 218–24. São Leopoldo: Sinodal.

"Bases bíblicas y teológicas de la comunicación." *Presencia Ecuménica* 5.12:3–9.

1988

"Luther and Liberation." *Tugón* 8.1:54–71.

1987

"Isaias 5.1–7." Homiletic study in *Proclamar Libertação*, vol. XIII, edited by Harald Malschitzky and Uwe Wegner 147–51. São Leopoldo: Sinodal.

1986

"Planejamento Familiar: Genocídio Planejado?" Homiletic study in *Proclamar Libertação*, vol. XII, edited by Harald Malschitzky and Uwe Wegner, 77–86. São Leopoldo: Sinodal.

"Labor: A Suggestion for Rethinking the Way of the Christian." *Word & World* 4.2:194–206.

"Luther and Liberation." *Dialog* 25:51–58.

"O desencontro entre a teologia Luterana e a teologia da libertação." In *Estudos teológicos* 26/1:37–58.

1985

"Filipenses 3.17–21." Homiletic study in *Proclamar Libertação*, vol. XI, edited by Harald Malschitzky and Uwe Wegner. São Leopoldo: Sinodal.

"Mito, alegoria y símbolo: la crítica y reconstrucción de las representaciones religiosas." *Eutopias: Teorias/Historia/Discurso* 1.1–2 (Winter–Spring) 201–24.

"Strauss and Bauer: Options for Contemporary Christology." *AAR-Currents in Contemporary Christology* 4.5:23–34.

1984

"Strauss: Pedagogy for a Theological Revolution." *Dialog* 23: 263–70.

"Paul's Reconstruction of Theology: Romans 9–14 in Context." *Word & World* 4.3:307–19.

1981

"Dependency Theory: Some Implications for Liberation Theology." *Dialog* 20:293–99.

"Pressupostos e Implicações do Conceito de Práxis em Hugo Assmann." *Estudos Teológicos* 18/2: 77–94.

1979

"Mateus 5.17–20." Homiletic study in *Proclamar Libertação*, vol. IV, edited by Baldur van Kaick, 125–32. São Leopoldo: Sinodal.

"Jeremias 29. 14–14a." Homiletic study in *Proclamar Libertação*, vol. III, edited by Baldur van Kaick, 48–61. São Leopoldo: Sinodal.

1978

"Considerações sobre o Etno-Luteranismo Latino-Americano." *Estudos Teológicos* 18.2:77–94.

www.ingramcontent.com/pod-product-compliance
Lightning Source LLC
Chambersburg PA
CBHW070257230426
43664CB00014B/2565